The Ultimate Ninja Foodi Digital Air Fryer Oven Cookbook

1200 Days Affordable, Quick and Easy Recipes
For Beginners to Bake, Air Fry,
Broil, Grill, Roast, Dehydrate

Johnny Browne

Copyright© 2021 By Johnny Browne All Rights Reserved

This book is copyright protected. It is only for personal use. You cannot amend, distribute, sell, use, quote or paraphrase any part of the content within this book, without the consent of the author or publisher.

Under no circumstances will any blame or legal responsibility be held against the publisher, or author, for any damages, reparation, or monetary loss due to the information contained within this book, either directly or indirectly.

Disclaimer Notice:

Please note the information contained within this document is for educational and entertainment purposes only. All effort has been executed to present accurate, up to date, reliable, complete information. No warranties of any kind are declared or implied. Readers acknowledge that the author is not engaged in the rendering of legal, financial, medical or professional advice. The content within this book has been derived from various sources. Please consult a licensed professional before attempting any techniques outlined in this book.

By reading this document, the reader agrees that under no circumstances is the author responsible for any losses, direct or indirect, that are incurred as a result of the use of the information contained within this document, including, but not limited to, errors, omissions, or inaccuracies.

Table of Contents

Introduction   **1**

All About Ninja Foodi Digital Air Fryer Oven 1
Components of the Ninja Foodi Digital Air fry Oven... 1
Benefits of Using the Ninja Digital Air Fry Oven 2
Proper Usage and Maintenance Tips.................... 3
Safety Tips 3
What Can Ninja Foodi Digital Air Fry Oven do? 4
Cooking Tips and Tricks 4

Chapter 1   Breakfasts   **5**

Fried Potatoes with Peppers and Onions 5
Asparagus and Cheese Strata 5
Carrot Banana Muffin 5
Breakfast Blueberry Cobbler 6
Egg and Avocado Burrito................................ 6
French Toast Sticks 6
Chicken Breakfast Sausages 7
Spicy Apple Turnovers 7
Cheesy Artichoke-Mushroom Frittata................... 7
Egg Florentine with Spinach 8
All-in-One Toast.. 8
Whole-Wheat Blueberry Scones 8
Mini Brown Rice Quiches............................... 9
Scotch Eggs 9
Whole-Wheat Muffins with Blueberries 9
Baked Avocado with Eggs 9
Creamy Cinnamon Rolls 10
Sweet Banana Bread Pudding 10
Spinach with Scrambled Eggs 10
Potatoes Lyonnaise 11
Apple and Walnut Muffins 11
Avocado Quesadillas 11
Kale and Potato Nuggets............................... 12
Ham and Corn Muffins................................. 12
Lush Vegetable Omelet 12

Blueberry Cake 12
Mushroom and Squash Toast 13
Banana Bread 13
Grit and Ham Fritters 13

Chapter 2   Vegetables   **14**

Ratatouille 14
Zucchini Crisps 14
Golden Garlicky Mushrooms 14
Mushroom and Pepper Pizza Squares 15
Cinnamon Celery Roots 15
Spicy Kung Pao Tofu 15
Maple and Pecan Granola 15
Lemony Brussels Sprouts and Tomatoes 16
Sweet and Spicy Broccoli 16
Stuffed Peppers with Beans and Rice 16
Spicy Thai-Style Vegetables 17
Cheesy Broccoli Tots 17
Sweet Potatoes with Zucchini 17
Paprika Cauliflower 18
Cream Cheese Stuffed Bell Peppers 18
Stuffed Portobellos with Peppers and Cheese 18
Cheese-Walnut Stuffed Mushrooms 19
Cheesy Rice and Olives Stuffed Peppers 19
Chermoula Beet 19
Stuffed Portobello Mushrooms with Vegetables 20
Ratatouille 20
Potatoes with Zucchinis 20
Air Fried Vegetables................................... 20
Potato and Broccoli with Tofu Scramble 21
Balsamic Brussels Sprouts 21
Lush Summer Rolls 21
Super Veg Rolls 21
Sweet Potatoes with Tofu 22
Cauliflower, Chickpea, and Avocado Mash 22

Basmati Risotto 22
Creamy and Cheesy Spinach 22
Mediterranean Air Fried Veggies 23
Rice and Eggplant Bowl 23
Jalapeño Poppers... 23
Black Bean and Tomato Chili 23
Mascarpone Mushrooms 24
Gold Ravioli 24
Ricotta Potatoes 24
Spicy Cauliflower 25

Chapter 3 Fish and Seafood   26

Coconut Chili Fish Curry 26
Spicy Orange Shrimp 26
Garlic Shrimp with Parsley 26
Seafood Spring Rolls 27
Caesar Shrimp Salad 27
Goat Cheese Shrimp 28
Coconut-Crusted Prawns.................................. 28
Garlic-Butter Shrimp with Vegetables 28
Fired Shrimp with Mayonnaise Sauce 29
Paprika Shrimp 29
Chili Prawns 29
Shrimp and Vegetable Paella 29
Herbed Scallops with Vegetables 30
Browned Shrimp Patties 30
Crispy Crab and Fish Cakes 30
Shrimp and Cherry Tomato Kebabs 31
Panko Crab Sticks with Mayo Sauce 31
Crab Cakes with Bell Peppers 31
Lemony Shrimp... 32
Easy Scallops 32
Piri-Piri King Prawns... 32
Breaded Calamari with Lemon 32
Breaded Scallops 33
Garlic Butter Shrimp Scampi 33
Classic Shrimp Empanadas 33
Bacon-Wrapped Scallops 34
Cajun-Style Fish Tacos 34

Tuna Patty Sliders... 34
Crispy Cod Cakes with Salad Greens 34
Air-Fried Scallops 35
Crispy Coconut Shrimp 35
Roasted Scallops with Snow Peas.................... 35
Green Curry Shrimp 36
Glazed Cod with Sesame Seeds 36
Salmon Burgers 36
Salmon Patty Bites 37
Blackened Salmon 37
Almond Crusted Fish 37
Blackened Shrimp Tacos 38
Air Fried Spring Rolls 38
Country Shrimp.. 38
Spicy Orange Shrimp 39
Homemade Fish Sticks 39
Seasoned Breaded Shrimp 39
Lemony Shrimp and Zucchini 40
Marinated Salmon Fillets 40
Lime-Chili Shrimp Bowl 40
Crab Cake Sandwich 41
Tortilla Shrimp Tacos 41

Chapter 4 Poultry   42

Air Fried Chicken Wings 42
Spanish Chicken and Pepper Baguette.................. 42
Turkey and Cauliflower Meatloaf 42
Deep Fried Duck Leg Quarters 43
Yakitori 43
Rosemary Turkey Breast................................... 43
Turkey and Mushroom Meatballs 44
Cheesy Turkey Burgers 44
Rosemary Turkey Scotch Eggs 45
Italian Chicken Breasts with Tomatoes 45
Duck Breasts with Balsamic Glaze.................. 45
Pineapple Chicken 46
Golden Chicken Fries 46
Peach and Cherry Chicken 46
Chicken Skewers with Corn Salad 47

Braised Chicken with Hot Peppers 47

Chicken Shawarma 48

Chicken Thighs with Radish Slaw 48

Chicken and Sweet Potato Curry 49

Super Lemon Chicken 49

Glazed Chicken Drumsticks 49

Herbed Hens 50

Chicken with Potatoes and Corn 50

Fajita Chicken Strips.. 50

Creole Hens 51

Gnocchi with Chicken and Spinach 51

Chicken Roast 51

Celery Chicken 52

Piri-Piri Chicken Thighs 52

Fried Chicken Tenders with Veggies 52

Chicken Satay with Peanut Sauce 53

Air Fried Naked Chicken Tenders 53

Israeli Chicken Schnitzel 53

Asian Turkey Meatballs 54

Potato Cheese Crusted Chicken 54

Sweet-and-Sour Drumsticks 54

Fried Buffalo Chicken Taquitos 55

Lemon Parmesan Chicken 55

Turkey Stuffed Bell Peppers 55

Nutty Chicken Tenders................................. 56

Blackened Chicken Breasts 56

Turkey and Cranberry Quesadillas...................... 56

Cajun Turkey 56

Crisp Paprika Chicken Drumsticks...................... 57

Orange and Honey Glazed Duck 57

Turkey, Hummus, and Cheese Wraps 57

Dill Chicken Strips... 58

Herbed Turkey Breast 58

Pecan-Crusted Turkey Cutlets 58

Honey Rosemary Chicken 59

Mini Turkey Meatloaves with Carrot 59

Turkey Hoisin Burgers 59

Chapter 5 Meats 60

Char Siu 60

Gold Cutlets with Aloha Salsa 60

Homemade Teriyaki Pork Ribs 61

Pork and Tricolor Vegetables Kebabs 61

Citrus Carnitas 61

Classic Walliser Schnitzel 62

Lechon Kawali 62

Macadamia Nuts Crusted Pork Rack.................... 62

Pork Meatballs with Red Chili 63

Pork Chops with Carrots and Mushrooms 63

Calf's Liver Golden Strips 63

Beef and Spinach Meatloaves 64

Dijon Pork Tenderloin 64

Italian Sausages and Red Grapes 64

Mushroom and Sausage Calzones 65

Sriracha Beef and Broccoli 65

Worcestershire Ribeye Steaks 66

Ravioli with Beef-Marinara Sauce 66

Spicy Pork Lettuce Wraps 66

Sirloin Steak and Pepper Fajitas 67

Pork with Butternut Squash and Apples 67

Pork Chop Roast 68

Fast Lamb Satay 68

Miso Marinated Steak 68

Spaghetti Squash Lasagna 68

Air Fried London Broil 69

Pepperoni and Bell Pepper Pockets 69

Air Fried Lamb Ribs 69

Classic Spring Rolls 69

Sumptuous Pizza Tortilla Rolls 70

Lollipop Lamb Chops 70

Orange Pork Tenderloin 70

Teriyaki Pork and Mushroom Rolls..................... 71

Lamb Meatballs....................................... 71

Beef and Vegetable Cubes 71

Pork with Aloha Salsa 72

Cheesy Beef Meatballs 72

Mongolian Flank Steak....................................72

Mushroom and Beef Meatloaf.........................73

Provolone Stuffed Beef and Pork Meatballs...........73

Pulled Pork 73

Potato and Prosciutto Salad 73

Pork and Pinto Bean Gorditas 74

Beef Schnitzel 74

Barbecue Pork Ribs 74

Citrus Pork Loin Roast 75

Beef Steak Fingers 75

Char Siew 75

Vietnamese Pork Chops 75

Rosemary Ribeye Steaks 76

Smoked Beef..76

Sweet and Sour Pork 76

Skirt Steak Fajitas...................................77

Swedish Beef Meatballs 77

Chapter 6   Appetizers and Snacks   78

Kale Chips with Sesame 78

Carrot Chips 78

Cinnamon Apple Wedges 78

Spiced Apple Chips 78

Corn and Black Bean Salsa 79

Sweet and Salty Snack Mix..........................79

Veggie Salmon Nachos 79

Avocado Chips 79

Tangy Fried Pickle Spears 80

Bruschetta with Tomato and Basil 80

Italian Rice Balls 80

Crispy Cod Fingers 81

Mushroom and Spinach Calzones 81

Lemony Endive in Curried Yogurt 81

Peppery Chicken Meatballs.........................82

Air Fried Chicken Wings 82

Cripsy Artichoke Bites 82

Crispy Spiced Chickpeas............................83

Honey Sriracha Chicken Wings 83

Tortilla Chips 83

Spicy Chicken Wings 83

Herbed Pita Chips...................................84

Sweet Bacon Tater Tots 84

Veggie Shrimp Toast................................84

Mozzarella Arancini 84

Lemony Pear Chips 85

Lemony Chicken Drumsticks 85

Pigs in a Blanket 85

Poutine with Waffle Fries 86

Tortellini with Spicy Dipping Sauce.................86

Chapter 7   Desserts   87

Crispy Pineapple Rings 87

Pineapple Sticks 87

Coconut Pineapple Sticks 87

Baked Peaches and Blueberries 87

Black and White Brownies 88

Chocolate Cheesecake 88

Apple Fritters 88

Blackberry and Peach Cobbler 89

Peanut Butter-Chocolate Bread Pudding 89

Ricotta Lemon Poppy Seed Cake 89

Coconut Chip Mixed Berry Crisp 90

Summer Berry Crisp.................................90

Lemony Blackberry Crisp............................90

Oatmeal and Carrot Cookie Cups 90

Pumpkin Pudding and Vanilla Wafers 91

Glazed Apples 91

Cinnamon S'mores 91

Oatmeal Raisin Bars 91

Jelly Doughnuts......................................92

Lemony Apple Butter 92

Pumpkin Pudding 92

Chocolate Pecan Pie 92

Caramelized Fruit Kebabs 93

Berry Crumble 93

Spice Cookies 93

Breaded Bananas with Chocolate Sauce 94

Pineapple Galette 94

Orange Cake 94

Fudgy Chocolate Brownies 95

Rich Chocolate Cookie................................. 95

Pear and Apple Crisp 95

Pecan and Cherry Stuffed Apples 96

Pineapple and Chocolate Cake 96

Apple Turnovers 96

Chapter 8   Casseroles, Frittatas, and Quiches   97

Greek Frittata 97

Sumptuous Beef and Bean Chili Casserole 97

Herbed Cheddar Frittata 97

Spinach and Chickpea Casserole 98

Chicken Divan 98

Creamy Pork Gratin 98

Chorizo, Corn, and Potato Frittata 99

Goat Cheese and Asparagus Frittata................... 99

Sumptuous Vegetable Frittata......................... 99

Kale Frittata 100

Shrimp Spinach Frittata 100

Keto Cheese Quiche 100

Mediterranean Quiche 101

Smoked Trout and Crème Fraiche Frittata 101

Mini Quiche Cups 101

Broccoli, Carrot, and Tomato Quiche 102

Vegetable Frittata 102

Mac and Cheese 102

Cheesy Bacon Quiche 102

Shrimp Quiche 103

Chapter 9   Wraps and Sandwiches   104

Chicken and Yogurt Taquitos 104

Pork Momos 104

Thai Pork Sliders 104

Crispy Crab and Cream Cheese Wontons 105

Crispy Chicken Egg Rolls 105

Bacon and Bell Pepper Sandwich 105

Sweet Potato and Black Bean Burritos 106

Air Fried Cream Cheese Wontons 106

Cheesy Chicken Sandwich 106

Lamb and Feta Hamburgers 107

Cabbage and Pork Gyoza 107

Montreal Steak and Seeds Burgers 107

Turkey, Leek, and Pepper Hamburger 108

Bulgogi Burgers..................................... 108

Eggplant Hoagies 108

Cheesy Shrimp Sandwich 109

Turkey Sliders with Chive Mayo 109

Smoky Chicken Sandwich 109

Salsa Verde Golden Chicken Empanadas 110

Mexican Flavor Chicken Burgers 110

Pea and Potato Samosas with Chutney 111

Classic Sloppy Joes 111

Veggie Pita Sandwich 112

Chicken Pita Sandwich 112

Chapter 10   Fast and Easy Everyday Favorites   113

Apple Fritters with Sugary Glaze 113

Hot Wings 113

Lemony and Garlicky Asparagus 113

Parsnip Fries with Garlic-Yogurt Dip 114

Air Fried Okra Chips................................. 114

Sweet and Sour Peanuts............................ 114

Cheesy Shrimps 114

Spanakopita 115

Spicy Air Fried Old Bay Shrimp 115

Garlicky Spiralized Zucchini and Squash 115

Southwest Corn and Bell Pepper Roast 116

Golden Salmon and Carrot Croquettes 116

Purple Potato Chips with Rosemary 116

Baked Cherry Tomatoes with Basil.................. 117

Air Fried Crispy Brussels Sprouts 117

Herb-Fried Veggies 117

Indian Masala Omelet 117

Peppery Brown Rice Fritters 118

South Carolina Shrimp and Corn Bake 118

Indian-Style Sweet Potato Fries 118

Pomegranate Avocado Fries 119

Rosemary and Orange Chickpeas 119

Scalloped Veggie Mix 119

Pea Delight 119

Croutons 120

Sweet Potato Soufflé 120

Chicken Wings 120

Spinach and Carrot Balls 120

Sweet Corn and Carrot Fritters 121

Traditional Queso Fundido 121

Chapter 11   Holiday Specials   122

Lush Snack Mix... 122

Jewish Blintzes 122

Air Fried Spicy Olives 122

Pão de Queijo 123

Classic Churros... 123

Pigs in a Blanket 123

Milky Pecan Tart 124

Garlicky Olive Stromboli 124

Supplì al Telefono (Risotto Croquettes).............. 125

Teriyaki Shrimp Skewers 125

Golden Nuggets 126

Bourbon Monkey Bread 126

Kale Salad Sushi Rolls with Sriracha Mayo 127

Honey Yeast Rolls.. 127

Chapter 12   Sauces, Dips, and Dressings   128

Lemony Tahini 128

Hummus... 128

Dijon and Balsamic Vinaigrette 128

Cashew Mayo 128

Classic Marinara Sauce 128

Pico de Gallo 129

Hemp Dressing 129

Cashew Ranch Dressing 129

Avocado Dressing.. 129

Mushroom Apple Gravy 129

Balsamic Dressing 129

Asian Dipping Sauce 130

Caesar Salad Dressing 130

Southwest Seasoning 130

Appendix 1 Measurement Conversion Chart   131

Appendix 2 Air Fryer Cooking Chart   132

Appendix 3 Index   133

Introduction

All About Ninja Foodi Digital Air Fryer Oven

Cooking food is becoming much easier with this digital air fryer oven. For roasting, baking, and air frying lovers, the Ninja Foodi digital air fryer oven is the ultimate oven to have. The Ninja Foodi Digital Air Fryer Oven is revolutionizing healthy cooking, and it is proved to be a beneficial device for anyone using it. You can use this oven for many purposes, such as cooking with the convenience and functionality of a air fryer, heating as a frying pan, and cooking like a convection oven.

The LCD screen on the air fryer oven makes it easy for both professional and novice chefs to use by displaying timers and instructions. Another excellent advantage is that it cooks food evenly thanks to its Digital Crisp Control Technology, which helps you precisely cook all types of food. The oven is ideal for air frying, roasting, baking, and broiling.

With each passing day and the advancement in innovation, there are many alternatives for an individual to appreciate food. Ninja Foodi Air Fryer Oven is perhaps the main machine for making an assortment of food. It reduces the amount of oil used, allowing people to enjoy healthier and lower-fat foods. For me, I really don't like to use too much oil when cooking. One of the principal benefits of the digital air fryer oven is that it readies the food in significantly less time, which means I don't need to wait too long to eat what I want when I'm hungry.

Components of the Ninja Foodi Digital Air fry Oven

The Ninja Foodi Digital Air fry Oven is a multi-purpose apparatus fit for executing about eight diverse cook procedures, i.e., performing multiple tasks. To make the cooking successful, the oven has several components that ensure it works at an optimum capacity. They include:

- **The Control Panel:** You would not think that it is hard to control your oven as the advanced control board on the Ninja Foodi Digital Air Fry Oven is not challenging to comprehend. The interface is genuinely natural to set and fixated on the surface of the oven to set the cooking temperature and time for each capacity. It additionally permits you to choose the quantity of slices and darkness. The Ninja Foodi Digital Air Fry Oven has a LED screen simply over the control board that shows the temperature in "F" just as the cooking time in minutes and hours. If the stove is preheating, you will see "Pre" showed on the screen or "Hot" if the unit is hot and will turn off when the oven is cool enough to be flipped up for storage or cleaning. Whenever it has cooled enough, the presentation will show "Flip" which implies that the air fry oven would now be able to be flipped and fit to be put away.
- **Sheet Pan:** This Oven accompanies a sheet pan that sits just underneath the air fryer basket, getting any falling scraps or trickling oil from the food cooking in the oven. There is no space to permit the pan to be moved without moving the air fryer basket and the other way around. So while eliminating the hot air fryer basket while cooking, you need to remember eliminating it along with the pan to try not to have it fall on your foot coincidentally.
- **Air Fry Basket:** Compared with the adjustment components currently available in most air fryer models, this component can hold more food. You can uniformly spread your food out to deliver even dissemination of hot air,

bringing about all around seared fresh air singed dishes. Contingent upon the recipe you use, it can hold foods up to 4 pounds.

- **The Digital Crisp Control Technology:** This component gives you programmable cooking presets, 60-second preheat time, temperature, airflow mechanism, and precision-controlled heat source for the ultimate cooking performance.
- **The Wire rack:** It is put at the base rail position and is essential for making bread, frozen waffles, and pizza, among others.
- **The main unit:** It is a box-like component with curve-edged and stainless steel paint. Inside it is the heating component and the fan that warms the air and courses it individually.

Benefits of Using the Ninja Digital Air Fry Oven

High-quality material

The oven comes with a classy and elegant look and is made of brushed stainless steel. The edges are well rounded and have an excellent coating. If you are looking for a solid and durable cooking appliance, then the Ninja Foodi Digital Air Fryer Oven is the perfect one to have. Proper use and maintenance additionally give it more years of service.

It consumes less counter space

A flexible flip capacity permits you to keep the oven in both vertical and level position on your counter or kitchen rack contingent upon accessible space. While cooking, it should be in an even position. Notwithstanding, when you are prepared to store it while not being used, flip it up, and it can remain in an upward position, leaving more space on your rack for your other kitchen devices. So it can take half less space on the ledge of the rack when flipped up.

Speed Cooking

The oven concocts to 60 percent quicker contrasted with a traditional oven. You can preheat the oven in 60 seconds and have a full supper in just 20 minutes.

Wonderful Design

- Excellent for sheet pan dinner
- It toasts evenly on proper slice and darkness settings
- It's soundless
- Easy to navigate as digital controls are basic and simple

Easy to Clean

It is not difficult to clean this cooking apparatus and it makes cleaning a fast and straightforward task to take care of. The Ninja Foodi Oven is additionally outfitted with a removable crumb tray that collects falling trash and deposits from the air fryer oven. It likewise shields the lower part of the oven from spills. You can likewise effectively access the backboard for proper cleaning. The oven is furnished with a huge opening at the back, so you will want to clean the whole surface appropriately. Use a cleanser and a soggy towel when cleaning.

Proper Usage and Maintenance Tips

- The Ninja Air fry Oven is not appropriate for outdoor use.
- Deeply clean at least once per week. Flip the oven to the upstanding position, eliminate the backboard, and wipe both the inside and outside using warm, soapy water and a soft cloth.
- Except for the air fryer basket and sheet pan, all other components are not dishwasher safe. That's to say, never clean the main unit in the dishwasher. Besides, try to clean after each utilization (after it should have cooled) to ensure they last longer.
- Study the user manual completely before use to prevent mishaps and unwanted outcomes. Fortunately, the Ninja Air fry Oven accompanies an essential and direct manual.
- Before the initial use, eliminate all bundling names and tapes. Then, hand-wash all components with warm, sudsy water, flush and dry completely.

Safety Tips

To ensure you are safe while cooking and the oven will keep going long, here are some significant hints you need to consider.

1. Material Paper and Foil

Sometimes cooking can make everything messy, especially when using sauces. Maybe everything will fall on the oven or stick to the crumb tray. It is smarter to line your air fryer basket or sheet pan with foil or material for simple eliminating once the dish is cooked. Notwithstanding, ensure that what you put on top is adequately substantial to hold down the paper and not fly around when the hot air begins to course.

2. Leave Enough Space Around the Ninja Foodi Digital Air Fry Oven

Since hot air needs to circle to keep food fresh, you should settle your oven on a level surface while cooking. So don't push your oven against the divider while cooking. It will keep hot air from circling appropriately and may rather bounce back on you while you are working the oven.

3. Remember Preheating

The Ninja Foodi Digital Air Fry Oven requires just 60 seconds to preheat. So please don't skip it. The oven needs to have its appropriate warmth temperature

before you push your food in there if you need to have its ideal advantage of cooking. Having the right wind stream and temperature level will guarantee that your food will have its fresh impact. Throwing your dish into the oven without preheating may not give you the ideal outcome you need.

4. Try not to Overload

You might need to cook your food quickly, yet if you need your food to come out flavorful and at its best appearance, don't attempt to lose your air fryer oven by overloading. Since the Ninja Digital Air Fry Oven works by circling hot air, leaving no sufficient room for air to course won't leave you with the ideal impact on your cooking. An extraordinary cook shows restraint.

What Can Ninja Foodi Digital Air Fry Oven do?

In case you do not know exactly what is Ninja Foodi and what it can do, below are some of the functionalities:

- **Dehydrate:** This function has come in handy whenever I want to dehydrate my beef and vegetables. This setting lowers the temperature and slows the fan speed to ensure your meals are adequately dehydrated.

- **Air Broil:** This cooking method works with temperature and it is ideal to have a golden-brown texture for your meal. If I want to have my lamb chops with garlic and olive oil, this is the method I use.

- **Air Roast:** You can roast your beef or chicken and prepare your seasoned vegetables on this function. You can have your roasted vegetables with chicken and turkey sausage. I am using this example because it is not only your proteins that you roast.

- **Bake:** This cooking method is quite limited to the fryer but it is not impossible. A perfect meal you can have here is the cauliflower casserole. You can also make dessert so, you are not stuck.

- **Air Fry:** The inbuilt temperature range makes it perfect for your fries. You can have your crispy fried chicken by simply adjusting the time. For your chicken tenders, you can set a temperature of 360°F and a time within the range of 8 to 10 minutes. If you are preparing frozen food, it will have extra time. Your frozen chicken will have 400°F for its temperature.

Cooking Tips and Tricks

- When using the bagel feature, organize bagels cut-side looking up on the wire rack.
- Halfway through cooking, either flip elements for crispier outcomes or turn the air fryer container 180 degrees.
- When utilizing a marinade that contains honey, sugar, and different other options, brush the marinade blend onto meat partially through cooking time to avoid burning.
- When dehydrating and air frying, organize food in a layer to guarantee proper cooking and crispier impact.
- Food cooks faster when using the Air Roast function. Therefore, if you are utilizing the customary oven plans, bring down the cooking time and temperature.
- Unlike other air fryer ovens, the unit preheats rapidly, ensuring that you have arranged all fixings and prepared to cook before preheating the Ninja Foodi Digital Air Fry Oven. When you had preheated the oven, the clock begins checking down. Essentially turn the dial to add additional time.

Chapter 1 Breakfasts

Fried Potatoes with Peppers and Onions

Prep time: 10 minutes | Cook time: 35 minutes | Serves 4

1 pound (454 g) red potatoes, cut into ½-inch dices
1 large red bell pepper, cut into ½-inch dices
1 large green bell pepper, cut into ½-inch dices
1 medium onion, cut into ½-inch dices
1½ tablespoons extra-virgin olive oil
1¼ teaspoons kosher salt
¾ teaspoon sweet paprika
¾ teaspoon garlic powder
Freshly ground black pepper, to taste

1. Mix together the potatoes, bell peppers, onion, oil, salt, paprika, garlic powder, and black pepper in a large mixing and toss to coat.
2. Transfer the potato mixture to the air fryer basket.
3. Put the air fryer basket on sheet pan and place into oven. Select Air Fry, set temperature to 350ºF (180ºC) and set time to 35 minutes.
4. Stir the potato mixture three times during cooking.
5. When done, the potatoes should be nicely browned.
6. Remove from the oven to a plate and serve warm.

Asparagus and Cheese Strata

Prep time: 10 minutes | Cook time: 17 minutes | Serves 4

6 asparagus spears, cut into 2-inch pieces
1 tablespoon water
2 slices whole-wheat bread, cut into ½-inch cubes
4 eggs
3 tablespoons whole milk
2 tablespoons chopped flat-leaf parsley
½ cup grated Havarti or Swiss cheese
Pinch salt
Freshly ground black pepper, to taste
Cooking spray

1. Add the asparagus spears and 1 tablespoon of water in the sheet pan.
2. Place the sheet pan on wire rack and slide into oven. Select Bake, set temperature to 330ºF (166ºC) and set time to 4 minutes.
3. When cooking is complete, the asparagus spears will be crisp-tender.
4. Remove the asparagus from the pan and drain on paper towels.
5. Spritz the pan with cooking spray. Place the bread and asparagus in the pan.
6. Whisk together the eggs and milk in a medium mixing bowl until creamy. Fold in the parsley, cheese, salt, and pepper and stir to combine. Pour this mixture into the sheet pan.
7. Select Bake and set time to 13 minutes. Put the pan back to the oven. When done, the eggs will be set and the top will be lightly browned.
8. Let cool for 5 minutes before slicing and serving.

Carrot Banana Muffin

Prep time: 10 minutes | Cook time: 20 minutes | Serves 12

1½ cups whole-wheat flour
1 cup grated carrot
1 cup mashed banana
½ cup bran
½ cup low-fat buttermilk
2 tablespoons agave nectar
2 teaspoons baking powder
1 teaspoon vanilla
1 teaspoon baking soda
½ teaspoon nutmeg
Pinch cloves
2 egg whites

1. Line a muffin pan with 12 paper liners.
2. In a large bowl, stir together all the ingredients. Mix well, but do not over beat.
3. Scoop the mixture into the muffin cups.
4. Put the muffin pan on wire rack and place into oven. Select Bake, set temperature to 400ºF (205ºC) and set time to 20 minutes.
5. When cooking is complete, remove from the oven and let rest for 5 minutes.
6. Serve warm or at room temperature.

Breakfast Blueberry Cobbler

Prep time: 5 minutes | Cook time: 15 minutes | Serves 4

¾ teaspoon baking powder
⅓ cup whole-wheat pastry flour
Dash sea salt
⅓ cup unsweetened nondairy milk
2 tablespoons maple syrup
½ teaspoon vanilla
Cooking spray
½ cup blueberries
¼ cup granola
Nondairy yogurt, for topping (optional)

1. Spritz the sheet pan with cooking spray.
2. Mix together the baking powder, flour, and salt in a medium bowl. Add the milk, maple syrup, and vanilla and whisk to combine.
3. Scrape the mixture into the prepared pan. Scatter the blueberries and granola on top.
4. Place the sheet pan on wire rack and slide into oven. Select Bake, set temperature to 347ºF (175ºC) and set time to 15 minutes.
5. When done, the top should begin to brown and a knife inserted in the center should come out clean.
6. Let the cobbler cool for 5 minutes and serve with a drizzle of nondairy yogurt.

Egg and Avocado Burrito

Prep time: 10 minutes | Cook time: 4 minutes | Serves 4

4 low-sodium whole-wheat flour tortillas
Filling:
1 hard-boiled egg, chopped
2 hard-boiled egg whites, chopped
1 ripe avocado, peeled, pitted, and chopped
1 red bell pepper, chopped
1 (1.2-ounce / 34-g) slice
low-sodium, low-fat American cheese, torn into pieces
3 tablespoons low-sodium salsa, plus additional for serving (optional)

Special Equipment:
4 toothpicks (optional), soaked in water for at least 30 minutes

1. Make the filling: Combine the egg, egg whites, avocado, red bell pepper, cheese, and salsa in a medium

bowl and stir until blended.
2. Assemble the burritos: Arrange the tortillas on a clean work surface and place ¼ of the prepared filling in the middle of each tortilla, leaving about 1½-inch on each end unfilled. Fold in the opposite sides of each tortilla and roll up. Secure with toothpicks through the center, if needed.
3. Transfer the burritos to the air fryer basket.
4. Put the air fryer basket on sheet pan and place into oven. Select Air Fry, set temperature to 390ºF (199ºC) and set time to 4 minutes.
5. When cooking is complete, the burritos should be crisp and golden brown.
6. Allow to cool for 5 minutes and serve with salsa, if desired.

French Toast Sticks

Prep time: 5 minutes | Cook time: 12 minutes | Serves 4

3 slices low-sodium whole-wheat bread, each cut into 4 strips
1 tablespoon unsalted butter, melted
1 tablespoon 2 percent milk
1 tablespoon sugar
1 egg, beaten
1 egg white
1 cup sliced fresh strawberries
1 tablespoon freshly squeezed lemon juice

1. Arrange the bread strips on a plate and drizzle with the melted butter.
2. In a bowl, whisk together the milk, sugar, egg and egg white.
3. Dredge the bread strips into the egg mixture and place on a wire rack to let the batter drip off. Arrange half the coated bread strips in the air fryer basket.
4. Put the air fryer basket on sheet pan and place into oven. Select Air Fry, set temperature to 380ºF (193ºC) and set time to 6 minutes.
5. After 3 minutes, remove from the oven and turn the strips over. Return to the oven to continue cooking.
6. When cooking is complete, the strips should be golden brown. Repeat with the remaining strips.
7. In a small bowl, mash the strawberries with a fork and stir in the lemon juice. Serve the French toast sticks with the strawberry sauce.

Chicken Breakfast Sausages

Prep time: 15 minutes | Cook time: 10 minutes | Makes 8 patties

1 Granny Smith apple, peeled and finely chopped
2 tablespoons apple juice
2 garlic cloves, minced
1 egg white
⅓ cup minced onion
3 tablespoons ground almonds
⅛ teaspoon freshly ground black pepper
1 pound (454 g) ground chicken breast

1. Combine all the ingredients except the chicken in a medium mixing bowl and stir well.
2. Add the chicken breast to the apple mixture and mix with your hands until well incorporated.
3. Divide the mixture into 8 equal portions and shape into patties. Arrange the patties in the air fryer basket.
4. Put the air fryer basket on sheet pan and place into oven. Select Air Fry, set temperature to 330°F (166°C) and set time to 10 minutes.
5. When done, a meat thermometer inserted in the center of the chicken should reach at least 165°F (74°C).
6. Remove from the oven to a plate. Let the chicken cool for 5 minutes and serve warm.

Spicy Apple Turnovers

Prep time: 10 minutes | Cook time: 20 minutes | Serves 4

1 cup diced apple
1 tablespoon brown sugar
1 teaspoon freshly squeezed lemon juice
1 teaspoon all-purpose flour, plus more for dusting
¼ teaspoon cinnamon
⅛ teaspoon allspice
½ package frozen puff pastry, thawed
1 large egg, beaten
2 teaspoons granulated sugar

1. Whisk together the apple, brown sugar, lemon juice, flour, cinnamon and allspice in a medium bowl.
2. On a clean work surface, lightly dust with the flour and lay the puff pastry sheet. Using a rolling pin, gently roll the dough to smooth out the folds, seal any tears and form it into a square. Cut the dough into four squares.
3. Spoon a quarter of the apple mixture into the center of each puff pastry square and spread it evenly in a triangle shape over half the pastry, leaving a border of about ½ inch around the edges of the pastry. Fold the pastry diagonally over the filling to form triangles. With a fork, crimp the edges to seal them. Place the turnovers in the sheet pan, spacing them evenly.
4. Cut two or three small slits in the top of each turnover. Brush with the egg. Sprinkle evenly with the granulated sugar.
5. Place the sheet pan on wire rack and slide into oven. Select Bake, set temperature to 350°F (180°C) and set time to 20 minutes.
6. When cooking is complete, remove the pan from the oven. The turnovers should be golden brown and the filling bubbling. Let cool for about 10 minutes before serving.

Cheesy Artichoke-Mushroom Frittata

Prep time: 10 minutes | Cook time: 15 minutes | Serves 6

8 eggs
½ teaspoon kosher salt
¼ cup whole milk
¾ cup shredded Mozzarella cheese, divided
2 tablespoons unsalted butter, melted
1 cup coarsely chopped artichoke hearts
¼ cup chopped onion
½ cup mushrooms
¼ cup grated Parmesan cheese
¼ teaspoon freshly ground black pepper

1. In a medium bowl, whisk together the eggs and salt. Let rest for a minute or two, then pour in the milk and whisk again. Stir in ½ cup of the Mozzarella cheese.
2. Grease the sheet pan with the butter. Stir in the artichoke hearts and onion and toss to coat with the butter.
3. Place the sheet pan on wire rack and slide into oven. Select Air Roast, set temperature to 375°F (190°C) and set time to 12 minutes.
4. After 5 minutes, remove from the oven. Spread the mushrooms over the vegetables. Pour the egg mixture on top. Stir gently just to distribute the vegetables evenly. Return the pan to the oven and continue cooking for 5 to 7 minutes, or until the edges are set. The center will still be quite liquid.
5. Select Air Broil, set temperature to Low and set time to 3 minutes. After 1 minute, remove the pan and sprinkle the remaining ¼ cup of the Mozzarella and Parmesan cheese over the frittata. Return the pan to the oven and continue cooking for 2 minutes.
6. When cooking is complete, the cheese should be melted with the top completely set but not browned. Sprinkle the black pepper on top and serve.

Chapter 1: Breakfasts | 7

Egg Florentine with Spinach

Prep time: 10 minutes | Cook time: 15 minutes | Serves 4

3 cups frozen spinach, thawed and drained
2 tablespoons heavy cream
¼ teaspoon kosher salt
⅛ teaspoon freshly ground black pepper
4 ounces (113 g) Ricotta cheese
2 garlic cloves, minced
½ cup panko bread crumbs
3 tablespoons grated Parmesan cheese
2 teaspoons unsalted butter, melted
4 large eggs

1. In a medium bowl, whisk together the spinach, heavy cream, salt, pepper, Ricotta cheese and garlic.
2. In a small bowl, whisk together the bread crumbs, Parmesan cheese and butter. Set aside.
3. Spoon the spinach mixture into the sheet pan and form four even circles.
4. Place the sheet pan on wire rack and slide into oven. Select Air Roast, set temperature to 375ºF (190ºC) and set time to 15 minutes.
5. After 8 minutes, remove the pan. The spinach should be bubbling. With the back of a large spoon, make indentations in the spinach for the eggs. Crack the eggs into the indentations and sprinkle the panko mixture over the surface of the eggs.
6. Return the pan to the oven and continue cooking.
7. When cooking is complete, remove the pan from the oven. Serve hot.

All-in-One Toast

Prep time: 10 minutes | Cook time: 10 minutes | Serves 1

1 strip bacon, diced
1 slice 1-inch thick bread
1 egg
Salt and freshly ground black pepper, to taste
¼ cup grated Colby cheese

1. Preheat the air fryer oven to 400ºF (204ºC).
2. Put the bacon in the air fryer basket.
3. Put the air fryer basket on sheet pan and place into oven. Select Air Fry and set time to 3 minutes, shaking the basket once or twice while it cooks.
4. Remove the bacon to a paper towel-lined plate and set aside.

5. Use a sharp paring knife to score a large circle in the middle of the slice of bread, cutting halfway through, but not all the way through to the cutting board. Press down on the circle in the center of the bread slice to create an indentation.
6. Transfer the slice of bread, hole-side up, to the air fryer basket. Crack the egg into the center of the bread, and season with salt and pepper.
7. Reduce the temperature to 380ºF (193ºC) and air fry for 5 minutes. Sprinkle the grated cheese around the edges of the bread, leaving the center of the yolk uncovered, and top with the cooked bacon. Press the cheese and bacon into the bread lightly.
8. Air fry for 1 or 2 more minutes, just to melt the cheese and finish cooking the egg. Serve immediately.

Whole-Wheat Blueberry Scones

Prep time: 5 minutes | Cook time: 20 minutes | Serves 14

½ cup low-fat buttermilk
¾ cup orange juice
Zest of 1 orange
2¼ cups whole-wheat pastry flour
⅓ cup agave nectar
¼ cup canola oil
1 teaspoon baking soda
1 teaspoon cream of tartar
1 cup fresh blueberries

1. In a small bowl, stir together the buttermilk, orange juice and orange zest.
2. In a large bowl, whisk together the flour, agave nectar, canola oil, baking soda and cream of tartar.
3. Add the buttermilk mixture and blueberries to the bowl with the flour mixture. Mix gently by hand until well combined.
4. Transfer the batter onto a lightly floured sheet pan. Pat into a circle about ¾ inch thick and 8 inches across. Use a knife to cut the circle into 14 wedges, cutting almost all the way through.
5. Place the sheet pan on wire rack and slide into oven. Select Bake, set temperature to 375ºF (190ºC) and set time to 20 minutes.
6. When cooking is complete, remove the pan and check the scones. They should be lightly browned.
7. Let rest for 5 minutes and cut completely through the wedges before serving.

8 | Chapter 1: Breakfasts

Mini Brown Rice Quiches

Prep time: 10 minutes | Cook time: 14 minutes | Serves 6

4 ounces (113 g) diced green chilies
3 cups cooked brown rice
1 cup shredded reduced-fat Cheddar cheese, divided
½ cup egg whites
⅓ cup fat-free milk
¼ cup diced pimiento
½ teaspoon cumin
1 small eggplant, cubed
1 bunch fresh cilantro, finely chopped
Cooking spray

1. Spritz a 12-cup muffin pan with cooking spray.
2. In a large bowl, stir together all the ingredients, except for ½ cup of the cheese.
3. Scoop the mixture evenly into the muffin cups and sprinkle the remaining ½ cup of the cheese on top.
4. Put the muffin pan on wire rack and slide into oven. Select Bake, set temperature to 400ºF (205ºC) and set time to 14 minutes.
5. When cooking is complete, remove from the oven and check the quiches. They should be set.
6. Carefully transfer the quiches to a platter and serve immediately.

Scotch Eggs

Prep time: 5 minutes | Cook time: 25 minutes | Serves 4

4 large hard boiled eggs
1 (12-ounce / 340-g)
package pork sausage
8 slices thick-cut bacon

Special Equipment:
4 wooden toothpicks, soaked in water for at least 30 minutes

1. Slice the sausage into four parts and place each part into a large circle.
2. Put an egg into each circle and wrap it in the sausage. Put in the refrigerator for 1 hour.
3. Preheat the air fryer oven to 450ºF (235ºC).
4. Make a cross with two pieces of thick-cut bacon. Put a wrapped egg in the center, fold the bacon over top of the egg, and secure with a toothpick. Transfer to the air fryer basket.
5. Put the air fryer basket on sheet pan and place into oven. Select Air Fry and set time to 25 minutes.
6. Serve immediately.

Whole-Wheat Muffins with Blueberries

Prep time: 5 minutes | Cook time: 25 minutes | Makes 8 muffins

½ cup unsweetened applesauce
½ cup plant-based milk
½ cup maple syrup
1 teaspoon vanilla extract
2 cups whole-wheat flour
½ teaspoon baking soda
1 cup blueberries
Cooking spray

1. Spritz a 8-cup muffin pan with cooking spray.
2. In a large bowl, stir together the applesauce, milk, maple syrup and vanilla extract. Whisk in the flour and baking soda until no dry flour is left and the batter is smooth. Gently mix in the blueberries until they are evenly distributed throughout the batter.
3. Spoon the batter into the muffin cups, three-quarters full.
4. Put the muffin pan on wire rack and slide into oven. Select Bake, set temperature to 375ºF (190ºC) and set time to 25 minutes.
5. When cooking is complete, remove from the oven and check the muffins. You can stick a knife into the center of a muffin and it should come out clean.
6. Let rest for 5 minutes before serving.

Baked Avocado with Eggs

Prep time: 5 minutes | Cook time: 9 minutes | Serves 2

1 large avocado, halved and pitted
2 large eggs
2 tomato slices, divided
½ cup nonfat Cottage cheese, divided
½ teaspoon fresh cilantro, for garnish

1. Line the sheet pan with aluminium foil.
2. Slice a thin piece from the bottom of each avocado half so they sit flat. Remove a small amount from each avocado half to make a bigger hole to hold the egg.
3. Arrange the avocado halves on the pan, hollow-side up. Break 1 egg into each half. Top each half with 1 tomato slice and ¼ cup of the Cottage cheese.
4. Place the sheet pan on wire rack and slide into oven. Select Bake, set temperature to 425ºF (220ºC) and set time to 9 minutes.
5. When cooking is complete, remove the pan from the oven. Garnish with the fresh cilantro and serve.

Chapter 1: Breakfasts | 9

Creamy Cinnamon Rolls

Prep time: 10 minutes | Cook time: 9 minutes | Serves 8

1 pound (454 g) frozen bread dough, thawed
¼ cup butter, melted
¾ cup brown sugar
1½ tablespoons ground cinnamon
Cream Cheese Glaze:
4 ounces (113 g) cream cheese, softened
2 tablespoons butter, softened
1¼ cups powdered sugar
½ teaspoon vanilla extract

1. Let the bread dough come to room temperature on the counter. On a lightly floured surface, roll the dough into a 13-inch by 11-inch rectangle. Position the rectangle so the 13-inch side is facing you. Brush the melted butter all over the dough, leaving a 1-inch border uncovered along the edge farthest away from you.
2. Combine the brown sugar and cinnamon in a small bowl. Sprinkle the mixture evenly over the buttered dough, keeping the 1-inch border uncovered. Roll the dough into a log, starting with the edge closest to you. Roll the dough tightly, rolling evenly, and push out any air pockets. When you get to the uncovered edge of the dough, press the dough onto the roll to seal it together.
3. Cut the log into 8 pieces, slicing slowly with a sawing motion so you don't flatten the dough. Turn the slices on their sides and cover with a clean kitchen towel. Let the rolls sit in the warmest part of the kitchen for 1½ to 2 hours to rise.
4. To make the glaze, place the cream cheese and butter in a microwave-safe bowl. Soften the mixture in the microwave for 30 seconds at a time until it is easy to stir. Gradually add the powdered sugar and stir to combine. Add the vanilla extract and whisk until smooth. Set aside.
5. When the rolls have risen, preheat the air fryer oven to 350°F (177°C).
6. Transfer the rolls to the air fryer basket.
7. Put the air fryer basket on sheet pan and place into oven. Select Air Fry and set time to 5 minutes.
8. Turn the rolls over and air fry for another 4 minutes.
9. Let the rolls cool for 2 minutes before glazing. Spread large dollops of cream cheese glaze on top of the warm cinnamon rolls, allowing some glaze to drip down the side of the rolls. Serve warm.

Sweet Banana Bread Pudding

Prep time: 10 minutes | Cook time: 18 minutes | Serves 4

2 medium ripe bananas, mashed
½ cup low-fat milk
2 tablespoons maple syrup
2 tablespoons peanut butter
1 teaspoon vanilla extract
Cooking spray
1 teaspoon ground cinnamon
2 slices whole-grain bread, torn into bite-sized pieces
¼ cup quick oats

1. Spritz the sheet pan with cooking spray.
2. In a large bowl, combine the bananas, milk, maple syrup, peanut butter, vanilla extract and cinnamon. Use an immersion blender to mix until well combined.
3. Stir in the bread pieces to coat well. Add the oats and stir until everything is combined.
4. Transfer the mixture to the sheet pan. Cover with the aluminum foil.
5. Put the sheet pan into oven. Select Air Fry, set temperature to 375°F (190°C) and set time to 18 minutes.
6. After 10 minutes, remove the foil and continue to cook for 8 minutes.
7. Serve immediately.

Spinach with Scrambled Eggs

Prep time: 10 minutes | Cook time: 10 minutes | Serves 2

2 tablespoons olive oil
4 eggs, whisked
5 ounces (142 g) fresh spinach, chopped
1 medium tomato, chopped
1 teaspoon fresh lemon
juice
½ teaspoon coarse salt
½ teaspoon ground black pepper
½ cup of fresh basil, roughly chopped

1. Preheat the air fryer oven to 280°F (138°C). Grease a sheet pan with the oil.
2. In the pan, mix the remaining ingredients, except for the basil leaves, whisking well until everything is completely combined.
3. Put the sheet pan on wire rack and slide into the oven. Select Bake and set time to 10 minutes.
4. Top with fresh basil leaves before serving.

Potatoes Lyonnaise

Prep time: 10 minutes | Cook time: 31 minutes | Serves 4

1 Vidalia onion, sliced
1 teaspoon butter, melted
1 teaspoon brown sugar
2 large russet potatoes
(about 1 pound / 454 g in
total), sliced ½-inch thick
1 tablespoon vegetable oil
Salt and freshly ground
black pepper, to taste

1. Preheat the air fryer oven to 370ºF (188ºC).
2. Toss the sliced onions, melted butter and brown sugar together in the air fryer basket.
3. Put the air fryer basket on sheet pan and place into oven. Select Air Fry and set time to 8 minutes, shaking the basket occasionally to help the onions cook evenly.
4. While the onions are cooking, bring a saucepan of salted water to a boil on the stovetop. Par-cook the potatoes in boiling water for 3 minutes. Drain the potatoes and pat them dry with a clean kitchen towel.
5. Add the potatoes to the onions in the air fryer basket and drizzle with vegetable oil. Toss to coat the potatoes with the oil and season with salt and freshly ground black pepper.
6. Increase the temperature to 400ºF (204ºC) and air fry for 20 minutes, tossing the vegetables a few times during the cooking time to help the potatoes brown evenly.
7. Season with salt and freshly ground black pepper and serve warm.

Apple and Walnut Muffins

Prep time: 15 minutes | Cook time: 10 minutes | Makes 8 muffins

1 cup flour
⅓ cup sugar
1 teaspoon baking powder
¼ teaspoon baking soda
¼ teaspoon salt
1 teaspoon cinnamon
¼ teaspoon ginger
¼ teaspoon nutmeg
1 egg
2 tablespoons pancake
syrup, plus 2 teaspoons
2 tablespoons melted
butter, plus 2 teaspoons
¾ cup unsweetened
applesauce
½ teaspoon vanilla extract
¼ cup chopped walnuts
¼ cup diced apple

1. Preheat the air fryer oven to 330ºF (166ºC).
2. In a large bowl, stir together the flour, sugar, baking powder, baking soda, salt, cinnamon, ginger, and nutmeg.
3. In a small bowl, beat egg until frothy. Add syrup, butter, applesauce, and vanilla and mix well.
4. Pour egg mixture into dry ingredients and stir just until moistened.
5. Gently stir in nuts and diced apple.
6. Divide batter among 8 parchment paper-lined muffin cups. Place the muffin cups in a sheet pan.
7. Put the sheet pan on wire rack and slide into the oven. Select Bake and set time to 10 minutes, or until a toothpick inserted in the center comes out clean.
8. Serve warm.

Avocado Quesadillas

Prep time: 10 minutes | Cook time: 11 minutes | Serves 4

4 eggs
2 tablespoons skim milk
Salt and ground black pepper, to taste
Cooking spray
4 flour tortillas
4 tablespoons salsa
2 ounces (57 g) Cheddar cheese, grated
½ small avocado, peeled and thinly sliced

1. Preheat the air fryer oven to 270ºF (132ºC).
2. Beat together the eggs, milk, salt, and pepper.
3. Spray a sheet pan lightly with cooking spray and add egg mixture.
4. Put the sheet pan on wire rack and slide into the oven. Select Bake and set time to 8 minutes, stirring every 1 to 2 minutes, or until eggs are scrambled to the liking. Remove and set aside.
5. Spray one side of each tortilla with cooking spray. Flip over.
6. Divide eggs, salsa, cheese, and avocado among the tortillas, covering only half of each tortilla.
7. Fold each tortilla in half and press down lightly. Increase the temperature to 390ºF (199ºC). Put the tortillas in air fryer basket.
8. Put the air fryer basket on sheet pan and place into oven. Select Air Fry and set time to 3 minutes, or until cheese melts and outside feels slightly crispy.
9. Cut each cooked tortilla into halves. Serve warm.

Kale and Potato Nuggets

Prep time: 10 minutes | Cook time: 18 minutes | Serves 4

1 teaspoon extra virgin olive oil
1 clove garlic, minced
4 cups kale, rinsed and chopped
2 cups potatoes, boiled and
mashed
⅛ cup milk
Salt and ground black pepper, to taste
Cooking spray

1. Preheat the air fryer oven to 390°F (199°C).
2. In a skillet over medium heat, sauté the garlic in the olive oil, until it turns golden brown. Sauté with the kale for an additional 3 minutes and remove from the heat.
3. Mix the mashed potatoes, kale and garlic in a bowl. Pour in the milk and sprinkle with salt and pepper.
4. Shape the mixture into nuggets and spritz with cooking spray. Put them in the air fryer basket.
5. Put the air fryer basket on sheet pan and place into oven. Select Air Fry and set time to 15 minutes, flipping the nuggets halfway through to make sure the nuggets fry evenly.
6. Serve immediately.

Ham and Corn Muffins

Prep time: 10 minutes | Cook time: 6 minutes | Makes 8 muffins

¾ cup yellow cornmeal
¼ cup flour
1½ teaspoons baking powder
¼ teaspoon salt
1 egg, beaten
2 tablespoons canola oil
½ cup milk
½ cup shredded sharp Cheddar cheese
½ cup diced ham

1. Preheat the air fryer oven to 390°F (199°C).
2. In a medium bowl, stir together the cornmeal, flour, baking powder, and salt.
3. Add the egg, oil, and milk to dry ingredients and mix well.
4. Stir in shredded cheese and diced ham.
5. Divide batter among 8 parchment paper-lined muffin cups. Place the muffin cups in a sheet pan.
6. Put the sheet pan on wire rack and slide into the oven. Select Bake and set time to 5 minutes.

7. Reduce the temperature to 330°F (166°C) and bake for 1 minute, or until a toothpick inserted in the center of the muffin comes out clean.
8. Serve warm.

Lush Vegetable Omelet

Prep time: 10 minutes | Cook time: 13 minutes | Serves 2

2 teaspoons and freshly ground black pepper, to
taste

1. Preheat the air fryer oven to 350°F (177°C).
2. Grease a sheet pan with canola oil.
3. Put the remaining ingredients in the sheet pan and stir well.
4. Put the sheet pan on wire rack and slide into the oven. Select Bake and set time to 13 minutes.
5. Serve warm.

Blueberry Cake

Prep time: 5 minutes | Cook time: 10 minutes | Serves 8

1½ cups Bisquick
¼ cup granulated sugar
2 large eggs, beaten
¾ cup whole milk
1 teaspoon vanilla extract
½ teaspoon lemon zest
Cooking spray
2 cups blueberries

1. Stir together the Bisquick and sugar in a medium bowl. Stir together the eggs, milk, vanilla and lemon zest. Add the wet ingredients to the dry ingredients and stir until well combined.
2. Spritz the sheet pan with cooking spray and line with parchment paper, pressing it into place. Spray the parchment paper with cooking spray. Pour the batter into the pan and spread it out evenly. Sprinkle the blueberries evenly over the top.
3. Place the sheet pan on wire rack and slide into oven. Select Bake, set temperature to 375°F (190°C) and set time to 10 minutes.
4. When cooking is complete, the cake should be pulling away from the edges of the pan and the top should be just starting to turn golden brown.
5. Let the cake rest for a minute before cutting into 16 squares. Serve immediately.

Mushroom and Squash Toast

Prep time: 10 minutes | Cook time: 10 minutes | Serves 4

1 tablespoon olive oil
1 red bell pepper, cut into strips
2 green onions, sliced
1 cup sliced button or cremini mushrooms
1 small yellow squash, sliced
2 tablespoons softened butter
4 slices bread
½ cup soft goat cheese

1. Preheat the air fryer oven to 350ºF (177ºC). Grease the air fryer basket with the olive oil.
2. Put the red pepper, green onions, mushrooms, and squash in the air fryer basket, stirring well.
3. Put the air fryer basket on sheet pan and place into oven. Select Air Fry and set time to 7 minutes, or the vegetables are tender, shaking the basket once throughout the cooking time.
4. Remove the vegetables and set them aside.
5. Spread the butter on the slices of bread and transfer to the air fryer basket, butter-side up.
6. Return to the oven and air fry for 3 minutes more.
7. Remove the toast and top with goat cheese and vegetables. Serve warm.

Banana Bread

Prep time: 10 minutes | Cook time: 22 minutes | Makes 3 loaves

3 ripe bananas, mashed
1 cup sugar
1 large egg
4 tablespoons (½ stick)
unsalted butter, melted
1½ cups all-purpose flour
1 teaspoon baking soda
1 teaspoon salt

1. Preheat the air fryer oven to 310ºF (154ºC).
2. Coat the insides of 3 mini loaf pans with cooking spray.
3. In a large mixing bowl, mix the bananas and sugar.
4. In a separate large mixing bowl, combine the egg, butter, flour, baking soda, and salt and mix well.
5. Add the banana mixture to the egg and flour mixture. Mix well.
6. Divide the batter evenly among the prepared pans.
7. Put the pans on wire rack and slide into oven. Select Bake and set time to 22 minutes. Insert a toothpick into the center of each loaf; if it comes out clean, they are done.
8. When the loaves are cooked through, remove the pans from the oven. Turn out the loaves onto a wire rack to cool.
9. Serve warm.

Grit and Ham Fritters

Prep time: 15 minutes | Cook time: 20 minutes | Serves 6 to 8

4 cups water
1 cup quick-cooking grits
¼ teaspoon salt
2 tablespoons butter
2 cups grated Cheddar cheese, divided
1 cup finely diced ham
1 tablespoon chopped chives
Salt and freshly ground black pepper, to taste
1 egg, beaten
2 cups panko bread crumbs
Cooking spray

1. Bring the water to a boil in a saucepan. Whisk in the grits and ¼ teaspoon of salt, and cook for 7 minutes until the grits are soft. Remove the pan from the heat and stir in the butter and 1 cup of the grated Cheddar cheese. Transfer the grits to a bowl and let them cool for 10 to 15 minutes.
2. Stir the ham, chives and the rest of the cheese into the grits and season with salt and pepper to taste. Add the beaten egg and refrigerate the mixture for 30 minutes.
3. Put the panko bread crumbs in a shallow dish. Measure out ¼-cup portions of the grits mixture and shape them into patties. Coat all sides of the patties with the panko bread crumbs, patting them with the hands so the crumbs adhere to the patties. You should have about 16 patties. Spritz both sides of the patties with cooking spray.
4. Preheat the air fryer oven to 400ºF (204ºC).
5. Working in batches, arrange the patties in the air fryer basket.
6. Put the air fryer basket on sheet pan and place into oven. Select Air Fry and set time to 8 minutes.
7. Using a flat spatula, flip the fritters over and air fry for another 4 minutes.
8. Serve hot.

Chapter 2   Vegetables

Ratatouille

Prep time: 10 minutes | Cook time: 12 minutes | Serves 6

1 medium zucchini, sliced ½-inch thick
1 small eggplant, peeled and sliced ½-inch thick
2 teaspoons kosher salt, divided
4 tablespoons extra-virgin olive oil, divided
3 garlic cloves, minced
1 small onion, chopped
1 small red bell pepper, cut into ½-inch chunks
1 small green bell pepper, cut into ½-inch chunks
½ teaspoon dried oregano
¼ teaspoon freshly ground black pepper
1 pint cherry tomatoes
2 tablespoons minced fresh basil
1 cup panko bread crumbs
½ cup grated Parmesan cheese (optional)

1. Season one side of the zucchini and eggplant slices with ¾ teaspoon of salt. Put the slices, salted side down, on a rack set over a baking sheet. Sprinkle the other sides with ¾ teaspoon of salt. Allow to sit for 10 minutes, or until the slices begin to exude water. When ready, rinse and dry them. Cut the zucchini slices into quarters and the eggplant slices into eighths.
2. Pour the zucchini and eggplant into a large bowl, along with 2 tablespoons of olive oil, garlic, onion, bell peppers, oregano, and black pepper. Toss to coat well. Arrange the vegetables in the air fryer basket.
3. Put the air fryer basket on sheet pan and place into oven. Select Air Roast, set temperature to 375°F (190°C), and set time to 12 minutes.
4. Meanwhile, add the tomatoes and basil to the large bowl. Sprinkle with the remaining ½ teaspoon of salt and 1 tablespoon of olive oil. Toss well and set aside.
5. Stir together the remaining 1 tablespoon of olive oil, panko, and Parmesan cheese (if desired) in a small bowl.
6. After 6 minutes, remove from the oven and add the tomato mixture and stir to mix well. Scatter the panko mixture on top. Return to the oven and continue cooking for 6 minutes, or until the vegetables are softened and the topping is golden brown.
7. Cool for 5 minutes before serving.

Zucchini Crisps

Prep time: 5 minutes | Cook time: 14 minutes | Serves 4

2 zucchini, sliced into ¼- to ½-inch-thick rounds (about 2 cups)
¼ teaspoon garlic granules
⅛ teaspoon sea salt
Freshly ground black pepper, to taste (optional)
Cooking spray

1. Spritz the air fryer basket with cooking spray.
2. Put the zucchini rounds in the basket, spreading them out as much as possible. Top with a sprinkle of garlic granules, sea salt, and black pepper (if desired). Spritz the zucchini rounds with cooking spray.
3. Put the air fryer basket on sheet pan and place into oven. Select Air Roast, set temperature to 392°F (200°C), and set time to 14 minutes.
4. Flip the zucchini rounds halfway through.
5. When cooking is complete, the zucchini rounds should be crisp-tender. Remove from the oven. Let them rest for 5 minutes and serve.

Golden Garlicky Mushrooms

Prep time: 10 minutes | Cook time: 10 minutes | Serves 4

6 small mushrooms
1 tablespoon bread crumbs
1 tablespoon olive oil
1 ounce (28 g) onion, peeled and diced
1 teaspoon parsley
1 teaspoon garlic purée
Salt and ground black pepper, to taste

1. Preheat the air fryer oven to 350°F (177°C).
2. Combine the bread crumbs, oil, onion, parsley, salt, pepper and garlic in a bowl. Cut out the mushrooms' stalks and stuff each cap with the crumb mixture. Transfer to the air fryer basket.
3. Put the air fryer basket on sheet pan and place into oven. Select Air Fry and set time to 10 minutes.
4. Serve hot.

Mushroom and Pepper Pizza Squares

Prep time: 10 minutes | Cook time: 10 minutes | Serves 10

1 pizza dough, cut into squares
1 cup chopped oyster mushrooms
1 shallot, chopped
¼ red bell pepper, chopped
2 tablespoons parsley
Salt and ground black pepper, to taste

1. Preheat the air fryer oven to 400ºF (204ºC).
2. In a bowl, combine the oyster mushrooms, shallot, bell pepper and parsley. Sprinkle some salt and pepper as desired.
3. Spread this mixture on top of the pizza squares, then transfer to a sheet pan.
4. Put the sheet pan on wire rack and slide into the oven. Select Bake and set time to 10 minutes.
5. Serve warm.

Cinnamon Celery Roots

Prep time: 10 minutes | Cook time: 20 minutes | Serves 4

2 celery roots, peeled and diced
1 teaspoon extra-virgin olive oil
1 teaspoon butter, melted
½ teaspoon ground cinnamon
Sea salt and freshly ground black pepper, to taste

1. Line the sheet pan with aluminum foil.
2. Toss the celery roots with the olive oil in a large bowl until well coated. Transfer them to the prepared sheet pan.
3. Place the sheet pan on wire rack and slide into oven. Select Air Roast, set temperature to 350ºF (180ºC), and set time to 20 minutes.
4. When done, the celery roots should be very tender. Remove from the oven to a serving bowl. Stir in the butter and cinnamon and mash them with a potato masher until fluffy.
5. Season with salt and pepper to taste. Serve immediately.

Spicy Kung Pao Tofu

Prep time: 10 minutes | Cook time: 10 minutes | Serves 4

⅓ cup Asian-Style sauce
1 teaspoon cornstarch
½ teaspoon red pepper flakes, or more to taste
1 pound (454 g) firm or extra-firm tofu, cut into 1-inch cubes
1 small carrot, peeled and
cut into ¼-inch-thick coins
1 small green bell pepper, cut into bite-size pieces
3 scallions, sliced, whites and green parts separated
3 tablespoons roasted unsalted peanuts

1. In a large bowl, whisk together the sauce, cornstarch, and red pepper flakes. Fold in the tofu, carrot, pepper, and the white parts of the scallions and toss to coat. Spread the mixture evenly in the sheet pan.
2. Place the sheet pan on wire rack and slide into oven. Select Air Roast, set temperature to 375ºF (190ºC), and set time to 10 minutes.
3. Stir the ingredients once halfway through the cooking time.
4. When done, remove from the oven. Serve sprinkled with the peanuts and scallion greens.

Maple and Pecan Granola

Prep time: 5 minutes | Cook time: 20 minutes | Serves 4

1½ cups rolled oats
¼ cup maple syrup
¼ cup pecan pieces
1 teaspoon vanilla extract
½ teaspoon ground cinnamon

1. Line a baking sheet with parchment paper.
2. Mix together the oats, maple syrup, pecan pieces, vanilla, and cinnamon in a large bowl and stir until the oats and pecan pieces are completely coated. Spread the mixture evenly in the sheet pan.
3. Place the sheet pan on wire rack and slide into oven. Select Bake, set temperature to 300ºF (150ºC), and set time to 20 minutes.
4. Stir once halfway through the cooking time.
5. When done, remove from the oven and cool for 30 minutes before serving. The granola may still be a bit soft right after removing, but it will gradually firm up as it cools.

Chapter 2: Vegetables 15

Lemony Brussels Sprouts and Tomatoes

Prep time: 15 minutes | Cook time: 20 minutes | Serves 4

1 pound (454 g) Brussels sprouts, trimmed and halved
1 tablespoon extra-virgin olive oil
Sea Salt and freshly ground
black pepper, to taste
½ cup sun-dried tomatoes, chopped
2 tablespoons freshly squeezed lemon juice
1 teaspoon lemon zest

1. Line the air fryer basket with aluminum foil.
2. Toss the Brussels sprouts with the olive oil in a large bowl. Sprinkle with salt and black pepper.
3. Spread the Brussels sprouts in a single layer in the basket.
4. Put the air fryer basket on sheet pan and place into oven. Select Air Roast, set temperature to 400°F (205°C), and set time to 20 minutes.
5. When done, the Brussels sprouts should be caramelized. Remove from the oven to a serving bowl, along with the tomatoes, lemon juice, and lemon zest. Toss to combine. Serve immediately.

Sweet and Spicy Broccoli

Prep time: 10 minutes | Cook time: 15 to 20 minutes | Serves 4

½ teaspoon olive oil, plus more for greasing
1 pound (454 g) fresh
Sauce:
1½ tablespoons soy sauce
2 teaspoons hot sauce or sriracha
1½ teaspoons honey
broccoli, cut into florets
½ tablespoon minced garlic
Salt, to taste

1 teaspoon white vinegar
Freshly ground black pepper, to taste

1. Grease the air fryer basket with olive oil.
2. Add the broccoli florets, ½ teaspoon of olive oil, and garlic to a large bowl and toss well. Season with salt to taste.
3. Put the broccoli in the basket in a single layer.
4. Put the air fryer basket on sheet pan and place into oven. Select Air Fry, set temperature to 400°F (205°C), and set time to 15 minutes.

5. Stir the broccoli florets three times during cooking.
6. Meanwhile, whisk together all the ingredients for the sauce in a small bowl until well incorporated. If the honey doesn't incorporate well, microwave the sauce for 10 to 20 seconds until the honey is melted.
7. When cooking is complete, the broccoli should be lightly browned and crispy. Continue cooking for 5 minutes, if desired. Remove from the oven to a serving bowl. Pour over the sauce and toss to combine. Add more salt and pepper, if needed. Serve warm.

Stuffed Peppers with Beans and Rice

Prep time: 10 minutes | Cook time: 18 minutes | Serves 4

4 medium red, green, or yellow bell peppers, halved and deseeded
4 tablespoons extra-virgin olive oil, divided
½ teaspoon kosher salt, divided
1 (15-ounce / 425-g) can chickpeas
1½ cups cooked white rice
½ cup diced roasted red peppers
¼ cup chopped parsley
½ small onion, finely chopped
3 garlic cloves, minced
½ teaspoon cumin
¼ teaspoon freshly ground black pepper
¾ cup panko bread crumbs

1. Brush the peppers inside and out with 1 tablespoon of olive oil. Season the insides with ¼ teaspoon of kosher salt. Arrange the peppers in the air fryer basket, cut side up.
2. Place the chickpeas with their liquid into a large bowl. Lightly mash the beans with a potato masher. Sprinkle with the remaining ¼ teaspoon of kosher salt and 1 tablespoon of olive oil. Add the rice, red peppers, parsley, onion, garlic, cumin, and black pepper to the bowl and stir to incorporate.
3. Divide the mixture among the bell pepper halves.
4. Stir together the remaining 2 tablespoons of olive oil and panko in a small bowl. Top the pepper halves with the panko mixture.
5. Put the air fryer basket on sheet pan and place into oven. Select Air Roast, set temperature to 375°F (190°C), and set time to 18 minutes.
6. When done, the peppers should be slightly wrinkled, and the panko should be golden brown.
7. Remove from the oven and serve on a plate.

Spicy Thai-Style Vegetables

Prep time: 10 minutes | Cook time: 8 minutes | Serves 4

1 small head Napa cabbage, shredded, divided
1 medium carrot, cut into thin coins
8 ounces (227 g) snow peas
1 red or green bell pepper, sliced into thin strips
1 tablespoon vegetable oil
2 tablespoons soy sauce
1 tablespoon sesame oil
2 tablespoons brown sugar
2 tablespoons freshly squeezed lime juice
2 teaspoons red or green Thai curry paste
1 serrano chile, deseeded and minced
1 cup frozen mango slices, thawed
½ cup chopped roasted peanuts or cashews

1. Put half the Napa cabbage in a large bowl, along with the carrot, snow peas, and bell pepper. Drizzle with the vegetable oil and toss to coat. Spread them evenly in the air fryer basket.
2. Put the air fryer basket on sheet pan and place into oven. Select Air Roast, set temperature to 375ºF (190ºC), and set time to 8 minutes.
3. Meanwhile, whisk together the soy sauce, sesame oil, brown sugar, lime juice, and curry paste in a small bowl.
4. When done, the vegetables should be tender and crisp. Remove from the oven and put the vegetables back into the bowl. Add the chile, mango slices, and the remaining cabbage. Pour over the dressing and toss to coat. Top with the roasted nuts and serve.

Cheesy Broccoli Tots

Prep time: 20 minutes | Cook time: 15 minutes | Serves 4

12 ounces (340 g) frozen broccoli, thawed, drained, and patted dry
1 large egg, lightly beaten
½ cup seasoned whole-wheat bread crumbs
¼ cup shredded reduced-fat
sharp Cheddar cheese
¼ cup grated Parmesan cheese
1½ teaspoons minced garlic
Salt and freshly ground black pepper, to taste
Cooking spray

1. Spritz the air fryer basket lightly with cooking spray.
2. Place the remaining ingredients into a food processor and process until the mixture resembles a coarse meal.

Transfer the mixture to a bowl.
3. Using a tablespoon, scoop out the broccoli mixture and form into 24 oval "tater tot" shapes with your hands.
4. Put the tots in the prepared basket in a single layer, spacing them 1 inch apart. Mist the tots lightly with cooking spray.
5. Put the air fryer basket on sheet pan and place into oven. Select Air Fry, set temperature to 375ºF (190ºC), and set time to 15 minutes.
6. Flip the tots halfway through the cooking time.
7. When done, the tots will be lightly browned and crispy. Remove from the oven and serve on a plate.

Sweet Potatoes with Zucchini

Prep time: 20 minutes | Cook time: 20 minutes | Serves 4

2 large-sized sweet potatoes, peeled and quartered
1 medium zucchini, sliced
1 Serrano pepper, deseeded and thinly sliced
1 bell pepper, deseeded and thinly sliced
1 to 2 carrots, cut into matchsticks
¼ cup olive oil
1½ tablespoons maple
syrup
½ teaspoon porcini powder
¼ teaspoon mustard powder
½ teaspoon fennel seeds
1 tablespoon garlic powder
½ teaspoon fine sea salt
¼ teaspoon ground black pepper
Tomato ketchup, for serving

1. Preheat the air fryer oven to 350ºF (177ºC).
2. Put the sweet potatoes, zucchini, peppers, and the carrot into the air fryer basket. Coat with a drizzling of olive oil.
3. Put the air fryer basket on sheet pan and place into oven. Select Air Fry and set time to 15 minutes.
4. In the meantime, prepare the sauce by vigorously combining the other ingredients, except for the tomato ketchup, with a whisk.
5. Lightly grease a baking dish.
6. Transfer the cooked vegetables to the baking dish, pour over the sauce and coat the vegetables well.
7. Increase the temperature to 390ºF (199ºC) and air fry the vegetables for an additional 5 minutes.
8. Serve warm with a side of ketchup.

Chapter 2: Vegetables 17

Paprika Cauliflower

Prep time: 10 minutes | Cook time: 20 minutes | Serves 4

1 large head cauliflower, broken into small florets
2 teaspoons smoked paprika

1 teaspoon garlic powder
Salt and freshly ground black pepper, to taste
Cooking spray

1. Spray the air fryer basket with cooking spray.
2. In a medium bowl, toss the cauliflower florets with the smoked paprika and garlic powder until evenly coated. Sprinkle with salt and pepper.
3. Place the cauliflower florets in the basket and lightly mist with cooking spray.
4. Put the air fryer basket on sheet pan and place into oven. Select Air Fry, set temperature to 400°F (205°C), and set time to 20 minutes.
5. Stir the cauliflower four times during cooking.
6. Remove the cauliflower from the oven and serve hot.

Cream Cheese Stuffed Bell Peppers

Prep time: 5 minutes | Cook time: 15 minutes | Serves 2

2 bell peppers, tops and seeds removed
Salt and pepper, to taste
⅔ cup cream cheese

2 tablespoons mayonnaise
1 tablespoon chopped fresh celery stalks
Cooking spray

1. Spritz the air fryer basket with cooking spray.
2. Place the peppers in the air fryer basket.
3. Put the air fryer basket on sheet pan and place into oven. Select Air Roast, set temperature to 400°F (205°C) and set time to 10 minutes.
4. Flip the peppers halfway through.
5. When cooking is complete, the peppers should be crisp-tender.
6. Remove from the oven to a plate and season with salt and pepper.
7. Mix the cream cheese, mayo, and celery in a small bowl and stir to incorporate. Evenly stuff the roasted peppers with the cream cheese mixture with a spoon. Serve immediately.

Stuffed Portobellos with Peppers and Cheese

Prep time: 15 minutes | Cook time: 15 minutes | Serves 4

4 tablespoons sherry vinegar or white wine vinegar
6 garlic cloves, minced, divided
1 tablespoon fresh thyme leaves
1 teaspoon Dijon mustard
1 teaspoon kosher salt, divided
¼ cup plus 3¼ teaspoons extra-virgin olive oil, divided

8 portobello mushroom caps, each about 3 inches across, patted dry
1 small red or yellow bell pepper, thinly sliced
1 small green bell pepper, thinly sliced
1 small onion, thinly sliced
¼ teaspoon red pepper flakes
Freshly ground black pepper, to taste
4 ounces (113 g) shredded Fontina cheese

1. Stir together the vinegar, 4 minced garlic cloves, thyme, mustard, and ½ teaspoon of kosher salt in a small bowl. Slowly pour in ¼ cup of olive oil, whisking constantly, or until an emulsion is formed. Reserve 2 tablespoons of the marinade and set aside.
2. Put the mushrooms in a resealable plastic bag and pour in the marinade. Seal and shake the bag, coating the mushrooms in the marinade. Transfer the mushrooms to the sheet pan, gill-side down.
3. Put the remaining 2 minced garlic cloves, bell peppers, onion, red pepper flakes, remaining ½ teaspoon of salt, and black pepper in a medium bowl. Drizzle with the remaining 3¼ teaspoons of olive oil and toss well. Transfer the bell pepper mixture to the pan.
4. Place the sheet pan on wire rack and slide into oven. Select Air Roast, set temperature to 375°F (190°C), and set time to 12 minutes.
5. After 7 minutes, remove the pan and stir the peppers and flip the mushrooms. Return the pan to the oven and continue cooking for 5 minutes.
6. Remove from the oven and place the pepper mixture onto a cutting board and coarsely chop.
7. Brush both sides of the mushrooms with the reserved 2 tablespoons marinade. Stuff the caps evenly with the pepper mixture. Scatter the cheese on top.
8. Select Air Broil, set temperature to High, and set time to 3 minutes.
9. When done, the mushrooms should be tender and the cheese should be melted.
10. Serve warm.

Cheese-Walnut Stuffed Mushrooms

Prep time: 5 minutes | Cook time: 10 minutes | Serves 4

4 large portobello mushrooms
1 tablespoon canola oil
½ cup shredded Mozzarella cheese
⅓ cup minced walnuts
2 tablespoons chopped fresh parsley
Cooking spray

1. Spritz the air fryer basket with cooking spray.
2. On a clean work surface, remove the mushroom stems. Scoop out the gills with a spoon and discard. Coat the mushrooms with canola oil. Top each mushroom evenly with the shredded Mozzarella cheese, followed by the minced walnuts.
3. Arrange the mushrooms in the basket.
4. Put the air fryer basket on sheet pan and place into oven. Select Air Roast, set temperature to 350°F (180°C) and set time to 10 minutes.
5. When cooking is complete, the mushroom should be golden brown.
6. Transfer the mushrooms to a plate and sprinkle the parsley on top for garnish before serving.

Cheesy Rice and Olives Stuffed Peppers

Prep time: 5 minutes | Cook time: 16 to 17 minutes | Serves 4

4 red bell peppers, tops sliced off
2 cups cooked rice
1 cup crumbled feta cheese
1 onion, chopped
¼ cup sliced kalamata olives
¾ cup tomato sauce
1 tablespoon Greek seasoning
Salt and black pepper, to taste
2 tablespoons chopped fresh dill, for serving

1. Microwave the red bell peppers for 1 to 2 minutes until tender.
2. When ready, transfer the red bell peppers to a plate to cool.
3. Mix the cooked rice, feta cheese, onion, kalamata olives, tomato sauce, Greek seasoning, salt, and pepper in a medium bowl and stir until well combined.
4. Divide the rice mixture among the red bell peppers and transfer to a greased sheet pan.
5. Place the sheet pan on wire rack and slide into oven. Select Bake, set temperature to 360°F (182°C) and set time to 15 minutes.
6. When cooking is complete, the rice should be heated through and the vegetables should be soft.
7. Remove from the oven and serve with the dill sprinkled on top.

Chermoula Beet

Prep time: 15 minutes | Cook time: 25 minutes | Serves 4

Chermoula:

1 cup packed fresh cilantro leaves
½ cup packed fresh parsley leaves
6 cloves garlic, peeled
2 teaspoons smoked paprika
2 teaspoons ground cumin
1 teaspoon ground coriander
½ to 1 teaspoon cayenne pepper
Pinch of crushed saffron (optional)
½ cup extra-virgin olive oil
Kosher salt, to taste

Beets:

3 medium beets, trimmed, peeled, and cut into 1-inch chunks
2 tablespoons chopped
fresh cilantro
2 tablespoons chopped fresh parsley

1. In a food processor, combine the cilantro, parsley, garlic, paprika, cumin, coriander, and cayenne. Pulse until coarsely chopped. Add the saffron, if using, and process until combined. With the food processor running, slowly add the olive oil in a steady stream; process until the sauce is uniform. Season with salt.
2. Preheat the air fryer oven to 375°F (191°C).
3. In a large bowl, drizzle the beets with ½ cup of the chermoula to coat. Arrange the beets in the air fryer basket.
4. Put the air fryer basket on sheet pan and place into oven. Select Air Fry and set time to 25 minutes, or until the beets are tender.
5. Transfer the beets to a serving platter. Sprinkle with the chopped cilantro and parsley and serve.

Chapter 2: Vegetables 19

Stuffed Portobello Mushrooms with Vegetables

Prep time: 5 minutes | Cook time: 8 minutes | Serves 4

4 portobello mushrooms, stem removed
1 tablespoon olive oil
1 tomato, diced
½ green bell pepper, diced
½ small red onion, diced
½ teaspoon garlic powder
Salt and black pepper, to taste
½ cup grated Mozzarella cheese

1. Using a spoon to scoop out the gills of the mushrooms and discard them. Brush the mushrooms with the olive oil.
2. In a mixing bowl, stir together the remaining ingredients except the Mozzarella cheese. Using a spoon to stuff each mushroom with the filling and scatter the Mozzarella cheese on top.
3. Arrange the mushrooms in the air fryer basket.
4. Put the air fryer basket on sheet pan and place into oven. Select Air Roast, set temperature to 330°F (166°C) and set time to 8 minutes.
5. When cooking is complete, the cheese should be melted.
6. Serve warm.

Ratatouille

Prep time: 20 minutes | Cook time: 25 minutes | Serves 4

1 sprig basil
1 sprig flat-leaf parsley
1 sprig mint
1 tablespoon coriander powder
1 teaspoon capers
½ lemon, juiced
Salt and ground black pepper, to taste
2 eggplants, sliced crosswise
2 red onions, chopped
4 cloves garlic, minced
2 red peppers, sliced crosswise
1 fennel bulb, sliced crosswise
3 large zucchinis, sliced crosswise
5 tablespoons olive oil
4 large tomatoes, chopped
2 teaspoons herbs de Provence

1. Blend the basil, parsley, coriander, mint, lemon juice and capers, with a little salt and pepper. Make sure all ingredients are well incorporated.
2. Preheat the air fryer oven to 400°F (204°C).
3. Coat the eggplant, onions, garlic, peppers, fennel, and zucchini with olive oil.
4. Transfer the vegetables into a baking dish and top with the tomatoes and herb purée. Sprinkle with more salt and pepper, and the herbs de Provence.
5. Place the baking dish on wire rack and slide into oven. Select Bake and set time to 25 minutes.
6. Serve immediately.

Potatoes with Zucchinis

Prep time: 10 minutes | Cook time: 45 minutes | Serves 4

2 potatoes, peeled and cubed
4 carrots, cut into chunks
1 head broccoli, cut into florets
4 zucchinis, sliced thickly
Salt and ground black pepper, to taste
¼ cup olive oil
1 tablespoon dry onion powder

1. Preheat the air fryer oven to 400°F (204°C).
2. In a baking dish, add all the ingredients and combine well.
3. Place the baking dish on wire rack and slide into oven. Select Bake and set time to 45 minutes, or until the vegetables are soft and the sides have browned. Serve warm.

Air Fried Vegetables

Prep time: 15 minutes | Cook time: 20 minutes | Serves 6

1⅓ cups small parsnips, peeled and cubed
1⅓ cups celery
2 red onions, sliced
1⅓ cups small butternut squash, cut in half,
deseeded and cubed
1 tablespoon fresh thyme
1 tablespoon olive oil
Salt and ground black pepper, to taste

1. Preheat the air fryer oven to 390°F (199°C).
2. Combine the vegetables with the thyme, olive oil, salt and pepper. Put the vegetables in the air fryer basket.
3. Put the air fryer basket on sheet pan and place into oven. Select Air Fry and set time to 20 minutes, stirring once during cooking, until the vegetables are nicely browned and cooked through.
4. Serve warm.

Potato and Broccoli with Tofu Scramble

Prep time: 15 minutes | Cook time: 30 minutes | Serves 3

2½ cups chopped red potato
2 tablespoons olive oil, divided
1 block tofu, chopped finely
2 tablespoons tamari
1 teaspoon turmeric powder
½ teaspoon onion powder
½ teaspoon garlic powder
½ cup chopped onion
4 cups broccoli florets

1. Preheat the air fryer oven to 400°F (204°C).
2. Toss together the potatoes and 1 tablespoon of the olive oil, then transfer to a baking dish.
3. Place the baking dish on wire rack and slide into oven. Select Bake and set time to 15 minutes. Stir the potatoes once during cooking.
4. Combine the tofu, the remaining 1 tablespoon of the olive oil, turmeric, onion powder, tamari, and garlic powder together, stirring in the onions, followed by the broccoli.
5. Top the potatoes with the tofu mixture and bake for an additional 15 minutes. Serve warm.

Balsamic Brussels Sprouts

Prep time: 5 minutes | Cook time: 13 minutes | Serves 2

2 cups Brussels sprouts, halved
1 tablespoon olive oil
1 tablespoon balsamic vinegar
1 tablespoon maple syrup
¼ teaspoon sea salt

1. Preheat the air fryer oven to 375°F (191°C).
2. Evenly coat the Brussels sprouts with the olive oil, balsamic vinegar, maple syrup, and salt. Transfer to the air fryer basket.
3. Put the air fryer basket on sheet pan and place into oven. Select Air Fry and set time to 5 minutes.
4. Give the basket a good shake, increase the temperature to 400°F (204°C) and continue to air fry for another 8 minutes.
5. Serve hot.

Lush Summer Rolls

Prep time: 15 minutes | Cook time: 15 minutes | Serves 4

1 cup shiitake mushroom, sliced thinly
1 celery stalk, chopped
1 medium carrot, shredded
½ teaspoon finely chopped ginger
1 teaspoon sugar
1 tablespoon soy sauce
1 teaspoon nutritional yeast
8 spring roll sheets
1 teaspoon corn starch
2 tablespoons water

1. Preheat the air fryer oven to 400°F (204°C).
2. In a bowl, combine the ginger, soy sauce, nutritional yeast, carrots, celery, mushroom, and sugar.
3. Mix the cornstarch and water to create an adhesive for the spring rolls.
4. Scoop a tablespoonful of the vegetable mixture into the middle of the spring roll sheets. Brush the edges of the sheets with the cornstarch adhesive and enclose around the filling to make spring rolls. Arrange the rolls in the air fryer basket.
5. Put the air fryer basket on sheet pan and place into oven. Select Air Fry and set time to 15 minutes, or until crisp.
6. Serve hot.

Super Veg Rolls

Prep time: 20 minutes | Cook time: 10 minutes | Serves 6

2 potatoes, mashed
¼ cup peas
¼ cup mashed carrots
1 small cabbage, sliced
¼ cups beans
2 tablespoons sweetcorn
1 small onion, chopped
½ cup bread crumbs
1 packet spring roll sheets
½ cup cornstarch slurry

1. Preheat the air fryer oven to 390°F (199°C).
2. Boil all the vegetables in water over a low heat. Rinse and allow to dry.
3. Unroll the spring roll sheets and spoon equal amounts of vegetable onto the center of each one. Fold into spring rolls and coat each one with the slurry and bread crumbs. Transfer to the air fryer basket.
4. Put the air fryer basket on sheet pan and place into oven. Select Air Fry and set time to 10 minutes.
5. Serve warm.

Chapter 2: Vegetables 21

Sweet Potatoes with Tofu

Prep time: 15 minutes | Cook time: 35 minutes | Serves 8

8 sweet potatoes, scrubbed
2 tablespoons olive oil
1 large onion, chopped
2 green chilies, deseeded and chopped
8 ounces (227 g) tofu, crumbled
2 tablespoons Cajun seasoning
1 cup chopped tomatoes
1 can kidney beans, drained and rinsed
Salt and ground black pepper, to taste

1. Preheat the air fryer oven to 400ºF (204ºC).
2. With a knife, pierce the skin of the sweet potatoes and transfer to the air fryer basket.
3. Put the air fryer basket on sheet pan and place into oven. Select Air Fry and set time to 30 minutes, or until soft.
4. Remove from the oven, halve each potato, and set to one side.
5. Over a medium heat, fry the onions and chilies in the olive oil in a skillet for 2 minutes until fragrant.
6. Add the tofu and Cajun seasoning and air fry for a further 3 minutes before incorporating the kidney beans and tomatoes. Sprinkle some salt and pepper as desire.
7. Top each sweet potato halve with a spoonful of the tofu mixture and serve.

Cauliflower, Chickpea, and Avocado Mash

Prep time: 10 minutes | Cook time: 25 minutes | Serves 4

1 medium head cauliflower, cut into florets
1 can chickpeas, drained and rinsed
1 tablespoon extra-virgin olive oil
2 tablespoons lemon juice
Salt and ground black pepper, to taste
4 flatbreads, toasted
2 ripe avocados, mashed

1. Preheat the air fryer oven to 425ºF (218ºC).
2. In a bowl, mix the chickpeas, cauliflower, lemon juice and olive oil. Sprinkle salt and pepper as desired. Transfer to the air fryer basket.
3. Put the air fryer basket on sheet pan and place into oven. Select Air Fry and set time to 25 minutes.
4. Spread on top of the flatbread along with the mashed avocado. Sprinkle with more pepper and salt and serve.

Basmati Risotto

Prep time: 10 minutes | Cook time: 30 minutes | Serves 2

1 onion, diced
1 small carrot, diced
2 cups vegetable broth, boiling
½ cup grated Cheddar cheese
1 clove garlic, minced
¾ cup long-grain basmati rice
1 tablespoon olive oil
1 tablespoon unsalted butter

1. Preheat the air fryer oven to 390ºF (199ºC).
2. Grease a baking tin with oil and stir in the butter, garlic, carrot, and onion.
3. Place the baking tin on wire rack and slide into oven. Select Bake and set time to 4 minutes.
4. Pour in the rice and bake for a further 4 minutes, stirring three times during cooking.
5. Reduce the temperature to 320ºF (160ºC).
6. Add the vegetable broth and give the dish a gentle stir. Bake, uncovered, for 22 minutes.
7. Pour in the cheese, stir once more and serve.

Creamy and Cheesy Spinach

Prep time: 10 minutes | Cook time: 15 minutes | Serves 4

Vegetable oil spray
1 (10-ounce / 283-g) package frozen spinach, thawed and squeezed dry
½ cup chopped onion
2 cloves garlic, minced
4 ounces (113 g) cream
cheese, diced
½ teaspoon ground nutmeg
1 teaspoon kosher salt
1 teaspoon black pepper
½ cup grated Parmesan cheese

1. Preheat the air fryer oven to 350ºF (177ºC). Spray a heatproof pan with vegetable oil spray.
2. In a medium bowl, combine the spinach, onion, garlic, cream cheese, nutmeg, salt, and pepper. Transfer to the prepared pan.
3. Place the pan on wire rack and slide into oven. Select Bake and set time to 10 minutes.
4. Stir, sprinkle the Parmesan cheese on top, and bake for 5 minutes, or until the cheese has melted and browned.
5. Serve hot.

Mediterranean Air Fried Veggies

Prep time: 10 minutes | Cook time: 6 minutes | Serves 4

1 large zucchini, sliced
1 cup cherry tomatoes, halved
1 parsnip, sliced
1 green pepper, sliced
1 carrot, sliced
1 teaspoon mixed herbs
1 teaspoon mustard
1 teaspoon garlic purée
6 tablespoons olive oil
Salt and ground black pepper, to taste

1. Preheat the air fryer oven to 400ºF (204ºC).
2. Combine all the ingredients in a bowl, making sure to coat the vegetables well. Transfer to the air fryer basket.
3. Put the air fryer basket on sheet pan and place into oven. Select Air Fry and set time to 6 minutes, ensuring the vegetables are tender and browned.
4. Serve immediately.

Rice and Eggplant Bowl

Prep time: 15 minutes | Cook time: 10 minutes | Serves 4

¼ cup sliced cucumber
1 teaspoon salt
1 tablespoon sugar
7 tablespoons Japanese rice vinegar
3 medium eggplants, sliced
3 tablespoons sweet white
miso paste
1 tablespoon mirin rice wine
4 cups cooked sushi rice
4 spring onions
1 tablespoon toasted sesame seeds

1. Coat the cucumber slices with the rice wine vinegar, salt, and sugar.
2. Put a dish on top of the bowl to weight it down completely.
3. In a bowl, mix the eggplants, mirin rice wine, and miso paste. Allow to marinate for half an hour.
4. Preheat the air fryer oven to 400ºF (204ºC).
5. Put the eggplant slices in the air fryer basket.
6. Put the air fryer basket on sheet pan and place into oven. Select Air Fry and set time to 10 minutes.
7. Fill the bottom of a serving bowl with rice and top with the eggplants and pickled cucumbers.
8. Add the spring onions and sesame seeds for garnish. Serve immediately.

Jalapeño Poppers

Prep time: 5 minutes | Cook time: 33 minutes | Serves 4

8 medium jalapeño peppers
5 ounces (142 g) cream cheese
¼ cup grated Mozzarella
cheese
½ teaspoon Italian seasoning mix
8 slices bacon

1. Preheat the air fryer oven to 400ºF (204ºC).
2. Cut the jalapeños in half.
3. Use a spoon to scrape out the insides of the peppers.
4. In a bowl, add together the cream cheese, Mozzarella cheese and Italian seasoning.
5. Pack the cream cheese mixture into the jalapeño halves and place the other halves on top.
6. Wrap each pepper in 1 slice of bacon, starting from the bottom and working up. Put the peppers in the air fryer basket.
7. Put the air fryer basket on sheet pan and place into oven. Select Air Fry and set time to 33 minutes.
8. Serve!

Black Bean and Tomato Chili

Prep time: 15 minutes | Cook time: 23 minutes | Serves 6

1 tablespoon olive oil
1 medium onion, diced
3 garlic cloves, minced
1 cup vegetable broth
3 cans black beans, drained and rinsed
2 cans diced tomatoes
2 chipotle peppers, chopped
2 teaspoons cumin
2 teaspoons chili powder
1 teaspoon dried oregano
½ teaspoon salt

1. Over a medium heat, fry the garlic and onions in the olive oil for 3 minutes.
2. Add the remaining ingredients, stirring constantly and scraping the bottom to prevent sticking.
3. Preheat the air fryer oven to 400ºF (204ºC).
4. Take a dish and place the mixture inside. Put a sheet of aluminum foil on top.
5. Place the dish on wire rack and slide into oven. Select Bake and set time to 20 minutes.
6. Serve immediately.

Mascarpone Mushrooms

Prep time: 10 minutes | Cook time: 15 minutes | Serves 4

Vegetable oil spray
4 cups sliced mushrooms
1 medium yellow onion, chopped
2 cloves garlic, minced
¼ cup heavy whipping cream or half-and-half
8 ounces (227 g) mascarpone cheese
1 teaspoon dried thyme
1 teaspoon kosher salt
1 teaspoon black pepper
½ teaspoon red pepper flakes
4 cups cooked konjac noodles, for serving
½ cup grated Parmesan cheese

1. Preheat the air fryer oven to 350ºF (177ºC). Spray a heatproof pan with vegetable oil spray.
2. In a medium bowl, combine the mushrooms, onion, garlic, cream, mascarpone, thyme, salt, black pepper, and red pepper flakes. Stir to combine. Transfer the mixture to the prepared pan.
3. Place the pan on wire rack and slide into oven. Select Bake and set time to 15 minutes, stirring halfway through the baking time.
4. Divide the pasta among four shallow bowls. Spoon the mushroom mixture evenly over the pasta. Sprinkle with Parmesan cheese and serve.

Gold Ravioli

Prep time: 10 minutes | Cook time: 6 minutes | Serves 4

½ cup panko bread crumbs
2 teaspoons nutritional yeast
1 teaspoon dried basil
1 teaspoon dried oregano
1 teaspoon garlic powder
Salt and ground black pepper, to taste
¼ cup aquafaba
8 ounces (227 g) ravioli
Cooking spray

1. Preheat the air fryer oven to 400ºF (204ºC). Line the air fryer basket with aluminum foil and lightly spray with cooking spray.
2. Combine the panko bread crumbs, nutritional yeast, basil, oregano, and garlic powder. Sprinkle with salt and pepper to taste.
3. Put the aquafaba in a separate bowl. Dip the ravioli in the aquafaba before coating it in the panko mixture. Spritz with cooking spray and transfer to the air fryer basket.
4. Put the air fryer basket on sheet pan and place into oven. Select Air Fry and set time to 6 minutes. Shake the basket halfway through the cooking time.
5. Serve hot.

Ricotta Potatoes

Prep time: 15 minutes | Cook time: 15 minutes | Serves 4

4 potatoes
2 tablespoons olive oil
½ cup Ricotta cheese, at room temperature
2 tablespoons chopped scallions
1 tablespoon roughly chopped fresh parsley
1 tablespoon minced coriander
2 ounces (57 g) Cheddar cheese, preferably freshly grated
1 teaspoon celery seeds
½ teaspoon salt
½ teaspoon garlic pepper

1. Preheat the air fryer oven to 350ºF (177ºC).
2. Pierce the skin of the potatoes with a knife, then transfer to the air fryer basket.
3. Put the air fryer basket on sheet pan and place into oven. Select Air Fry and set time to 13 minutes. If they are not cooked through by this time, leave for 2 to 3 minutes longer.
4. In the meantime, make the stuffing by combining all the other ingredients.
5. Cut halfway into the cooked potatoes to open them.
6. Spoon equal amounts of the stuffing into each potato and serve hot.

Spicy Cauliflower

Prep time: 15 minutes | Cook time: 20 minutes | Serves 4

Cauliflower:

5 cups cauliflower florets

3 tablespoons vegetable oil

½ teaspoon ground cumin

½ teaspoon ground coriander

½ teaspoon kosher salt

Sauce:

½ cup Greek yogurt or sour cream

¼ cup chopped fresh cilantro

1 jalapeño, coarsely chopped

4 cloves garlic, peeled

½ teaspoon kosher salt

2 tablespoons water

1. Preheat the air fryer oven to 400°F (204°C).
2. In a large bowl, combine the cauliflower, oil, cumin, coriander, and salt. Toss to coat.
3. Put the cauliflower in the air fryer basket. Put the air fryer basket on sheet pan and place into oven. Select Air Fry and set time to 20 minutes, stirring halfway through the cooking time.
4. Meanwhile, in a blender, combine the yogurt, cilantro, jalapeño, garlic, and salt. Blend, adding the water as needed to keep the blades moving and to thin the sauce.
5. Transfer the cauliflower to a large serving bowl. Pour the sauce over and toss gently to coat. Serve immediately.

Chapter 3　Fish and Seafood

Coconut Chili Fish Curry

Prep time: 10 minutes | Cook time: 22 minutes | Serves 4

2 tablespoons sunflower oil, divided
1 pound (454 g) fish, chopped
1 ripe tomato, pureéd
2 red chilies, chopped
1 shallot, minced
1 garlic clove, minced
1 cup coconut milk
1 tablespoon coriander powder
1 teaspoon red curry paste
½ teaspoon fenugreek seeds
Salt and white pepper, to taste

1. Coat the air fryer basket with 1 tablespoon of sunflower oil. Place the fish in the basket.
2. Put the air fryer basket on sheet pan and place into oven. Select Air Fry, set temperature to 380ºF (193ºC), and set time to 10 minutes.
3. Flip the fish halfway through the cooking time.
4. When cooking is complete, transfer the cooked fish to the sheet pan greased with the remaining 1 tablespoon of sunflower oil. Stir in the remaining ingredients.
5. Put the air fryer basket on sheet pan and place into oven. Select Air Fry, set temperature to 350ºF (180ºC), and set time to 12 minutes.
6. When cooking is complete, they should be heated through. Cool for 5 to 8 minutes before serving.

Spicy Orange Shrimp

Prep time: 40 minutes | Cook time: 12 minutes | Serves 4

⅓ cup orange juice
3 teaspoons minced garlic
1 teaspoon Old Bay seasoning
¼ to ½ teaspoon cayenne pepper
1 pound (454 g) medium shrimp, thawed, deveined, peeled, with tails off, and patted dry
Cooking.spray

1. Stir together the orange juice, garlic, Old Bay seasoning, and cayenne pepper in a medium bowl. Add the shrimp to the bowl and toss to coat well.
2. Cover the bowl with plastic wrap and marinate in the refrigerator for 30 minutes.
3. Spritz the air fryer basket with cooking spray. Place the shrimp in the pan and spray with cooking spray.
4. Put the air fryer basket on sheet pan and place into oven. Select Air Fry, set temperature to 400ºF (205ºC), and set time to 12 minutes.
5. Flip the shrimp halfway through the cooking time.
6. When cooked, the shrimp should be opaque and crisp. Remove from the oven and serve hot.

Garlic Shrimp with Parsley

Prep time: 10 minutes | Cook time: 5 minutes | Serves 4

18 shrimp, shelled and deveined
2 garlic cloves, peeled and minced
2 tablespoons extra-virgin olive oil
2 tablespoons freshly squeezed lemon juice
½ cup fresh parsley, coarsely chopped
1 teaspoon onion powder
1 teaspoon lemon-pepper seasoning
½ teaspoon hot paprika
½ teaspoon salt
¼ teaspoon cumin powder

1. Toss all the ingredients in a mixing bowl until the shrimp are well coated.
2. Cover and allow to marinate in the refrigerator for 30 minutes.
3. When ready, transfer the shrimp to the air fryer basket.
4. Put the air fryer basket on sheet pan and place into oven. Select Air Fry, set temperature to 400ºF (205ºC), and set time to 5 minutes.
5. When cooking is complete, the shrimp should be pink on the outside and opaque in the center. Remove from the oven and serve warm.

Seafood Spring Rolls

Prep time: 10 minutes | Cook time: 20 minutes | Serves 4

1 tablespoon olive oil	tiny shrimp, drained
2 teaspoons minced garlic	4 teaspoons soy sauce
1 cup matchstick cut carrots	Salt and freshly ground black pepper, to taste
2 cups finely sliced cabbage	16 square spring roll wrappers
2 (4-ounce / 113-g) cans	Cooking spray

1. Spray the air fryer basket with cooking spray. Set aside.
2. Heat the olive oil in a medium skillet over medium heat until it shimmers.
3. Add the garlic to the skillet and cook for 30 seconds. Stir in the cabbage and carrots and sauté for about 5 minutes, stirring occasionally, or until the vegetables are lightly tender.
4. Fold in the shrimp and soy sauce and sprinkle with salt and pepper, then stir to combine. Sauté for another 2 minutes, or until the moisture is evaporated. Remove from the heat and set aside to cool.
5. Put a spring roll wrapper on a work surface and spoon 1 tablespoon of the shrimp mixture onto the lower end of the wrapper.
6. Roll the wrapper away from you halfway, and then fold in the right and left sides, like an envelope. Continue to roll to the very end, using a little water to seal the edge. Repeat with the remaining wrappers and filling.
7. Place the spring rolls in the air fryer basket in a single layer, leaving space between each spring roll. Mist them lightly with cooking spray.
8. Put the air fryer basket on sheet pan and place into oven. Select Air Fry, set temperature to 375°F (190°C), and set time to 10 minutes.
9. Flip the rolls halfway through the cooking time.
10. When cooking is complete, the spring rolls will be heated through and start to brown. If necessary, continue cooking for 5 minutes more. Remove from the oven and cool for a few minutes before serving.

Caesar Shrimp Salad

Prep time: 10 minutes | Cook time: 15 minutes | Serves 4

½ baguette, cut into 1-inch cubes (about 2½ cups)	2 romaine lettuce hearts, cut in half lengthwise and ends trimmed
4 tablespoons extra-virgin olive oil, divided	1 pound (454 g) medium shrimp, peeled and deveined
¼ teaspoon granulated garlic	
¼ teaspoon kosher salt	2 ounces (57 g) Parmesan cheese, coarsely grated
¾ cup Caesar dressing, divided	

1. Make the croutons: Put the bread cubes in a medium bowl and drizzle 3 tablespoons of olive oil over top. Season with granulated garlic and salt and toss to coat. Transfer to the air fryer basket in a single layer.
2. Put the air fryer basket on sheet pan and place into oven. Select Air Fry, set temperature to 400°F (205°C), and set time to 4 minutes.
3. Toss the croutons halfway through the cooking time.
4. When done, remove from the oven and set aside.
5. Brush 2 tablespoons of Caesar dressing on the cut side of the lettuce. Set aside.
6. Toss the shrimp with the ¼ cup of Caesar dressing in a large bowl until well coated. Set aside.
7. Coat the sheet pan with the remaining 1 tablespoon of olive oil. Arrange the romaine halves on the coated pan, cut side down. Brush the tops with the remaining 2 tablespoons of Caesar dressing.
8. Place the sheet pan on wire rack and slide into oven. Select Air Roast, set temperature to 375°F (190°C), and set time to 10 minutes.
9. After 5 minutes, remove from the oven and flip the romaine halves. Spoon the shrimp around the lettuce. Return the pan to the oven and continue cooking.
10. When done, remove from the oven. If they are not quite cooked through, roast for another 1 minute.
11. On each of four plates, put a romaine half. Divide the shrimp among the plates and top with croutons and grated Parmesan cheese. Serve immediately.

Goat Cheese Shrimp

Prep time: 15 minutes | Cook time: 8 minutes | Serves 2

1 pound (454 g) shrimp, deveined
1½ tablespoons olive oil
1½ tablespoons balsamic vinegar
1 tablespoon coconut aminos
½ tablespoon fresh parsley, roughly chopped
Sea salt flakes, to taste
1 teaspoon Dijon mustard
½ teaspoon smoked cayenne pepper
½ teaspoon garlic powder
Salt and ground black peppercorns, to taste
1 cup shredded goat cheese

1. Except for the cheese, stir together all the ingredients in a large bowl until the shrimp are evenly coated.
2. Place the shrimp in the air fryer basket.
3. Put the air fryer basket on sheet pan and place into oven. Select Air Roast, set temperature to 385ºF (196ºC), and set time to 8 minutes.
4. When cooking is complete, the shrimp should be pink and cooked through. Remove from the oven and serve with the shredded goat cheese sprinkled on top.

Coconut-Crusted Prawns

Prep time: 15 minutes | Cook time: 8 minutes | Serves 4

12 prawns, cleaned and deveined
1 teaspoon fresh lemon juice
½ teaspoon cumin powder
Salt and ground black pepper, to taste
1 medium egg
⅓ cup beer
½ cup flour, divided
1 tablespoon curry powder
1 teaspoon baking powder
½ teaspoon grated fresh ginger
1 cup flaked coconut

1. In a large bowl, toss the prawns with the lemon juice, cumin powder, salt, and pepper until well coated. Set aside.
2. In a shallow bowl, whisk together the egg, beer, ¼ cup of flour, curry powder, baking powder, and ginger until combined.
3. In a separate shallow bowl, put the remaining ¼ cup of flour, and on a plate, place the flaked coconut.
4. Dip the prawns in the flour, then in the egg mixture,

finally roll in the flaked coconut to coat well. Transfer the prawns to air fryer basket.
5. Put the air fryer basket on sheet pan and place into oven. Select Air Fry, set temperature to 350ºF (180ºC), and set time to 8 minutes.
6. After 5 minutes, remove from the oven and flip the prawns. Return to the oven and continue cooking for 3 minutes more.
7. When cooking is complete, remove from the oven and serve warm.

Garlic-Butter Shrimp with Vegetables

Prep time: 10 minutes | Cook time: 15 minutes | Serves 4

1 pound (454 g) small red potatoes, halved
2 ears corn, shucked and cut into rounds, 1 to 1½ inches thick
2 tablespoons Old Bay or similar seasoning
½ cup unsalted butter, melted
1 (12- to 13-ounce / 340- to 369-g) package kielbasa or other smoked sausages
3 garlic cloves, minced
1 pound (454 g) medium shrimp, peeled and deveined

1. Place the potatoes and corn in a large bowl.
2. Stir together the butter and Old Bay seasoning in a small bowl. Drizzle half the butter mixture over the potatoes and corn, tossing to coat. Spread out the vegetables in the sheet pan.
3. Place the sheet pan on wire rack and slide into oven. Select Air Roast, set temperature to 350ºF (180ºC), and set time to 15 minutes.
4. Meanwhile, cut the sausages into 2-inch lengths, then cut each piece in half lengthwise. Put the sausages and shrimp in a medium bowl and set aside.
5. Add the garlic to the bowl of remaining butter mixture and stir well.
6. After 10 minutes, remove the pan and pour the vegetables into the large bowl. Drizzle with the garlic butter and toss until well coated. Arrange the vegetables, sausages, and shrimp in the pan.
7. Return to the oven and continue cooking. After 5 minutes, check the shrimp for doneness. The shrimp should be pink and opaque. If they are not quite cooked through, roast for an additional 1 minute.
8. When done, remove from the oven and serve on a plate.

Fired Shrimp with Mayonnaise Sauce

Prep time: 5 minutes | Cook time: 7 minutes | Serves 4

Shrimp
12 jumbo shrimp

Sauce:
4 tablespoons mayonnaise
1 teaspoon grated lemon rind

½ teaspoon garlic salt
¼ teaspoon freshly cracked mixed peppercorns

1 teaspoon Dijon mustard
1 teaspoon chipotle powder
½ teaspoon cumin powder

1. In a medium bowl, season the shrimp with garlic salt and cracked mixed peppercorns.
2. Place the shrimp in the air fryer basket.
3. Put the air fryer basket on sheet pan and place into oven. Select Air Fry, set temperature to 395°F (202°C), and set time to 7 minutes.
4. After 5 minutes, remove from the oven and flip the shrimp. Return to the oven and continue cooking for 2 minutes more, or until they are pink and no longer opaque.
5. Meanwhile, stir together all the ingredients for the sauce in a small bowl until well mixed.
6. When cooking is complete, remove the shrimp from the oven and serve alongside the sauce.

Paprika Shrimp

Prep time: 5 minutes | Cook time: 10 minutes | Serves 4

1 pound (454 g) tiger shrimp
2 tablespoons olive oil
½ tablespoon old bay seasoning

¼ tablespoon smoked paprika
¼ teaspoon cayenne pepper
A pinch of sea salt

1. Toss all the ingredients in a large bowl until the shrimp are evenly coated.
2. Arrange the shrimp in the air fryer basket.
3. Put the air fryer basket on sheet pan and place into oven. Select Air Fry, set temperature to 380°F (193°C), and set time to 10 minutes.
4. When cooking is complete, the shrimp should be pink and cooked through. Remove from the oven and serve hot.

Chili Prawns

Prep time: 10 minutes | Cook time: 8 minutes | Serves 2

8 prawns, cleaned
Salt and black pepper, to taste
½ teaspoon ground cayenne

pepper
½ teaspoon garlic powder
½ teaspoon ground cumin
½ teaspoon red chili flakes
Cooking spray

1. Spritz the air fryer basket with cooking spray.
2. Toss the remaining ingredients in a large bowl until the prawns are well coated.
3. Spread the coated prawns evenly in the basket and spray them with cooking spray.
4. Put the air fryer basket on sheet pan and place into oven. Select Air Fry, set temperature to 340°F (171°C), and set time to 8 minutes.
5. Flip the prawns halfway through the cooking time.
6. When cooking is complete, the prawns should be pink. Remove the prawns from the oven to a plate.

Shrimp and Vegetable Paella

Prep time: 5 minutes | Cook time: 16 minutes | Serves 4

1 (10-ounce / 284-g) package frozen cooked rice, thawed
1 (6-ounce / 170-g) jar artichoke hearts, drained and chopped
¼ cup vegetable broth

½ teaspoon dried thyme
½ teaspoon turmeric
1 cup frozen cooked small shrimp
½ cup frozen baby peas
1 tomato, diced

1. Mix together the cooked rice, chopped artichoke hearts, vegetable broth, thyme, and turmeric in the sheet pan and stir to combine.
2. Place the sheet pan on wire rack and slide into oven. Select Bake, set temperature to 340°F (171°C), and set time to 16 minutes.
3. After 9 minutes, remove from the oven and add the shrimp, baby peas, and diced tomato to the sheet pan. Mix well. Return the pan to the oven and continue cooking for 7 minutes more, or until the shrimp are done and the paella is bubbling.
4. When cooking is complete, remove from the oven. Cool for 5 minutes before serving.

Chapter 3: Fish and Seafood | 29

Herbed Scallops with Vegetables

Prep time: 15 minutes | Cook time: 9 minutes | Serves 4

1 cup frozen peas
1 cup green beans
1 cup frozen chopped broccoli
2 teaspoons olive oil
½ teaspoon dried oregano
½ teaspoon dried basil
12 ounces (340 g) sea scallops, rinsed and patted dry

1. Put the peas, green beans, and broccoli in a large bowl. Drizzle with the olive oil and toss to coat well. Transfer the vegetables to the air fryer basket.
2. Put the air fryer basket on sheet pan and place into oven. Select Air Fry, set temperature to 400°F (205°C), and set time to 5 minutes.
3. When cooking is complete, the vegetables should be fork-tender. Transfer the vegetables to a serving bowl. Scatter with the oregano and basil and set aside.
4. Place the scallops in the basket.
5. Put the air fryer basket on sheet pan and place into oven. Select Air Fry, set temperature to 400°F (205°C), and set time to 4 minutes.
6. When cooking is complete, the scallops should be firm and just opaque in the center. Remove from the oven to the bowl of vegetables and toss well. Serve warm.

Browned Shrimp Patties

Prep time: 15 minutes | Cook time: 12 minutes | Serves 4

½ pound (227 g) raw shrimp, shelled, deveined, and chopped finely
2 cups cooked sushi rice
¼ cup chopped red bell pepper
¼ cup chopped celery
¼ cup chopped green onion
2 teaspoons Worcestershire sauce
½ teaspoon salt
½ teaspoon garlic powder
½ teaspoon Old Bay seasoning
½ cup plain bread crumbs
Cooking spray

1. Put all the ingredients except the bread crumbs and oil in a large bowl and stir to incorporate.
2. Scoop out the shrimp mixture and shape into 8 equal-sized patties with your hands, no more than ½-inch thick. Roll the patties in the bread crumbs on a plate and spray both sides with cooking spray. Place the patties in the air fryer basket.
3. Put the air fryer basket on sheet pan and place into oven. Select Air Fry, set temperature to 390°F (199°C), and set time to 12 minutes.
4. Flip the patties halfway through the cooking time.
5. When cooking is complete, the outside should be crispy brown. Divide the patties among four plates and serve warm.

Crispy Crab and Fish Cakes

Prep time: 20 minutes | Cook time: 12 minutes | Serves 4

8 ounces (227 g) imitation crab meat
4 ounces (113 g) leftover cooked fish (such as cod, pollock, or haddock)
2 tablespoons minced celery
2 tablespoons minced green onion
2 tablespoons light mayonnaise
1 tablespoon plus 2 teaspoons Worcestershire
sauce
¾ cup crushed saltine cracker crumbs
2 teaspoons dried parsley flakes
1 teaspoon prepared yellow mustard
½ teaspoon garlic powder
½ teaspoon dried dill weed, crushed
½ teaspoon Old Bay seasoning
½ cup panko bread crumbs
Cooking spray

1. Pulse the crab meat and fish in a food processor until finely chopped.
2. Transfer the meat mixture to a large bowl, along with the celery, green onion, mayo, Worcestershire sauce, cracker crumbs, parsley flakes, mustard, garlic powder, dill weed, and Old Bay seasoning. Stir to mix well.
3. Scoop out the meat mixture and form into 8 equal-sized patties with your hands.
4. Place the panko bread crumbs on a plate. Roll the patties in the bread crumbs until they are evenly coated on both sides. Put the patties in the sheet pan and spritz them with cooking spray.
5. Place the sheet pan on wire rack and slide into oven. Select Bake, set temperature to 390°F (199°C), and set time to 12 minutes.
6. Flip the patties halfway through the cooking time.
7. When cooking is complete, they should be golden brown and cooked through. Remove the pan from the oven. Divide the patties among four plates and serve.

Shrimp and Cherry Tomato Kebabs

Prep time: 15 minutes | Cook time: 5 minutes | Serves 4

1½ pounds (680 g) jumbo shrimp, cleaned, shelled and deveined
1 pound (454 g) cherry tomatoes
2 tablespoons butter, melted
1 tablespoons Sriracha sauce
Sea salt and ground black pepper, to taste
1 teaspoon dried parsley flakes
½ teaspoon dried basil
½ teaspoon dried oregano
½ teaspoon mustard seeds
½ teaspoon marjoram

Special Equipment:
4 to 6 wooden skewers, soaked in water for 30 minutes

1. Put all the ingredients in a large bowl and toss to coat well.
2. Make the kebabs: Thread, alternating jumbo shrimp and cherry tomatoes, onto the wooden skewers. Place the kebabs in the air fryer basket.
3. Put the air fryer basket on sheet pan and place into oven. Select Air Fry, set temperature to 400ºF (205ºC), and set time to 5 minutes.
4. When cooking is complete, the shrimp should be pink and the cherry tomatoes should be softened. Remove from the oven. Let the shrimp and cherry tomato kebabs cool for 5 minutes and serve hot.

Panko Crab Sticks with Mayo Sauce

Prep time: 5 minutes | Cook time: 12 minutes | Serves 4

Crab Sticks:
2 eggs
1 cup flour
⅓ cup panko bread crumbs
1 tablespoon old bay
seasoning
1 pound (454 g) crab sticks
Cooking spray

Mayo Sauce:
½ cup mayonnaise
1 lime, juiced
2 garlic cloves, minced

1. In a bowl, beat the eggs. In a shallow bowl, place the flour. In another shallow bowl, thoroughly combine the panko bread crumbs and old bay seasoning.
2. Dredge the crab sticks in the flour, shaking off any excess, then in the beaten eggs, finally press them in the bread crumb mixture to coat well.
3. Arrange the crab sticks in the air fryer basket and spray with cooking spray.
4. Put the air fryer basket on sheet pan and place into oven. Select Air Fry, set temperature to 390ºF (199ºC), and set time to 12 minutes.
5. Flip the crab sticks halfway through the cooking time.
6. Meanwhile, make the sauce by whisking together the mayo, lime juice, and garlic in a small bowl.
7. When cooking is complete, remove from the oven. Serve the crab sticks with the mayo sauce on the side.

Crab Cakes with Bell Peppers

Prep time: 5 minutes | Cook time: 10 minutes | Serves 4

8 ounces (227 g) jumbo lump crab meat
1 egg, beaten
Juice of ½ lemon
⅓ cup bread crumbs
¼ cup diced green bell pepper
¼ cup diced red bell pepper
¼ cup mayonnaise
1 tablespoon Old Bay seasoning
1 teaspoon flour
Cooking spray

1. Make the crab cakes: Place all the ingredients except the flour and oil in a large bowl and stir until well incorporated.
2. Divide the crab mixture into four equal portions and shape each portion into a patty with your hands. Top each patty with a sprinkle of ¼ teaspoon of flour.
3. Arrange the crab cakes in the air fryer basket and spritz them with cooking spray.
4. Put the air fryer basket on sheet pan and place into oven. Select Air Fry, set temperature to 375ºF (190ºC), and set time to 10 minutes.
5. Flip the crab cakes halfway through.
6. When cooking is complete, the cakes should be cooked through. Remove from the oven and divide the crab cakes among four plates and serve.

Chapter 3: Fish and Seafood | 31

Lemony Shrimp

Prep time: 10 minutes | Cook time: 8 minutes | Serves 4

1 pound (454 g) shrimp, deveined
4 tablespoons olive oil
1½ tablespoons lemon juice
1½ tablespoons fresh parsley, roughly chopped
2 cloves garlic, finely minced
1 teaspoon crushed red pepper flakes, or more to taste
Garlic pepper, to taste
Sea salt flakes, to taste

1. Toss all the ingredients in a large bowl until the shrimp are coated on all sides.
2. Arrange the shrimp in the air fryer basket.
3. Put the air fryer basket on sheet pan and place into oven. Select Air Fry, set temperature to 385°F (196°C), and set time to 8 minutes.
4. When cooking is complete, the shrimp should be pink and cooked through. Remove from the oven and serve warm.

Easy Scallops

Prep time: 5 minutes | Cook time: 4 minutes | Serves 2

12 medium sea scallops, rinsed and patted dry
1 teaspoon fine sea salt
¾ teaspoon ground black pepper, plus more for garnish
Fresh thyme leaves, for garnish (optional)
Avocado oil spray

1. Coat the air fryer basket with avocado oil spray.
2. Place the scallops in a medium bowl and spritz with avocado oil spray. Sprinkle the salt and pepper to season.
3. Transfer the seasoned scallops to the basket, spacing them apart.
4. Put the air fryer basket on sheet pan and place into oven. Select Air Fry, set temperature to 390°F (199°C), and set time to 4 minutes.
5. Flip the scallops halfway through the cooking time.
6. When cooking is complete, the scallops should reach an internal temperature of just 145°F (63°C) on a meat thermometer. Sprinkle the pepper and thyme leaves on top for garnish, if desired. Serve immediately.

Piri-Piri King Prawns

Prep time: 10 minutes | Cook time: 8 minutes | Serves 2

12 king prawns, rinsed
1 tablespoon coconut oil
Salt and ground black pepper, to taste
1 teaspoon onion powder
1 teaspoon garlic paste
1 teaspoon curry powder
½ teaspoon piri piri powder
½ teaspoon cumin powder

1. Combine all the ingredients in a large bowl and toss until the prawns are completely coated. Place the prawns in the air fryer basket.
2. Put the air fryer basket on sheet pan and place into oven. Select Air Fry, set temperature to 360°F (182°C), and set time to 8 minutes.
3. Flip the prawns halfway through the cooking time.
4. When cooking is complete, the prawns will turn pink. Remove from the oven and serve hot.

Breaded Calamari with Lemon

Prep time: 5 minutes | Cook time: 12 minutes | Serves 4

2 large eggs
2 garlic cloves, minced
½ cup cornstarch
1 cup bread crumbs
1 pound (454 g) calamari rings
Cooking spray
1 lemon, sliced

1. In a small bowl, whisk the eggs with minced garlic. Place the cornstarch and bread crumbs into separate shallow dishes.
2. Dredge the calamari rings in the cornstarch, then dip in the egg mixture, shaking off any excess, finally roll them in the bread crumbs to coat well. Let the calamari rings sit for 10 minutes in the refrigerator.
3. Spritz the air fryer basket with cooking spray. Transfer the calamari rings to the basket.
4. Put the air fryer basket on sheet pan and place into oven. Select Air Fry, set temperature to 390°F (199°C), and set time to 12 minutes.
5. Stir the calamari rings once halfway through the cooking time.
6. When cooking is complete, remove from the oven. Serve the calamari rings with the lemon slices sprinkled on top.

Breaded Scallops

Prep time: 5 minutes | Cook time: 7 minutes | Serves 4

1 egg
3 tablespoons flour
1 cup bread crumbs
1 pound (454 g) fresh scallops
2 tablespoons olive oil
Salt and black pepper, to taste

1. In a bowl, lightly beat the egg. Place the flour and bread crumbs into separate shallow dishes.
2. Dredge the scallops in the flour and shake off any excess. Dip the flour-coated scallops in the beaten egg and roll in the bread crumbs.
3. Brush the scallops generously with olive oil and season with salt and pepper, to taste. Transfer the scallops to the air fryer basket.
4. Put the air fryer basket on sheet pan and place into oven. Select Air Fry, set temperature to 360°F (182°C), and set time to 7 minutes.
5. Flip the scallops halfway through the cooking time.
6. When cooking is complete, the scallops should reach an internal temperature of just 145°F (63°C) on a meat thermometer. Remove from the oven. Let the scallops cool for 5 minutes and serve.

Garlic Butter Shrimp Scampi

Prep time: 5 minutes | Cook time: 8 minutes | Serves 4

Sauce:
¼ cup unsalted butter
2 tablespoons fish stock or chicken broth
2 cloves garlic, minced
2 tablespoons chopped fresh basil leaves
Shrimp:
1 pound (454 g) large shrimp, peeled and deveined, tails removed
1 tablespoon lemon juice
1 tablespoon chopped fresh parsley, plus more for garnish
1 teaspoon red pepper flakes

Fresh basil sprigs, for garnish

1. Put all the ingredients for the sauce in the sheet pan and stir to incorporate.
2. Put the air fryer basket on sheet pan and place into oven. Select Air Fry, set temperature to 350°F (180°C), and set time to 8 minutes.
3. After 3 minutes, remove from the oven and add the shrimp to the sheet pan, flipping to coat in the sauce. Return to the oven and continue cooking for 5 minutes until the shrimp are pink and opaque. Stir the shrimp twice during cooking.
4. When cooking is complete, remove from the oven. Serve garnished with the parsley and basil sprigs.

Classic Shrimp Empanadas

Prep time: 10 minutes | Cook time: 8 minutes | Serves 5

½ pound (227g) raw shrimp, peeled, deveined and chopped
¼ cup chopped red onion
1 scallion, chopped
2 garlic cloves, minced
2 tablespoons minced red bell pepper
2 tablespoons chopped fresh cilantro
½ tablespoon fresh lime juice
¼ teaspoon sweet paprika
⅛ teaspoon kosher salt
⅛ teaspoon crushed red pepper flakes (optional)
1 large egg, beaten
10 frozen Goya Empanada Discos, thawed
Cooking spray

1. In a medium bowl, combine the shrimp, red onion, scallion, garlic, bell pepper, cilantro, lime juice, paprika, salt, and pepper flakes (if using).
2. In a small bowl, beat the egg with 1 teaspoon water until smooth.
3. Place an empanada disc on a work surface and put 2 tablespoons of the shrimp mixture in the center. Brush the outer edges of the disc with the egg wash. Fold the disc over and gently press the edges to seal. Use a fork and press around the edges to crimp and seal completely. Brush the tops of the empanadas with the egg wash.
4. Preheat the air fryer oven to 380°F (193°C). Spray the air fryer basket with cooking spray.
5. Arrange a single layer of the empanadas in the air fryer basket.
6. Put the air fryer basket on sheet pan and place into oven. Select Air Fry and set time to 8 minutes, flipping halfway through, or until golden brown and crispy. Serve hot.

Chapter 3: Fish and Seafood | 33

Bacon-Wrapped Scallops

Prep time: 5 minutes | Cook time: 10 minutes | Serves 4

8 slices bacon, cut in half
16 sea scallops, patted dry
Cooking spray
Salt and freshly ground
black pepper, to taste
16 toothpicks, soaked
in water for at least 30
minutes

1. On a clean work surface, wrap half of a slice of bacon around each scallop and secure with a toothpick.
2. Lay the bacon-wrapped scallops in the air fryer basket in a single layer.
3. Spritz the scallops with cooking spray and sprinkle the salt and pepper to season.
4. Put the air fryer basket on sheet pan and place into oven. Select Air Fry, set temperature to 370ºF (188ºC), and set time to 10 minutes.
5. Flip the scallops halfway through the cooking time.
6. When cooking is complete, the bacon should be cooked through and the scallops should be firm. Remove the scallops from the oven to a plate Serve warm.

Cajun-Style Fish Tacos

Prep time: 5 minutes | Cook time: 15 minutes | Serves 6

2 teaspoons avocado oil
1 tablespoon Cajun
seasoning
4 tilapia fillets
1 (14-ounce / 397-g)
package coleslaw mix
12 corn tortillas
2 limes, cut into wedges

1. Preheat the air fryer oven to 380ºF (193ºC). Line the air fryer basket with parchment paper.
2. In a medium, shallow bowl, mix the avocado oil and the Cajun seasoning to make a marinade. Add the tilapia fillets and coat evenly.
3. Place the fillets in the basket in a single layer, leaving room between each fillet.
4. Put the air fryer basket on sheet pan and place into oven. Select Air Fry and set time to 15 minutes, or until the fish is cooked and easily flakes with a fork.
5. Assemble the tacos by placing some of the coleslaw mix in each tortilla. Add ⅓ of a tilapia fillet to each tortilla. Squeeze some lime juice over the top of each taco and serve.

Tuna Patty Sliders

Prep time: 15 minutes | Cook time: 12 to 15 minutes | Serves 4

3 (5-ounce / 142-g) cans
tuna, packed in water
⅔ cup whole-wheat panko
bread crumbs
⅓ cup shredded Parmesan
cheese
1 tablespoon sriracha
¾ teaspoon black pepper
10 whole-wheat slider buns
Cooking spray

1. Preheat the air fryer oven to 350ºF (177ºC).
2. Spray the air fryer basket lightly with cooking spray.
3. In a medium bowl combine the tuna, bread crumbs, Parmesan cheese, sriracha, and black pepper and stir to combine.
4. Form the mixture into 10 patties.
5. Place the patties in the air fryer basket in a single layer. Spray the patties lightly with cooking spray.
6. Put the air fryer basket on sheet pan and place into oven. Select Air Fry and set time to 8 minutes.
7. Turn the patties over and lightly spray with cooking spray. Air fry until golden brown and crisp, another 4 to 7 more minutes. Serve warm.

Crispy Cod Cakes with Salad Greens

Prep time: 15 minutes | Cook time: 12 minutes | Serves 4

1 pound (454 g) cod fillets,
cut into chunks
⅓ cup packed fresh basil
leaves
3 cloves garlic, crushed
½ teaspoon smoked paprika
¼ teaspoon salt
¼ teaspoon pepper
1 large egg, beaten
1 cup panko bread crumbs
Cooking spray
Salad greens, for serving

1. In a food processor, pulse cod, basil, garlic, smoked paprika, salt, and pepper until cod is finely chopped, stirring occasionally. Form into 8 patties, about 2 inches in diameter. Dip each first into the egg, then into the panko, patting to adhere. Spray with oil on one side.
2. Preheat the air fryer oven to 400ºF (204ºC).
3. Place the cakes in the air fryer basket, oil-side down; spray with oil.
4. Put the air fryer basket on sheet pan and place into oven. Select Air Fry and set time to 12 minutes, until golden brown and cooked through.
5. Serve cod cakes with salad greens.

34 | Chapter 3: Fish and Seafood

Air-Fried Scallops

Prep time: 10 minutes | Cook time: 12 minutes | Serves 2

⅓ cup shallots, chopped
1½ tablespoons olive oil
1½ tablespoons coconut aminos
1 tablespoon Mediterranean seasoning mix
½ tablespoon balsamic vinegar
½ teaspoon ginger, grated
1 clove garlic, chopped
1 pound (454 g) scallops, cleaned
Cooking spray
Belgian endive, for garnish

1. Place all the ingredients except the scallops and Belgian endive in a small skillet over medium heat and stir to combine. Let this mixture simmer for about 2 minutes.
2. Remove the mixture from the skillet to a large bowl and set aside to cool.
3. Add the scallops, coating them all over, then transfer to the refrigerator to marinate for at least 2 hours.
4. When ready, place the scallops in the air fryer basket in a single layer and spray with cooking spray.
5. Put the air fryer basket on sheet pan and place into oven. Select Air Fry, set temperature to 345°F (174°C), and set time to 10 minutes.
6. Flip the scallops halfway through the cooking time.
7. When cooking is complete, the scallops should be tender and opaque. Remove from the oven and serve garnished with the Belgian endive.

Crispy Coconut Shrimp

Prep time: 15 minutes | Cook time: 8 minutes | Serves 4

Sweet Chili Mayo:
3 tablespoons mayonnaise
3 tablespoons Thai sweet chili sauce
1 tablespoon Sriracha sauce
Shrimp:
⅔ cup sweetened shredded coconut
⅔ cup panko bread crumbs
Kosher salt, to taste
2 tablespoons all-purpose or gluten-free flour
2 large eggs
24 extra-jumbo shrimp (about 1 pound / 454 g), peeled and deveined
Cooking spray

1. In a medium bowl, combine the mayonnaise, Thai sweet chili sauce, and Sriracha and mix well.
2. In a medium bowl, combine the coconut, panko,

and ¼ teaspoon salt. Place the flour in a shallow bowl. Whisk the eggs in another shallow bowl.
3. Season the shrimp with ⅛ teaspoon salt. Dip the shrimp in the flour, shaking off any excess, then into the egg. Coat in the coconut-panko mixture, gently pressing to adhere, then transfer to a large plate. Spray both sides of the shrimp with oil.
4. Preheat the air fryer oven to 360°F (182°C).
5. Working in batches, arrange a single layer of the shrimp in the air fryer basket.
6. Put the air fryer basket on sheet pan and place into oven. Select Air Fry and set time to 8 minutes, flipping halfway through, or until the crust is golden brown and the shrimp are cooked through.
7. Serve with the sweet chili mayo for dipping.

Roasted Scallops with Snow Peas

Prep time: 10 minutes | Cook time: 8 minutes | Serves 4

1 pound (454 g) sea scallops
3 tablespoons hoisin sauce
½ cup toasted sesame seeds
6 ounces (170 g) snow peas, trimmed
3 teaspoons vegetable oil, divided
1 teaspoon soy sauce
1 teaspoon sesame oil
1 cup roasted mushrooms

1. Brush the scallops with the hoisin sauce. Put the sesame seeds in a shallow dish. Roll the scallops in the sesame seeds until evenly coated.
2. Combine the snow peas with 1 teaspoon of vegetable oil, the sesame oil, and soy sauce in a medium bowl and toss to coat.
3. Grease the sheet pan with the remaining 2 teaspoons of vegetable oil. Put the scallops in the middle of the pan and arrange the snow peas around the scallops in a single layer.
4. Place the sheet pan on wire rack and slide into oven. Select Air Roast, set temperature to 375°F (190°C), and set time to 8 minutes.
5. After 5 minutes, remove the pan and flip the scallops. Fold in the mushrooms and stir well. Return the pan to the oven and continue cooking.
6. When done, remove from the oven and cool for 5 minutes. Serve warm.

Chapter 3: Fish and Seafood | 35

Green Curry Shrimp

Prep time: 15 minutes | Cook time: 5 minutes | Serves 4

1 to 2 tablespoons Thai green curry paste
2 tablespoons coconut oil, melted
1 tablespoon half-and-half or coconut milk
1 teaspoon fish sauce
1 teaspoon soy sauce
1 teaspoon minced fresh ginger
1 clove garlic, minced
1 pound (454 g) jumbo raw shrimp, peeled and deveined
¼ cup chopped fresh Thai basil or sweet basil
¼ cup chopped fresh cilantro

1. In a sheet pan, combine the curry paste, coconut oil, half-and-half, fish sauce, soy sauce, ginger, and garlic. Whisk until well combined.
2. Add the shrimp and toss until well coated. Marinate at room temperature for 15 to 30 minutes.
3. Preheat the air fryer oven to 400°F (204°C).
4. Put the sheet pan on wire rack and slide into the oven. Select Bake and set time to 5 minutes, stirring halfway through the cooking time.
5. Transfer the shrimp to a serving bowl or platter. Garnish with the basil and cilantro. Serve immediately.

Glazed Cod with Sesame Seeds

Prep time: 5 minutes | Cook time: 8 minutes | Makes 1 fillet

1 tablespoon reduced-sodium soy sauce
2 teaspoons honey
Cooking spray
6 ounces (170 g) fresh cod fillet
1 teaspoon sesame seeds

1. Preheat the air fryer oven to 360°F (182°C).
2. In a small bowl, combine the soy sauce and honey.
3. Spray the air fryer basket with cooking spray, then place the cod in the basket, brush with the soy mixture, and sprinkle sesame seeds on top.
4. Put the air fryer basket on sheet pan and place into oven. Select Air Fry and set time to 8 minutes, or until opaque.
5. Remove the fish and allow to cool on a wire rack for 5 minutes before serving.

Salmon Burgers

Prep time: 15 minutes | Cook time: 12 minutes | Serves 5

Lemon-Caper Rémoulade:
½ cup mayonnaise
2 tablespoons minced drained capers
2 tablespoons chopped
fresh parsley
2 teaspoons fresh lemon juice

Salmon Patties:
1 pound (454 g) wild salmon fillet, skinned and pin bones removed
6 tablespoons panko bread crumbs
¼ cup minced red onion plus ¼ cup slivered for serving
1 garlic clove, minced
1 large egg, lightly beaten
1 tablespoon Dijon mustard
1 teaspoon fresh lemon juice
1 tablespoon chopped fresh parsley
½ teaspoon kosher salt

For Serving:
5 whole wheat potato buns or gluten-free buns
10 butter lettuce leaves

1. For the lemon-caper rémoulade: In a small bowl, combine the mayonnaise, capers, parsley, and lemon juice and mix well.
2. For the salmon patties: Cut off a 4-ounce / 113-g piece of the salmon and transfer to a food processor. Pulse until it becomes pasty. With a sharp knife, chop the remaining salmon into small cubes.
3. In a medium bowl, combine the chopped and processed salmon with the panko, minced red onion, garlic, egg, mustard, lemon juice, parsley, and salt. Toss gently to combine. Form the mixture into 5 patties about ¾ inch thick. Refrigerate for at least 30 minutes.
4. Preheat the air fryer oven to 400°F (204°C).
5. Place the patties in the air fryer basket.
6. Put the air fryer basket on sheet pan and place into oven. Select Air Fry and set time to 12 minutes, gently flipping halfway through, until golden and cooked through.
7. To serve, transfer each patty to a bun. Top each with 2 lettuce leaves, 2 tablespoons of the rémoulade, and the slivered red onions.

Salmon Patty Bites

Prep time: 15 minutes | Cook time: 15 minutes | Serves 4

4 (5-ounce / 142-g) cans pink salmon, skinless, boneless in water, drained
2 eggs, beaten
1 cup whole-wheat panko bread crumbs

4 tablespoons finely minced red bell pepper
2 tablespoons parsley flakes
2 teaspoons Old Bay seasoning
Cooking spray

1. Preheat the air fryer oven to 360°F (182°C).
2. Spray the air fryer basket lightly with cooking spray.
3. In a medium bowl, mix the salmon, eggs, panko bread crumbs, red bell pepper, parsley flakes, and Old Bay seasoning.
4. Using a small cookie scoop, form the mixture into 20 balls.
5. Place the salmon bites in the air fryer basket in a single layer and spray lightly with cooking spray.
6. Put the air fryer basket on sheet pan and place into oven. Select Air Fry and set time to 15 minutes, shaking the basket a couple of times for even cooking.
7. Serve immediately.

Blackened Salmon

Prep time: 10 minutes | Cook time: 6 minutes | Serves 4

Salmon:

1 tablespoon sweet paprika
½ teaspoon cayenne pepper
1 teaspoon garlic powder
1 teaspoon dried oregano
1 teaspoon dried thyme
¾ teaspoon kosher salt
⅛ teaspoon freshly ground black pepper
Cooking spray
4 (6 ounces / 170 g each) wild salmon fillets
Cucumber-Avocado Salsa:
2 tablespoons chopped red

onion
1½ tablespoons fresh lemon juice
1 teaspoon extra-virgin olive oil
¼ teaspoon plus ⅛ teaspoon kosher salt
Freshly ground black pepper, to taste
4 Persian cucumbers, diced
6 ounces (170 g) Hass avocado, diced

1. For the salmon: In a small bowl, combine the paprika, cayenne, garlic powder, oregano, thyme, salt, and black pepper. Spray both sides of the fish with oil and rub all over. Coat the fish all over with the spices.
2. For the cucumber-avocado salsa: In a medium bowl, combine the red onion, lemon juice, olive oil, salt, and pepper. Let stand for 5 minutes, then add the cucumbers and avocado.
3. Preheat the air fryer oven to 400°F (204°C).
4. Arrange the salmon fillets skin-side down in the air fryer basket.
5. Put the air fryer basket on sheet pan and place into oven. Select Air Fry and set time to 6 minutes, or until the fish flakes easily with a fork, depending on the thickness of the fish.
6. Serve topped with the salsa.

Almond Crusted Fish

Prep time: 10 minutes | Cook time: 8 minutes | Serves 4

½ cup raw whole almonds
1 scallion, finely chopped
Grated zest and juice of 1 lemon
½ tablespoon extra-virgin olive oil
¾ teaspoon kosher salt,

divided
Freshly ground black pepper, to taste
4 (6 ounces / 170 g each) skinless fish fillets
Cooking spray
1 teaspoon Dijon mustard

1. In a food processor, pulse the almonds to coarsely chop. Transfer to a small bowl and add the scallion, lemon zest, and olive oil. Season with ¼ teaspoon of the salt and pepper to taste and mix to combine.
2. Spray the top of the fish with oil and squeeze the lemon juice over the fish. Season with the remaining ½ teaspoon salt and pepper to taste. Spread the mustard on top of the fish. Dividing evenly, press the almond mixture onto the top of the fillets to adhere.
3. Preheat the air fryer oven to 375°F (191°C).
4. Place the fillets in the air fryer basket in a single layer.
5. Put the air fryer basket on sheet pan and place into oven. Select Air Fry and set time to 8 minutes, until the crumbs start to brown and the fish is cooked through.
6. Serve immediately.

Chapter 3: Fish and Seafood | 37

Blackened Shrimp Tacos

Prep time: 10 minutes | Cook time: 10 to 15 minutes | Serves 4

12 ounces (340 g) medium shrimp, deveined, with tails off
1 teaspoon olive oil
1 to 2 teaspoons Blackened seasoning
8 corn tortillas, warmed
1 (14-ounce / 397-g) bag coleslaw mix
2 limes, cut in half
Cooking spray

1. Preheat the air fryer oven to 400°F (204°C).
2. Spray the air fryer basket lightly with cooking spray.
3. Dry the shrimp with a paper towel to remove excess water.
4. In a medium bowl, toss the shrimp with olive oil and Blackened seasoning.
5. Place the shrimp in the air fryer basket.
6. Put the air fryer basket on sheet pan and place into oven. Select Air Fry and set time to 5 minutes.
7. Shake the basket, lightly spray with cooking spray, and cook until the shrimp are cooked through and starting to brown, 5 to 10 more minutes.
8. Fill each tortilla with the coleslaw mix and top with the blackened shrimp. Squeeze fresh lime juice over top and serve.

Air Fried Spring Rolls

Prep time: 10 minutes | Cook time: 17 to 22 minutes | Serves 4

2 teaspoons minced garlic
2 cups finely sliced cabbage
1 cup matchstick cut carrots
2 (4-ounce / 113-g) cans tiny shrimp, drained
4 teaspoons soy sauce
Salt and freshly ground black pepper, to taste
16 square spring roll wrappers
Cooking spray

1. Preheat the air fryer oven to 370°F (188°C).
2. Spray the air fryer basket lightly with cooking spray. Spray a medium sauté pan with cooking spray.
3. Add the garlic to the sauté pan and cook over medium heat until fragrant, 30 to 45 seconds. Add the cabbage and carrots and sauté until the vegetables are slightly tender, about 5 minutes.

4. Add the shrimp and soy sauce and season with salt and pepper, then stir to combine. Sauté until the moisture has evaporated, 2 more minutes. Set aside to cool.
5. Place a spring roll wrapper on a work surface so it looks like a diamond. Place 1 tablespoon of the shrimp mixture on the lower end of the wrapper.
6. Roll the wrapper away from you halfway, then fold in the right and left sides, like an envelope. Continue to roll to the very end, using a little water to seal the edge. Repeat with the remaining wrappers and filling.
7. Place the spring rolls in the air fryer basket in a single layer, leaving room between each roll. Lightly spray with cooking spray. You may need to cook them in batches.
8. Put the air fryer basket on sheet pan and place into oven. Select Air Fry and set time to 5 minutes.
9. Turn the rolls over, lightly spray with cooking spray, and air fry until heated through and the rolls start to brown, 5 to 10 more minutes. Cool for 5 minutes before serving.

Country Shrimp

Prep time: 10 minutes | Cook time: 15 minutes | Serves 4

1 pound (454 g) large shrimp, deveined, with tails on
1 pound (454 g) smoked turkey sausage, cut into thick slices
2 corn cobs, quartered
1 zucchini, cut into bite-sized pieces
1 red bell pepper, cut into chunks
1 tablespoon Old Bay seasoning
2 tablespoons olive oil
Cooking spray

1. Preheat the air fryer oven to 400°F (204°C). Spray the air fryer basket lightly with cooking spray.
2. In a large bowl, mix the shrimp, turkey sausage, corn, zucchini, bell pepper, and Old Bay seasoning, and toss to coat with the spices. Add the olive oil and toss again until evenly coated.
3. Spread the mixture in the air fryer basket in a single layer.
4. Put the air fryer basket on sheet pan and place into oven. Select Air Fry and set time to 15 minutes, or until cooked through, shaking the basket every 5 minutes for even cooking.
5. Serve immediately.

38 | Chapter 3: Fish and Seafood

Spicy Orange Shrimp

Prep time: 20 minutes | Cook time: 10 to 15 minutes | Serves 4

⅓ cup orange juice
3 teaspoons minced garlic
1 teaspoon Old Bay seasoning
¼ to ½ teaspoon cayenne

pepper
1 pound (454 g) medium shrimp, peeled and deveined, with tails off
Cooking spray

1. In a medium bowl, combine the orange juice, garlic, Old Bay seasoning, and cayenne pepper.
2. Dry the shrimp with paper towels to remove excess water.
3. Add the shrimp to the marinade and stir to evenly coat. Cover with plastic wrap and place in the refrigerator for 30 minutes so the shrimp can soak up the marinade.
4. Preheat the air fryer oven to 400°F (204°C). Spray the air fryer basket lightly with cooking spray.
5. Place the shrimp into the air fryer basket.
6. Put the air fryer basket on sheet pan and place into oven. Select Air Fry and set time to 5 minutes.
7. Shake the basket and lightly spray with olive oil. Air fry until the shrimp are opaque and crisp, 5 to 10 more minutes.
8. Serve immediately.

Homemade Fish Sticks

Prep time: 15 minutes | Cook time: 13 to 15 minutes | Serves 4

4 fish fillets
½ cup whole-wheat flour
1 teaspoon seasoned salt
2 eggs
1½ cups whole-wheat

panko bread crumbs
½ tablespoon dried parsley flakes
Cooking spray

1. Preheat the air fryer oven to 400°F (204°C). Spray the air fryer basket lightly with cooking spray.
2. Cut the fish fillets lengthwise into "sticks."
3. In a shallow bowl, mix the whole-wheat flour and seasoned salt.
4. In a small bowl, whisk the eggs with 1 teaspoon of water.
5. In another shallow bowl, mix the panko bread crumbs and parsley flakes.
6. Coat each fish stick in the seasoned flour, then in the egg mixture, and dredge them in the panko bread crumbs.
7. Place the fish sticks in the air fryer basket in a single layer and lightly spray the fish sticks with cooking spray.
8. Put the air fryer basket on sheet pan and place into oven. Select Air Fry and set time to 8 minutes.
9. Flip the fish sticks over and lightly spray with cooking spray. Air fry until golden brown and crispy, 5 to 7 more minutes.
10. Serve warm.

Seasoned Breaded Shrimp

Prep time: 15 minutes | Cook time: 15 minutes | Serves 4

2 teaspoons Old Bay seasoning, divided
½ teaspoon garlic powder
½ teaspoon onion powder
1 pound (454 g) large shrimp, deveined, with tails

on
2 large eggs
½ cup whole-wheat panko bread crumbs
Cooking spray

1. Preheat the air fryer oven to 380°F (193°C).
2. Spray the air fryer basket lightly with cooking spray.
3. In a medium bowl, mix together 1 teaspoon of Old Bay seasoning, garlic powder, and onion powder. Add the shrimp and toss with the seasoning mix to lightly coat.
4. In a separate small bowl, whisk the eggs with 1 teaspoon water.
5. In a shallow bowl, mix together the remaining 1 teaspoon Old Bay seasoning and the panko bread crumbs.
6. Dip each shrimp in the egg mixture and dredge in the bread crumb mixture to evenly coat.
7. Place the shrimp in the air fryer basket in a single layer. Lightly spray the shrimp with cooking spray. You many need to cook the shrimp in batches.
8. Put the air fryer basket on sheet pan and place into oven. Select Air Fry and set time to 15 minutes, or until the shrimp is cooked through and crispy, shaking the basket at 5-minute intervals to redistribute and evenly cook.
9. Serve immediately.

Chapter 3: Fish and Seafood | 39

Lemony Shrimp and Zucchini

Prep time: 15 minutes | Cook time: 8 minutes | Serves 4

1¼ pounds (567 g) extra-large raw shrimp, peeled and deveined
2 medium zucchini (about 8 ounces / 227 g each), halved lengthwise and cut into ½-inch-thick slices
1½ tablespoons olive oil
½ teaspoon garlic salt
1½ teaspoons dried oregano
⅛ teaspoon crushed red pepper flakes (optional)
Juice of ½ lemon
1 tablespoon chopped fresh mint
1 tablespoon chopped fresh dill

1. Preheat the air fryer oven to 350°F (177°C).
2. In a large bowl, combine the shrimp, zucchini, oil, garlic salt, oregano, and pepper flakes (if using) and toss to coat.
3. Working in batches, arrange a single layer of the shrimp and zucchini in the air fryer basket.
4. Put the air fryer basket on sheet pan and place into oven. Select Air Fry and set time to 8 minutes, shaking the basket halfway through, until the zucchini is golden and the shrimp are cooked through.
5. Transfer to a serving dish and tent with foil while you air fry the remaining shrimp and zucchini.
6. Top with the lemon juice, mint, and dill and serve.

Marinated Salmon Fillets

Prep time: 10 minutes | Cook time: 18 minutes | Serves 4

¼ cup soy sauce
¼ cup rice wine vinegar
1 tablespoon brown sugar
1 tablespoon olive oil
1 teaspoon mustard powder
1 teaspoon ground ginger
½ teaspoon freshly ground black pepper
½ teaspoon minced garlic
4 (6-ounce / 170-g) salmon fillets, skin-on
Cooking spray

1. In a small bowl, combine the soy sauce, rice wine vinegar, brown sugar, olive oil, mustard powder, ginger, black pepper, and garlic to make a marinade.
2. Place the fillets in a shallow baking dish and pour the marinade over them. Cover the baking dish and marinate for at least 1 hour in the refrigerator, turning the fillets occasionally to keep them coated in the marinade.
3. Preheat the air fryer oven to 370°F (188°C). Spray the air fryer basket lightly with cooking spray.
4. Shake off as much marinade as possible from the fillets and place them, skin-side down, in the air fryer basket in a single layer.
5. Put the air fryer basket on sheet pan and place into oven. Select Air Fry and set time to 18 minutes. The minimum internal temperature should be 145°F (63°C) at the thickest part of the fillets.
6. Serve hot.

Lime-Chili Shrimp Bowl

Prep time: 10 minutes | Cook time: 10 to 15 minutes | Serves 4

2 teaspoons lime juice
1 teaspoon olive oil
1 teaspoon honey
1 teaspoon minced garlic
1 teaspoon chili powder
Salt, to taste
12 ounces (340 g) medium shrimp, peeled and deveined
2 cups cooked brown rice
1 (15-ounce / 425-g) can seasoned black beans, warmed
1 large avocado, chopped
1 cup sliced cherry tomatoes
Cooking spray

1. Preheat the air fryer oven to 400°F (204°C). Spray the air fryer basket lightly with cooking spray.
2. In a medium bowl, mix together the lime juice, olive oil, honey, garlic, chili powder, and salt to make a marinade.
3. Add the shrimp and toss to coat evenly in the marinade.
4. Place the shrimp in the air fryer basket.
5. Put the air fryer basket on sheet pan and place into oven. Select Air Fry and set time to 5 minutes.
6. Shake the basket and air fry until the shrimp are cooked through and starting to brown, an additional 5 to 10 minutes.
7. To assemble the bowls, spoon ¼ of the rice, black beans, avocado, and cherry tomatoes into each of four bowls. Top with the shrimp and serve.

Crab Cake Sandwich

Prep time: 15 minutes | Cook time: 10 minutes | Serves 4

Crab Cakes:

½ cup panko bread crumbs
1 large egg, beaten
1 large egg white
1 tablespoon mayonnaise
1 teaspoon Dijon mustard
¼ cup minced fresh parsley
1 tablespoon fresh lemon juice
½ teaspoon Old Bay seasoning
⅛ teaspoon sweet paprika
⅛ teaspoon kosher salt
Freshly ground black pepper, to taste
10 ounces (283 g) lump crab meat
Cooking spray

Cajun Mayo:

¼ cup mayonnaise
1 tablespoon minced dill pickle
1 teaspoon fresh lemon juice
¾ teaspoon Cajun seasoning

For Serving:

4 Boston lettuce leaves
4 whole wheat potato buns
or gluten-free buns

1. For the crab cakes: In a large bowl, combine the panko, whole egg, egg white, mayonnaise, mustard, parsley, lemon juice, Old Bay, paprika, salt, and pepper to taste and mix well. Fold in the crab meat, being careful not to over mix. Gently shape into 4 round patties, about ½ cup each, ¾ inch thick. Spray both sides with oil.
2. Preheat the air fryer oven to 370°F (188°C).
3. Place the crab cakes in the air fryer basket.
4. Put the air fryer basket on sheet pan and place into oven. Select Air Fry and set time to 10 minutes, flipping halfway through, until the edges are golden.
5. Meanwhile, for the Cajun mayo: In a small bowl, combine the mayonnaise, pickle, lemon juice, and Cajun seasoning.
6. Place a lettuce leaf on each bun bottom and top with a crab cake and a generous tablespoon of Cajun mayonnaise. Add the bun top and serve.

Tortilla Shrimp Tacos

Prep time: 10 minutes | Cook time: 6 minutes | Serves 4

Spicy Mayo:

3 tablespoons mayonnaise
1 tablespoon Louisiana-style hot pepper sauce
Cilantro-Lime Slaw:
2 cups shredded green cabbage
½ small red onion, thinly sliced
1 small jalapeño, thinly sliced
2 tablespoons chopped fresh cilantro
Juice of 1 lime
¼ teaspoon kosher salt

Shrimp:

1 large egg, beaten
1 cup crushed tortilla chips
24 jumbo shrimp (about 1 pound / 454 g), peeled and deveined
⅛ teaspoon kosher salt
Cooking spray
8 corn tortillas, for serving

1. For the spicy mayo: In a small bowl, mix the mayonnaise and hot pepper sauce.
2. For the cilantro-lime slaw: In a large bowl, toss together the cabbage, onion, jalapeño, cilantro, lime juice, and salt to combine. Cover and refrigerate to chill.
3. For the shrimp: Place the egg in a shallow bowl and the crushed tortilla chips in another. Season the shrimp with the salt. Dip the shrimp in the egg, then in the crumbs, pressing gently to adhere. Place on a work surface and spray both sides with oil.
4. Preheat the air fryer oven to 360°F (182°C).
5. Working in batches, arrange a single layer of the shrimp in the air fryer basket.
6. Put the air fryer basket on sheet pan and place into oven. Select Air Fry and set time to 6 minutes, flipping halfway through, or until golden and cooked through in the center.
7. To serve, place 2 tortillas on each plate and top each with 3 shrimp. Top each taco with ¼ cup slaw, then drizzle with spicy mayo.

Chapter 4   Poultry

Air Fried Chicken Wings

Prep time: 10 minutes | Cook time: 15 minutes | Serves 4

1 tablespoon olive oil
8 whole chicken wings
Chicken seasoning or rub, to taste
1 teaspoon garlic powder
Freshly ground black pepper, to taste

1. Grease the basket with olive oil.
2. On a clean work surface, rub the chicken wings with chicken seasoning and rub, garlic powder, and ground black pepper.
3. Arrange the well-coated chicken wings in the basket.
4. Put the air fryer basket on sheet pan and place into oven. Select Air Fry, set temperature to 400°F (205°C) and set time to 15 minutes.
5. Flip the chicken wings halfway through.
6. When cooking is complete, the internal temperature of the chicken wings should reach at least 165°F (74°C).
7. Remove the chicken wings from the oven. Serve immediately.

Spanish Chicken and Pepper Baguette

Prep time: 10 minutes | Cook time: 20 minutes | Serves 2

1¼ pounds (567 g) assorted small chicken parts, breasts cut into halves
¼ teaspoon salt
¼ teaspoon ground black pepper
2 teaspoons olive oil
½ pound (227 g) mini sweet peppers
¼ cup light mayonnaise
¼ teaspoon smoked paprika
½ clove garlic, crushed
Baguette, for serving
Cooking spray

1. Spritz the air fryer basket with cooking spray.
2. Toss the chicken with salt, ground black pepper, and olive oil in a large bowl.

3. Arrange the sweet peppers and chicken in the basket.
4. Put the air fryer basket on sheet pan and place into oven. Select Air Fry, set temperature to 375°F (190°C) and set time to 20 minutes.
5. Flip the chicken and transfer the peppers on a plate halfway through.
6. When cooking is complete, the chicken should be well browned.
7. Meanwhile, combine the mayo, paprika, and garlic in a small bowl. Stir to mix well.
8. Assemble the baguette with chicken and sweet pepper, then spread with mayo mixture and serve.

Turkey and Cauliflower Meatloaf

Prep time: 15 minutes | Cook time: 50 minutes | Serves 6

2 pounds (907 g) lean ground turkey
1⅓ cups riced cauliflower
2 large eggs, lightly beaten
¼ cup almond flour
⅔ cup chopped yellow or white onion
1 teaspoon ground dried turmeric
1 teaspoon ground cumin
1 teaspoon ground coriander
1 tablespoon minced garlic
1 teaspoon salt
1 teaspoon ground black pepper
Cooking spray

1. Spritz the sheet pan with cooking spray.
2. Combine all the ingredients in a large bowl. Stir to mix well. Pour half of the mixture in the prepared pan and press with a spatula to coat the bottom evenly. Spritz the mixture with cooking spray.
3. Place the sheet pan on wire rack and slide into oven. Select Bake, set temperature to 350°F (180°C) and set time to 25 minutes.
4. When cooking is complete, the meat should be well browned and the internal temperature should reach at least 165°F (74°C).
5. Remove the pan from the oven and serve immediately.

42 | Chapter 4: Poultry

Deep Fried Duck Leg Quarters

Prep time: 5 minutes | Cook time: 45 minutes | Serves 4

4 (½-pound / 227-g) skin-on duck leg quarters
2 medium garlic cloves, minced
½ teaspoon salt
½ teaspoon ground black pepper

1. Spritz the air fryer basket with cooking spray.
2. On a clean work surface, rub the duck leg quarters with garlic, salt, and black pepper.
3. Arrange the leg quarters in the basket and spritz with cooking spray.
4. Put the air fryer basket on sheet pan and place into oven. Select Air Fry, set temperature to 300ºF (150ºC) and set time to 30 minutes.
5. After 30 minutes, remove from the oven. Flip the leg quarters. Increase temperature to 375ºF (190ºC) and set time to 15 minutes. Return to the oven and continue cooking.
6. When cooking is complete, the leg quarters should be well browned and crispy.
7. Remove the duck leg quarters from the oven and allow to cool for 10 minutes before serving.

Yakitori

Prep time: 10 minutes | Cook time: 15 minutes | Serves 4

½ cup mirin
¼ cup dry white wine
½ cup soy sauce
1 tablespoon light brown sugar
1½ pounds (680 g) boneless, skinless chicken
thighs, cut into 1½-inch pieces, fat trimmed
4 medium scallions, trimmed, cut into 1½-inch pieces
Cooking spray

Special Equipment:
4 (4-inch) bamboo skewers, soaked in water for at least 30 minutes

1. Combine the mirin, dry white wine, soy sauce, and brown sugar in a saucepan. Bring to a boil over medium heat. Keep stirring.
2. Boil for another 2 minutes or until it has a thick consistency. Turn off the heat.
3. Spritz the air fryer basket with cooking spray.
4. Run the bamboo skewers through the chicken pieces and scallions alternatively.
5. Arrange the skewers in the basket, then brush with mirin mixture on both sides. Spritz with cooking spray.
6. Put the air fryer basket on sheet pan and place into oven. Select Air Fry, set temperature to 400ºF (205ºC) and set time to 10 minutes.
7. Flip the skewers halfway through.
8. When cooking is complete, the chicken and scallions should be glossy.
9. Serve immediately.

Rosemary Turkey Breast

Prep time: 2 hours 20 minutes | Cook time: 30 minutes | Serves 6

½ teaspoon dried rosemary
2 minced garlic cloves
2 teaspoons salt
1 teaspoon ground black pepper
¼ cup olive oil
2½ pounds (1.1 kg) turkey
breast
¼ cup pure maple syrup
1 tablespoon stone-ground brown mustard
1 tablespoon melted vegan butter

1. Combine the rosemary, garlic, salt, ground black pepper, and olive oil in a large bowl. Stir to mix well.
2. Dunk the turkey breast in the mixture and wrap the bowl in plastic. Refrigerate for 2 hours to marinate.
3. Remove the bowl from the refrigerator and let sit for half an hour before cooking.
4. Spritz the air fryer basket with cooking spray.
5. Remove the turkey from the marinade and place in the basket.
6. Put the air fryer basket on sheet pan and place into oven. Select Air Fry, set temperature to 400ºF (205ºC) and set time to 20 minutes.
7. Flip the breast halfway through.
8. When cooking is complete, the breast should be well browned.
9. Meanwhile, combine the remaining ingredients in a small bowl. Stir to mix well.
10. Pour half of the butter mixture over the turkey breast in the oven and air fry for 10 more minutes. Flip the breast and pour the remaining half of butter mixture over halfway through.
11. Transfer the turkey on a plate and slice to serve.

Turkey and Mushroom Meatballs

Prep time: 10 minutes | Cook time: 15 minutes | Serves 6

Sauce:

2 tablespoons tamari

2 tablespoons tomato sauce

1 tablespoon lime juice

¼ teaspoon peeled and grated fresh ginger

1 clove garlic, smashed to a paste

½ cup chicken broth

⅓ cup sugar

2 tablespoons toasted sesame oil

Cooking spray

Meatballs:

2 pounds (907 g) ground turkey

¾ cup finely chopped button mushrooms

2 large eggs, beaten

1½ teaspoons tamari

¼ cup finely chopped green onions, plus more for garnish

2 teaspoons peeled and grated fresh ginger

1 clove garlic, smashed

2 teaspoons toasted sesame oil

2 tablespoons sugar

For Serving:

Lettuce leaves, for serving

Sliced red chiles, for garnish (optional)

Toasted sesame seeds, for garnish (optional)

1. Spritz the air fryer basket with cooking spray.
2. Combine the ingredients for the sauce in a small bowl. Stir to mix well. Set aside.
3. Combine the ingredients for the meatballs in a large bowl. Stir to mix well, then shape the mixture in twelve 1½-inch meatballs.
4. Arrange the meatballs in the basket, then baste with the sauce.
5. Put the air fryer basket on sheet pan and place into oven. Select Air Fry, set temperature to 350ºF (180ºC) and set time to 15 minutes.
6. Flip the balls halfway through.
7. When cooking is complete, the meatballs should be golden brown.
8. Unfold the lettuce leaves on a large serving plate, then transfer the cooked meatballs on the leaves. Spread the red chiles and sesame seeds over the balls, then serve.

Cheesy Turkey Burgers

Prep time: 10 minutes | Cook time: 25 minutes | Serves 4

2 medium yellow onions

1 tablespoon olive oil

1½ teaspoons kosher salt, divided

1¼ pound (567 g) ground turkey

⅓ cup mayonnaise

1 tablespoon Dijon mustard

2 teaspoons Worcestershire sauce

4 slices sharp Cheddar cheese (about 4 ounces / 113 g in total)

4 hamburger buns, sliced

1. Trim the onions and cut them in half through the root. Cut one of the halves in half. Grate one quarter. Place the grated onion in a large bowl. Thinly slice the remaining onions and place in a medium bowl with the oil and ½ teaspoon of kosher salt. Toss to coat. Place the onions in a single layer in the sheet pan.
2. Place the sheet pan on wire rack and slide into oven. Select Air Roast, set temperature to 350ºF (180ºC), and set time to 10 minutes.
3. While the onions are cooking, add the turkey to the grated onion. Add the remaining kosher salt, mayonnaise, mustard, and Worcestershire sauce. Mix just until combined, being careful not to overwork the turkey. Divide the mixture into 4 patties, each about ¾-inch thick.
4. When cooking is complete, remove from the oven. Move the onions to one side of the pan and place the burgers on the pan. Poke your finger into the center of each burger to make a deep indentation.
5. Select Air Broil, set temperature to High, and set time to 12 minutes.
6. After 6 minutes, remove the pan. Turn the burgers and stir the onions. Return the pan to the oven and continue cooking. After about 4 minutes, remove the pan and place the cheese slices on the burgers. Return the pan to the oven and continue cooking for about 1 minute, or until the cheese is melted and the center of the burgers has reached at least 165ºF (74ºC) on a meat thermometer.
7. When cooking is complete, remove from the oven. Loosely cover the burgers with foil.
8. Lay out the buns, cut-side up, on the oven rack. Select Air Broil; set temperature to High, and set time to 3 minutes. Check the buns after 2 minutes; they should be lightly browned.
9. Remove the buns from the oven. Assemble the burgers and serve.

44 | Chapter 4: Poultry

Rosemary Turkey Scotch Eggs

Prep time: 15 minutes | Cook time: 12 minutes | Serves 4

1 egg
1 cup panko bread crumbs
½ teaspoon rosemary
1 pound (454 g) ground turkey
4 hard-boiled eggs, peeled
Salt and ground black pepper, to taste
Cooking spray

1. Spritz the air fryer basket with cooking spray.
2. Whisk the egg with salt in a bowl. Combine the bread crumbs with rosemary in a shallow dish.
3. Stir the ground turkey with salt and ground black pepper in a separate large bowl, then divide the ground turkey into four portions.
4. Wrap each hard-boiled egg with a portion of ground turkey. Dredge in the whisked egg, then roll over the breadcrumb mixture.
5. Place the wrapped eggs in the basket and spritz with cooking spray.
6. Put the air fryer basket on sheet pan and place into oven. Select Air Fry, set temperature to 400°F (205°C) and set time to 12 minutes.
7. Flip the eggs halfway through.
8. When cooking is complete, the scotch eggs should be golden brown and crunchy.
9. Serve immediately.

Italian Chicken Breasts with Tomatoes

Prep time: 10 minutes | Cook time: 35 minutes | Serves 8

3 pounds (1.4 kg) chicken breasts, bone-in
1 teaspoon minced fresh basil
1 teaspoon minced fresh rosemary
2 tablespoons minced fresh parsley
1 teaspoon cayenne pepper
½ teaspoon salt
½ teaspoon freshly ground black pepper
4 medium Roma tomatoes, halved
Cooking spray

1. Spritz the air fryer basket with cooking spray.
2. Combine all the ingredients, except for the chicken breasts and tomatoes, in a large bowl. Stir to mix well.
3. Dunk the chicken breasts in the mixture and press to coat well.
4. Transfer the chicken breasts in the basket.
5. Put the air fryer basket on sheet pan and place into oven. Select Air Fry, set temperature to 370°F (188°C) and set time to 20 minutes.
6. Flip the breasts halfway through the cooking time.
7. When cooking is complete, the internal temperature of the thickest part of the breasts should reach at least 165°F (74°C).
8. Remove the cooked chicken breasts from the oven and adjust the temperature to 350°F (180°C).
9. Place the tomatoes in the basket and spritz with cooking spray. Sprinkle with a touch of salt.
10. Set time to 10 minutes. Stir the tomatoes halfway through the cooking time.
11. When cooking is complete, the tomatoes should be tender.
12. Serve the tomatoes with chicken breasts on a large serving plate.

Duck Breasts with Balsamic Glaze

Prep time: 5 minutes | Cook time: 13 minutes | Serves 4

4 (6-ounce / 170-g) skin-on duck breasts
1 teaspoon salt
¼ cup orange marmalade
1 tablespoon white balsamic vinegar
¾ teaspoon ground black pepper

1. Cut 10 slits into the skin of the duck breasts, then sprinkle with salt on both sides.
2. Place the breasts in the air fryer basket, skin side up.
3. Put the air fryer basket on sheet pan and place into oven. Select Air Fry, set temperature to 400°F (205°C) and set time to 10 minutes.
4. Meanwhile, combine the remaining ingredients in a small bowl. Stir to mix well.
5. When cooking is complete, brush the duck skin with the marmalade mixture. Flip the breast and air fry for 3 more minutes or until the skin is crispy and the breast is well browned.
6. Serve immediately.

Chapter 4: Poultry | 45

Pineapple Chicken

Prep time: 10 minutes | Cook time: 10 minutes | Serves 6

1½ pounds (680 g) boneless, skinless chicken breasts, cut into 1-inch chunks
¾ cup soy sauce
2 tablespoons ketchup
2 tablespoons brown sugar
2 tablespoons rice vinegar
1 red bell pepper, cut into 1-inch chunks
1 green bell pepper, cut into 1-inch chunks
6 scallions, cut into 1-inch pieces
1 cup (¾-inch chunks) fresh pineapple, rinsed and drained
Cooking spray

1. Place the chicken in a large bowl. Add the soy sauce, ketchup, brown sugar, vinegar, red and green peppers, and scallions. Toss to coat.
2. Spritz the sheet pan with cooking spray and place the chicken and vegetables on the pan.
3. Place the sheet pan on wire rack and slide into oven. Select Air Roast, set temperature to 375°F (190°C), and set time to 10 minutes.
4. After 6 minutes, remove from the oven. Add the pineapple chunks to the pan and stir. Return the pan to the oven and continue cooking.
5. When cooking is complete, remove from the oven. Serve with steamed rice, if desired.

Golden Chicken Fries

Prep time: 20 minutes | Cook time: 6 minutes | Serves 4 to 6

1 pound (454 g) chicken tenders, cut into about ½-inch-wide strips
Salt, to taste
¼ cup all-purpose flour
Seasonings:
½ teaspoon garlic powder
1 tablespoon chili powder
2 eggs
¾ cup panko bread crumbs
¾ cup crushed organic nacho cheese tortilla chips
Cooking spray
½ teaspoon onion powder
1 teaspoon ground cumin

1. Stir together all seasonings in a small bowl and set aside.
2. Sprinkle the chicken with salt. Place strips in a large bowl and sprinkle with 1 tablespoon of the seasoning mix. Stir well to distribute seasonings.
3. Add flour to chicken and stir well to coat all sides.
4. Beat eggs in a separate bowl.
5. In a shallow dish, combine the panko, crushed chips, and the remaining 2 teaspoons of seasoning mix.
6. Dip chicken strips in eggs, then roll in crumbs. Mist with oil or cooking spray. Arrange the chicken strips in a single layer in the basket.
7. Put the air fryer basket on sheet pan and place into oven. Select Air Fry, set the temperature to 400°F (205°C) and set the time to 6 minutes.
8. After 4 minutes, remove from the oven. Flip the strips with tongs. Return to the oven and continue cooking.
9. When cooking is complete, the chicken should be crispy and its juices should be run clear.
10. Allow to cool under room temperature before serving.

Peach and Cherry Chicken

Prep time: 8 minutes | Cook time: 15 minutes | Serves 4

⅓ cup peach preserves
1 teaspoon ground rosemary
½ teaspoon black pepper
½ teaspoon salt
½ teaspoon marjoram
1 teaspoon light olive oil
1 pound (454 g) boneless chicken breasts, cut in 1½-inch chunks
1 (10-ounce / 284-g) package frozen dark cherries, thawed and drained
Cooking spray

1. In a medium bowl, mix peach preserves, rosemary, pepper, salt, marjoram, and olive oil.
2. Stir in chicken chunks and toss to coat well with the preserve mixture.
3. Spritz the sheet pan with cooking spray and lay chicken chunks in the pan.
4. Place the sheet pan on wire rack and slide into oven. Select Bake, set the temperature to 400°F (205°C) and set the time to 15 minutes.
5. After 7 minutes, remove from the oven and flip the chicken chunks. Return the pan to the oven and continue cooking.
6. When cooking is complete, the chicken should no longer pink and the juices should run clear.
7. Scatter the cherries over and cook for an additional minute to heat cherries.
8. Serve immediately.

Chicken Skewers with Corn Salad

Prep time: 17 minutes | Cook time: 10 minutes | Serves 4

1 pound (454 g) boneless, skinless chicken breast, cut into 1½-inch chunks
1 green bell pepper, deseeded and cut into 1-inch pieces
1 red bell pepper, deseeded and cut into 1-inch pieces
1 large onion, cut into large chunks
2 tablespoons fajita seasoning
3 tablespoons vegetable oil, divided
2 teaspoons kosher salt, divided
2 cups corn, drained
¼ teaspoon granulated garlic
1 teaspoon freshly squeezed lime juice
1 tablespoon mayonnaise
3 tablespoons grated Parmesan cheese

Special Equipment:
12 wooden skewers, soaked in water for at least 30 minutes

1. Place the chicken, bell peppers, and onion in a large bowl. Add the fajita seasoning, 2 tablespoons of vegetable oil, and 1½ teaspoons of kosher salt. Toss to coat evenly.
2. Alternate the chicken and vegetables on the skewers, making about 12 skewers.
3. Place the corn in a medium bowl and add the remaining vegetable oil. Add the remaining kosher salt and the garlic, and toss to coat. Place the corn in an even layer in the sheet pan and place the skewers on top.
4. Place the sheet pan on wire rack and slide into oven. Select Air Roast, set temperature to 375ºF (190ºC), and set time to 10 minutes.
5. After about 5 minutes, remove from the oven and turn the skewers. Return to the oven and continue cooking.
6. When cooking is complete, remove from the oven. Place the skewers on a platter. Put the corn back to the bowl and combine with the lime juice, mayonnaise, and Parmesan cheese. Stir to mix well. Serve the skewers with the corn.

Braised Chicken with Hot Peppers

Prep time: 10 minutes | Cook time: 27 minutes | Serves 4

4 bone-in, skin-on chicken thighs (about 1½ pounds / 680 g)
1½ teaspoon kosher salt, divided
1 link sweet Italian sausage (about 4 ounces / 113 g), whole
8 ounces (227 g) miniature bell peppers, halved and deseeded
1 small onion, thinly sliced
2 garlic cloves, minced
1 tablespoon olive oil
4 hot pickled cherry peppers, deseeded and quartered, along with 2 tablespoons pickling liquid from the jar
¼ cup chicken stock
Cooking spray

1. Salt the chicken thighs on both sides with 1 teaspoon of kosher salt. Spritz the sheet pan with cooking spray and place the thighs skin-side down on the pan. Add the sausage.
2. Place the sheet pan on wire rack and slide into oven. Select Air Roast, set temperature to 375ºF (190ºC), and set time to 27 minutes.
3. While the chicken and sausage cook, place the bell peppers, onion, and garlic in a large bowl. Sprinkle with the remaining kosher salt and add the olive oil. Toss to coat.
4. After 10 minutes, remove from the oven and flip the chicken thighs and sausage. Add the pepper mixture to the pan. Return the pan to the oven and continue cooking.
5. After another 10 minutes, remove from the oven and add the pickled peppers, pickling liquid, and stock. Stir the pickled peppers into the peppers and onion. Return the pan to the oven and continue cooking.
6. When cooking is complete, the peppers and onion should be soft and the chicken should read 165ºF (74ºC) on a meat thermometer. Remove from the oven. Slice the sausage into thin pieces and stir it into the pepper mixture. Spoon the peppers over four plates. Top with a chicken thigh.

Chapter 4: Poultry | 47

Chicken Shawarma

Prep time: 10 minutes | Cook time: 18 minutes | Serves 4

1½ pounds (680 g) boneless, skinless chicken thighs
1¼ teaspoon kosher salt, divided
2 tablespoons plus 1 teaspoon olive oil, divided
⅔ cup plus 2 tablespoons plain Greek yogurt, divided
2 tablespoons freshly squeezed lemon juice
(about 1 medium lemon)
4 garlic cloves, minced, divided
1 tablespoon Shawarma Seasoning
4 pita breads, cut in half
2 cups cherry tomatoes
½ small cucumber, peeled, deseeded, and chopped
1 tablespoon chopped fresh parsley

1. Sprinkle the chicken thighs on both sides with 1 teaspoon of kosher salt. Place in a resealable plastic bag and set aside while you make the marinade.
2. In a small bowl, mix 2 tablespoons of olive oil, 2 tablespoons of yogurt, the lemon juice, 3 garlic cloves, and Shawarma Seasoning until thoroughly combined. Pour the marinade over the chicken. Seal the bag, squeezing out as much air as possible. And massage the chicken to coat it with the sauce. Set aside.
3. Wrap 2 pita breads each in two pieces of aluminum foil and place in the sheet pan.
4. Place the sheet pan on wire rack and slide into oven. Select Bake, set temperature to 300ºF (150ºC), and set time to 6 minutes.
5. After 3 minutes, remove the pan from the oven and turn over the foil packets. Return the pan to the oven and continue cooking. When cooking is complete, remove the pan from the oven and place the foil-wrapped pitas on the top of the oven to keep warm.
6. Remove the chicken from the marinade, letting the excess drip off into the bag. Place them in the sheet pan. Arrange the tomatoes around the sides of the chicken. Discard the marinade.
7. Place the pan back to the oven. Select Air Broil, set temperature to High, and set time to 12 minutes.
8. After 6 minutes, remove the pan from the oven and turn over the chicken. Return the pan to the oven and continue cooking.
9. Wrap the cucumber in a paper towel to remove as much moisture as possible. Place them in a small bowl. Add the remaining yogurt, kosher salt, olive oil, garlic clove, and parsley. Whisk until combined.
10. When cooking is complete, the chicken should be browned, crisp along its edges, and sizzling. Remove from the oven and place the chicken on a cutting board.

Cut each thigh into several pieces. Unwrap the pitas. Spread a tablespoon of sauce into a pita half. Add some chicken and add 2 roasted tomatoes. Serve.

Chicken Thighs with Radish Slaw

Prep time: 10 minutes | Cook time: 27 minutes | Serves 4

4 bone-in, skin-on chicken thighs
1½ teaspoon kosher salt, divided
1 tablespoon smoked paprika
½ teaspoon granulated garlic
½ teaspoon dried oregano
¼ teaspoon freshly ground black pepper
3 cups shredded cabbage
½ small red onion, thinly sliced
4 large radishes, julienned
3 tablespoons red wine vinegar
2 tablespoons olive oil
Cooking spray

1. Salt the chicken thighs on both sides with 1 teaspoon of kosher salt. In a small bowl, combine the paprika, garlic, oregano, and black pepper. Sprinkle half this mixture over the skin sides of the thighs. Spritz the sheet pan with cooking spray and place the thighs skin-side down in the pan. Sprinkle the remaining spice mixture over the other sides of the chicken pieces.
2. Place the sheet pan on wire rack and slide into oven. Select Air Roast, set temperature to 375ºF (190ºC), and set time to 27 minutes.
3. After 10 minutes, remove from the oven and turn over the chicken thighs. Return to the oven and continue cooking.
4. While the chicken cooks, place the cabbage, onion, and radishes in a large bowl. Sprinkle with the remaining kosher salt, vinegar, and olive oil. Toss to coat.
5. After another 9 to 10 minutes, remove from the oven and place the chicken thighs on a cutting board. Place the cabbage mixture in the pan and toss with the chicken fat and spices.
6. Spread the cabbage in an even layer on the pan and place the chicken on it, skin-side up. Return the pan to the oven and continue cooking. Roast for another 7 to 8 minutes.
7. When cooking is complete, the cabbage is just becoming tender. Remove from the oven. Taste and adjust the seasoning if necessary. Serve.

Chicken and Sweet Potato Curry

Prep time: 10 minutes | Cook time: 20 minutes | Serves 4

1 pound (454 g) boneless, skinless chicken thighs	1 tablespoon curry powder
1 teaspoon kosher salt, divided	2 medium sweet potatoes, peeled and cut in 1-inch cubes
¼ cup unsalted butter, melted	12 ounces (340 g) Brussels sprouts, halved

1. Sprinkle the chicken thighs with ½ teaspoon of kosher salt. Place them in the single layer in the sheet pan.
2. In a small bowl, stir together the butter and curry powder.
3. Place the sweet potatoes and Brussels sprouts in a large bowl. Drizzle half the curry butter over the vegetables and add the remaining kosher salt. Toss to coat. Transfer the vegetables to the sheet pan and place in a single layer around the chicken. Brush half of the remaining curry butter over the chicken.
4. Place the sheet pan on wire rack and slide into oven. Select Air Roast, set temperature to 400ºF (205ºC), and set time to 20 minutes.
5. After 10 minutes, remove from the oven and turn over the chicken thighs. Baste them with the remaining curry butter. Return to the oven and continue cooking.
6. Cooking is complete when the sweet potatoes are tender and the chicken is cooked through and reads 165ºF (74ºC) on a meat thermometer.

Super Lemon Chicken

Prep time: 5 minutes | Cook time: 35 minutes | Serves 6

3 (8-ounce / 227-g) boneless, skinless chicken breasts, halved, rinsed	½ cup fresh lemon juice
	½ cup water
1 cup dried bread crumbs	¼ cup minced fresh oregano
¼ cup olive oil	
¼ cup chicken broth	1 medium lemon, cut into wedges
Zest of 1 lemon	
3 medium garlic cloves, minced	¼ cup minced fresh parsley, divided
	Cooking spray

1. Pour the bread crumbs in a shadow dish, then roll the chicken breasts in the bread crumbs to coat.
2. Spritz a skillet with cooking spray, and brown the coated chicken breasts over medium heat about 3 minutes on each side. Transfer the browned chicken to the sheet pan.
3. In a small bowl, combine the remaining ingredients, except the lemon and parsley. Pour the sauce over the chicken.
4. Place the sheet pan on wire rack and slide into oven. Select Bake, set the temperature to 325ºF (163ºC) and set the time to 30 minutes.
5. After 15 minutes, remove the pan from the oven. Flip the breasts. Return the pan to the oven and continue cooking.
6. When cooking is complete, the chicken should no longer pink.
7. Transfer to a serving platter, and spoon the sauce over the chicken. Garnish with the lemon and parsley.

Glazed Chicken Drumsticks

Prep time: 5 minutes | Cook time: 20 minutes | Serves 2

4 chicken drumsticks	1 teaspoon toasted sesame oil
3 tablespoons soy sauce	
2 tablespoons brown sugar	½ teaspoon red pepper flakes
1 teaspoon minced garlic	
1 teaspoon minced fresh ginger	½ teaspoon kosher salt
	½ teaspoon black pepper

1. Preheat the air fryer oven to 400ºF (204ºC).
2. Line a round sheet pan with aluminum foil. (If you don't do this, you'll either end up scrubbing forever or throwing out the pan.) Arrange the drumsticks in the prepared pan.
3. In a medium bowl, stir together the soy sauce, brown sugar, garlic, ginger, sesame oil, red pepper flakes, salt, and black pepper. Pour the sauce over the drumsticks and toss to coat.
4. Put the sheet pan on wire rack and slide into the oven. Select Bake and set time to 20 minutes, turning the drumsticks halfway through the cooking time. Use a meat thermometer to ensure the chicken has reached an internal temperature of 165ºF (74ºC).
5. Cool for 5 minutes before serving.

Chapter 4: Poultry | 49

Herbed Hens

Prep time: 2 hours 15 minutes | Cook time: 30 minutes | Serves 8

4 (1¼-pound / 567-g) Cornish hens, giblets removed, split lengthwise
2 cups white wine, divided
2 garlic cloves, minced
1 small onion, minced
½ teaspoon celery seeds
½ teaspoon poultry seasoning
½ teaspoon paprika
½ teaspoon dried oregano
¼ teaspoon freshly ground black pepper

1. Place the hens, cavity side up, in the sheet pan. Pour 1½ cups of the wine over the hens. Set aside.
2. In a shallow bowl, combine the garlic, onion, celery seeds, poultry seasoning, paprika, oregano, and pepper. Sprinkle half of the combined seasonings over the cavity of each split half. Cover and refrigerate. Allow the hens to marinate for 2 hours.
3. Transfer the hens to the pan. Place the sheet pan on wire rack and slide into oven. Select Bake, set temperature to 350°F (180°C) and set time to 90 minutes.
4. Flip the breast halfway through and remove the skin. Pour the remaining ½ cup of wine over the top, and sprinkle with the remaining seasonings.
5. When cooking is complete, the inner temperature of the hens should be at least 165°F (74°C). Transfer the hens to a serving platter and serve hot.

Chicken with Potatoes and Corn

Prep time: 10 minutes | Cook time: 25 minutes | Serves 4

4 bone-in, skin-on chicken thighs
2 teaspoons kosher salt, divided
1 cup Bisquick baking mix
½ cup butter, melted, divided
1 pound (454 g) small red
potatoes, quartered
3 ears corn, shucked and cut into rounds 1- to 1½-inches thick
⅓ cup heavy whipping cream
½ teaspoon freshly ground black pepper

1. Sprinkle the chicken on all sides with 1 teaspoon of kosher salt. Place the baking mix in a shallow dish.

Brush the thighs on all sides with ¼ cup of butter, then dredge them in the baking mix, coating them all on sides. Place the chicken in the center of the sheet pan.
2. Place the potatoes in a large bowl with 2 tablespoons of butter and toss to coat. Place them on one side of the chicken on the pan.
3. Place the corn in a medium bowl and drizzle with the remaining butter. Sprinkle with ¼ teaspoon of kosher salt and toss to coat. Place on the pan on the other side of the chicken.
4. Place the sheet pan on wire rack and slide into oven. Select Air Roast, set temperature to 375°F (190°C), and set time to 25 minutes.
5. After 20 minutes, remove from the oven and put the potatoes back to the bowl. Return the pan to oven and continue cooking.
6. As the chicken continues cooking, add the cream, black pepper, and remaining kosher salt to the potatoes. Lightly mash the potatoes with a potato masher.
7. When cooking is complete, the corn should be tender and the chicken cooked through, reading 165°F (74°C) on a meat thermometer. Remove from the oven. Serve the chicken with the smashed potatoes and corn on the side.

Fajita Chicken Strips

Prep time: 10 minutes | Cook time: 15 minutes | Serves 4

1 pound (454 g) boneless, skinless chicken tenderloins, cut into strips
3 bell peppers, any color, cut into chunks
1 onion, cut into chunks
1 tablespoon olive oil
1 tablespoon fajita seasoning mix
Cooking spray

1. Preheat the air fryer oven to 370°F (188°C).
2. In a large bowl, mix together the chicken, bell peppers, onion, olive oil, and fajita seasoning mix until completely coated.
3. Spray the air fryer basket lightly with cooking spray.
4. Place the chicken and vegetables in the air fryer basket and lightly spray with cooking spray.
5. Put the air fryer basket on sheet pan and place into oven. Select Air Fry and set time to 7 minutes.
6. Shake the basket and air fry for an additional 5 to 8 minutes, until the chicken is cooked through and the veggies are starting to char.
7. Serve warm.

Creole Hens

Prep time: 10 minutes | Cook time: 40 minutes | Serves 4

½ tablespoon Creole seasoning
½ tablespoon garlic powder
½ tablespoon onion powder
½ tablespoon freshly
ground black pepper
½ tablespoon paprika
2 tablespoons olive oil
2 Cornish hens
Cooking spray

1. Spritz the air fryer basket with cooking spray.
2. In a small bowl, mix the Creole seasoning, garlic powder, onion powder, pepper, and paprika.
3. Pat the Cornish hens dry and brush each hen all over with the olive oil. Rub each hen with the seasoning mixture. Place the Cornish hens in the basket.
4. Put the air fryer basket on sheet pan and place into oven. Select Air Fry, set the temperature to 375ºF (190ºC) and set the time to 30 minutes.
5. After 15 minutes, remove from the oven. Flip the hens over and baste it with any drippings collected in the bottom drawer of the oven. Return to the oven and continue cooking.
6. When cooking is complete, a thermometer inserted into the thickest part of the hens should reach at least 165ºF (74ºC).
7. Let the hens rest for 10 minutes before carving.

Gnocchi with Chicken and Spinach

Prep time: 10 minutes | Cook time: 13 minutes | Serves 4

1 (1-pound / 454-g) package shelf-stable gnocchi
1¼ cups chicken stock
½ teaspoon kosher salt
1 pound (454 g) chicken breast, cut into 1-inch chunks
1 cup heavy whipping cream
2 tablespoons sun-dried tomato purée
1 garlic clove, minced
1 cup frozen spinach, thawed and drained
1 cup grated Parmesan cheese

1. Place the gnocchi in an even layer in the sheet pan. Pour the chicken stock over the gnocchi.
2. Place the sheet pan on wire rack and slide into oven. Select Bake, set temperature to 450ºF (235ºC), and set time to 7 minutes.
3. While the gnocchi are cooking, sprinkle the salt over the chicken pieces. In a small bowl, mix the cream, tomato purée, and garlic.
4. When cooking is complete, blot off any remaining stock, or drain the gnocchi and return it to the pan. Top the gnocchi with the spinach and chicken. Pour the cream mixture over the ingredients in the pan.
5. Place the sheet pan on wire rack and slide into oven. Select Air Roast, set temperature to 400ºF (205ºC), and set time to 6 minutes.
6. After 4 minutes, remove from the oven and gently stir the ingredients. Return to the oven and continue cooking.
7. When cooking is complete, the gnocchi should be tender and the chicken should be cooked through. Remove from the oven. Stir in the Parmesan cheese until it's melted and serve.

Chicken Roast

Prep time: 15 minutes | Cook time: 1 hour | Serves 6

1 teaspoon Italian seasoning
½ teaspoon garlic powder
½ teaspoon paprika
1 teaspoon salt
½ teaspoon freshly ground black pepper
½ teaspoon onion powder
2 tablespoons olive oil
1 (3-pound / 1.4-kg) whole chicken, giblets removed, pat dry
Cooking spray

1. Spritz the air fryer basket with cooking spray.
2. In a small bowl, mix the Italian seasoning, garlic powder, paprika, salt, pepper, and onion powder.
3. Brush the chicken with the olive oil and rub it with the seasoning mixture.
4. Tie the chicken legs with butcher's twine. Place the chicken in the basket, breast side down.
5. Put the air fryer basket on sheet pan and place into oven. Select Air Fry, set the temperature to 350ºF (180ºC) and set the time to an hour.
6. After 30 minutes, remove from the oven. Flip the chicken over and baste it with any drippings collected in the bottom drawer of the oven. Return to the oven and continue cooking.
7. When cooking is complete, a thermometer inserted into the thickest part of the thigh should reach at least 165ºF (74ºC).
8. Let the chicken rest for 10 minutes before carving and serving.

Chapter 4: Poultry | 51

Celery Chicken

Prep time: 10 minutes | Cook time: 15 minutes | Serves 4

½ cup soy sauce
2 tablespoons hoisin sauce
4 teaspoons minced garlic
1 teaspoon freshly ground black pepper
8 boneless, skinless

chicken tenderloins
1 cup chopped celery
1 medium red bell pepper, diced
Olive oil spray

1. Preheat the air fryer oven to 375°F (191°C). Spray the air fryer basket lightly with olive oil spray.
2. In a large bowl, mix together the soy sauce, hoisin sauce, garlic, and black pepper to make a marinade. Add the chicken, celery, and bell pepper and toss to coat.
3. Shake the excess marinade off the chicken, place it and the vegetables in the air fryer basket, and lightly spray with olive oil spray. Reserve the remaining marinade.
4. Put the air fryer basket on sheet pan and place into oven. Select Air Fry and set time to 8 minutes.
5. Turn the chicken over and brush with some of the remaining marinade. Air fry for an additional 5 to 7 minutes, or until the chicken reaches an internal temperature of at least 165°F (74°C). Rest for 5 minutes before serving.

Piri-Piri Chicken Thighs

Prep time: 5 minutes | Cook time: 23 minutes | Serves 4

¼ cup piri-piri sauce
1 tablespoon freshly squeezed lemon juice
2 tablespoons brown sugar, divided
2 cloves garlic, minced
1 tablespoon extra-virgin

olive oil
4 bone-in, skin-on chicken thighs, each weighing approximately 7 to 8 ounces (198 to 227 g)
½ teaspoon cornstarch

1. To make the marinade, whisk together the piri-piri sauce, lemon juice, 1 tablespoon of brown sugar, and the garlic in a small bowl. While whisking, slowly pour in the oil in a steady stream and continue to whisk until emulsified. Using a skewer, poke holes in the chicken thighs and place them in a small glass dish. Pour the marinade over the chicken and turn the thighs to coat them with the sauce. Cover the dish and refrigerate for at least 15 minutes and up to 1 hour.
2. Preheat the air fryer oven to 375°F (191°C). Remove the chicken thighs from the dish, reserving the marinade, and place them skin-side down in the air fryer basket.
3. Put the air fryer basket on sheet pan and place into oven. Select Air Fry and set time to 18 minutes, or until the internal temperature reaches 165°F (74°C).
4. Meanwhile, whisk the remaining brown sugar and the cornstarch into the marinade and microwave it on high power for 1 minute until it is bubbling and thickened to a glaze.
5. Once the chicken is cooked, turn the thighs over and brush them with the glaze. Air fry for a few additional minutes until the glaze browns and begins to char in spots.
6. Remove the chicken to a platter and serve with additional piri-piri sauce, if desired.

Fried Chicken Tenders with Veggies

Prep time: 10 minutes | Cook time: 20 minutes | Serves 4

1 pound (454 g) chicken tenders
1 tablespoon honey
Pinch salt
Freshly ground black pepper, to taste

½ cup soft fresh bread crumbs
½ teaspoon dried thyme
1 tablespoon olive oil
2 carrots, sliced
12 small red potatoes

1. Preheat the air fryer oven to 380°F (193°C).
2. In a medium bowl, toss the chicken tenders with the honey, salt, and pepper.
3. In a shallow bowl, combine the bread crumbs, thyme, and olive oil, and mix.
4. Coat the tenders in the bread crumbs, pressing firmly onto the meat.
5. Place the carrots and potatoes in the air fryer basket and top with the chicken tenders.
6. Put the air fryer basket on sheet pan and place into oven. Select Air Fry and set time to 20 minutes, or until the chicken is cooked to 165°F (74°C) and the vegetables are tender. Shake the basket halfway during the cooking time.
7. Serve warm.

Chicken Satay with Peanut Sauce

Prep time: 12 minutes | Cook time: 9 minutes | Serves 4

½ cup crunchy peanut butter

⅓ cup chicken broth

3 tablespoons low-sodium soy sauce

2 tablespoons lemon juice

2 cloves garlic, minced

2 tablespoons olive oil

1 teaspoon curry powder

1 pound (454 g) chicken tenders

1. Preheat the air fryer oven to 390°F (199°C).
2. In a medium bowl, combine the peanut butter, chicken broth, soy sauce, lemon juice, garlic, olive oil, and curry powder, and mix well with a wire whisk until smooth. Remove 2 tablespoons of this mixture to a small bowl. Put remaining sauce into a serving bowl and set aside.
3. Add the chicken tenders to the bowl with the 2 tablespoons sauce and stir to coat. Let stand for a few minutes to marinate, then run a bamboo skewer through each chicken tender lengthwise. Put the chicken in the air fryer basket.
4. Put the air fryer basket on sheet pan and place into oven. Select Air Fry and set time to 9 minutes, or until the chicken reaches 165°F (74°C) on a meat thermometer. Serve the chicken with the reserved sauce.

Air Fried Naked Chicken Tenders

Prep time: 5 minutes | Cook time: 7 minutes | Serves 4

Seasoning:

1 teaspoon kosher salt

½ teaspoon garlic powder

½ teaspoon onion powder

½ teaspoon chili powder

¼ teaspoon sweet paprika

¼ teaspoon freshly ground black pepper

Chicken:

8 chicken breast tenders (1 pound / 454 g total)

2 tablespoons mayonnaise

1. Preheat the air fryer oven to 375°F (191°C).
2. For the seasoning: In a small bowl, combine the salt, garlic powder, onion powder, chili powder, paprika, and pepper.
3. For the chicken: Place the chicken in a medium bowl and add the mayonnaise. Mix well to coat all over, then sprinkle with the seasoning mix.
4. Arrange a single layer of the chicken in the air fryer basket.
5. Put the air fryer basket on sheet pan and place into oven. Select Air Fry and set time to 7 minutes. Flip the chicken halfway through the cooking time, or until cooked through in the center.
6. Serve immediately.

Israeli Chicken Schnitzel

Prep time: 5 minutes | Cook time: 10 minutes | Serves 4

2 large boneless, skinless chicken breasts, each weighing about 1 pound (454 g)

1 cup all-purpose flour

2 teaspoons garlic powder

2 teaspoons kosher salt

1 teaspoon black pepper

1 teaspoon paprika

2 eggs beaten with 2 tablespoons water

2 cups panko bread crumbs

Vegetable oil spray

Lemon juice, for serving

1. Preheat the air fryer oven to 375°F (191°C).
2. Place 1 chicken breast between 2 pieces of plastic wrap. Use a mallet or a rolling pin to pound the chicken until it is ¼ inch thick. Set aside. Repeat with the second breast. Whisk together the flour, garlic powder, salt, pepper, and paprika on a large plate. Place the panko in a separate shallow bowl or pie plate.
3. Dredge 1 chicken breast in the flour, shaking off any excess, then dip it in the egg mixture. Dredge the chicken breast in the panko, making sure to coat it completely. Shake off any excess panko. Place the battered chicken breast on a plate. Repeat with the second chicken breast.
4. Spray the air fryer basket with oil spray. Put the battered chicken breasts in the basket and spray the top with oil spray.
5. Put the air fryer basket on sheet pan and place into oven. Select Air Fry and set time to 5 minutes.
6. Flip the chicken and spray with oil spray. Air fry until the second side is browned and crispy and the internal temperature reaches 165°F (74°C).
7. Serve hot with lemon juice.

Chapter 4: Poultry | 53

Asian Turkey Meatballs

Prep time: 10 minutes | Cook time: 14 minutes | Serves 4

2 tablespoons peanut oil, divided	2 tablespoons low-sodium soy sauce
1 small onion, minced	¼ cup panko bread crumbs
¼ cup water chestnuts, finely chopped	1 egg, beaten
½ teaspoon ground ginger	1 pound (454 g) ground turkey

1. Preheat the air fryer oven to 400ºF (204ºC).
2. In a small bowl, combine 1 tablespoon of peanut oil and onion. Transfer the onion to the air fryer basket.
3. Put the air fryer basket on sheet pan and place into oven. Select Air Fry and set time to 2 minutes, or until crisp and tender. Transfer the onion to a medium bowl.
4. Add the water chestnuts, ground ginger, soy sauce, and bread crumbs to the onion and mix well. Add egg and stir well. Mix in the ground turkey until combined.
5. Form the mixture into 1-inch meatballs. Drizzle the remaining 1 tablespoon of oil over the meatballs. Put the meatballs in the air fryer basket.
6. Put the air fryer basket on sheet pan and place into oven. Select Air Fry and set time to 12 minutes, or until the meatballs register 165ºF (74ºC) on a meat thermometer.
7. Rest for 5 minutes before serving.

Potato Cheese Crusted Chicken

Prep time: 15 minutes | Cook time: 24 minutes | Serves 4

¼ cup buttermilk	½ teaspoon freshly ground black pepper
1 large egg, beaten	
1 cup instant potato flakes	2 whole boneless, skinless chicken breasts (about 1 pound / 454 g each), halved
¼ cup grated Parmesan cheese	
1 teaspoon salt	Cooking spray

1. Preheat the air fryer oven to 325ºF (163ºC). Line a sheet pan with parchment paper.
2. In a shallow bowl, whisk the buttermilk and egg until blended. In another shallow bowl, stir together the potato flakes, cheese, salt, and pepper.
3. One at a time, dip the chicken pieces in the buttermilk mixture and the potato flake mixture, coating thoroughly.
4. Place the coated chicken on the parchment and spritz with cooking spray.
5. Put the sheet pan on wire rack and slide into the oven. Select Bake and set time to 24 minutes, flipping the chicken and spritzing it with cooking spray during cooking, or until the outside is crispy and the inside is no longer pink.
6. Serve immediately.

Sweet-and-Sour Drumsticks

Prep time: 5 minutes | Cook time: 24 minutes | Serves 4

6 chicken drumsticks	1 tablespoon peanut oil
3 tablespoons lemon juice, divided	3 tablespoons honey
	3 tablespoons brown sugar
3 tablespoons low-sodium soy sauce, divided	2 tablespoons ketchup
	¼ cup pineapple juice

1. Preheat the air fryer oven to 350ºF (177ºC).
2. Sprinkle the chicken drumsticks with 1 tablespoon of lemon juice and 1 tablespoon of soy sauce.
3. Place them in a sheet pan and drizzle with the peanut oil. Toss to coat.
4. Put the sheet pan on wire rack and slide into the oven. Select Bake and set time to 18 minutes, or until the chicken is almost done.
5. Meanwhile, in a large bowl, combine the remaining 2 tablespoons of lemon juice, the remaining 2 tablespoons of soy sauce, honey, brown sugar, ketchup, and pineapple juice.
6. Add the cooked chicken to the bowl and stir to coat the chicken well with the sauce.
7. Place the sheet pan with the coated chicken back into oven and bake for 6 minutes more, or until the chicken is glazed and registers 165ºF (74ºC) on a meat thermometer.
8. Serve warm.

Fried Buffalo Chicken Taquitos

Prep time: 15 minutes | Cook time: 8 minutes | Serves 6

8 ounces (227 g) fat-free cream cheese, softened
⅛ cup Buffalo sauce
2 cups shredded cooked chicken
12 (7-inch) low-carb flour tortillas
Olive oil spray

1. Preheat the air fryer oven to 360ºF (182ºC). Spray the air fryer basket lightly with olive oil spray.
2. In a large bowl, mix together the cream cheese and Buffalo sauce until well combined. Add the chicken and stir until combined.
3. Place the tortillas on a clean work surface. Spoon 2 to 3 tablespoons of the chicken mixture in a thin line down the center of each tortilla. Roll up the tortillas.
4. Place the tortillas in the air fryer basket, seam-side down. Spray each tortilla lightly with olive oil spray. You may need to cook the taquitos in batches.
5. Put the air fryer basket on sheet pan and place into oven. Select Air Fry and set time to 8 minutes, or until golden brown.
6. Serve hot.

Lemon Parmesan Chicken

Prep time: 10 minutes | Cook time: 20 minutes | Serves 4

1 egg
2 tablespoons lemon juice
2 teaspoons minced garlic
½ teaspoon salt
½ teaspoon freshly ground black pepper
4 boneless, skinless chicken breasts, thin cut
Olive oil spray
½ cup whole-wheat bread crumbs
¼ cup grated Parmesan cheese

1. In a medium bowl, whisk together the egg, lemon juice, garlic, salt, and pepper. Add the chicken breasts, cover, and refrigerate for up to 1 hour.
2. In a shallow bowl, combine the bread crumbs and Parmesan cheese.
3. Preheat the air fryer oven to 360ºF (182ºC). Spray the air fryer basket lightly with olive oil spray.
4. Remove the chicken breasts from the egg mixture, then dredge them in the bread crumb mixture, and place in the air fryer basket in a single layer. Lightly spray the chicken breasts with olive oil spray.
5. Put the air fryer basket on sheet pan and place into oven. Select Air Fry and set time to 8 minutes.
6. Flip the chicken, lightly spray with olive oil spray, and air fry until the chicken reaches an internal temperature of 165ºF (74ºC), for an additional 7 to 12 minutes.
7. Serve warm.

Turkey Stuffed Bell Peppers

Prep time: 20 minutes | Cook time: 15 minutes | Serves 4

½ pound (227 g) lean ground turkey
4 medium bell peppers
1 (15-ounce / 425-g) can black beans, drained and rinsed
1 cup shredded reduced-fat Cheddar cheese
1 cup cooked long-grain brown rice
1 cup mild salsa
1¼ teaspoons chili powder
1 teaspoon salt
½ teaspoon ground cumin
½ teaspoon freshly ground black pepper
Olive oil spray
Chopped fresh cilantro, for garnish

1. Preheat the air fryer oven to 360ºF (182ºC).
2. In a large skillet over medium-high heat, cook the turkey, breaking it up with a spoon, until browned, about 5 minutes. Drain off any excess fat.
3. Cut about ½ inch off the tops of the peppers and then cut in half lengthwise. Remove and discard the seeds and set the peppers aside.
4. In a large bowl, combine the browned turkey, black beans, Cheddar cheese, rice, salsa, chili powder, salt, cumin, and black pepper. Spoon the mixture into the bell peppers.
5. Lightly spray the air fryer basket with olive oil spray. Place the stuffed peppers in the air fryer basket.
6. Put the air fryer basket on sheet pan and place into oven. Select Air Fry and set time to 15 minutes, or until heated through.
7. Garnish with cilantro and serve.

Chapter 4: Poultry | 55

Nutty Chicken Tenders

Prep time: 5 minutes | Cook time: 12 minutes | Serves 4

1 pound (454 g) chicken tenders
1 teaspoon kosher salt
1 teaspoon black pepper
½ teaspoon smoked paprika
¼ cup coarse mustard
2 tablespoons honey
1 cup finely crushed pecans

1. Preheat the air fryer oven to 350ºF (177ºC).
2. Place the chicken in a large bowl. Sprinkle with the salt, pepper, and paprika. Toss until the chicken is coated with the spices. Add the mustard and honey and toss until the chicken is coated.
3. Place the pecans on a plate. Working with one piece of chicken at a time, roll the chicken in the pecans until both sides are coated. Lightly brush off any loose pecans. Place the chicken in a sheet pan.
4. Put the sheet pan on wire rack and slide into the oven. Select Bake and set time to 12 minutes, or until the chicken is cooked through and the pecans are golden brown.
5. Serve warm.

Blackened Chicken Breasts

Prep time: 10 minutes | Cook time: 20 minutes | Serves 4

1 large egg, beaten
¾ cup Blackened seasoning
2 whole boneless, skinless
chicken breasts (about 1 pound / 454 g each), halved
Cooking spray

1. Preheat the air fryer oven to 360ºF (182ºC). Line the air fryer basket with parchment paper.
2. Place the beaten egg in one shallow bowl and the Blackened seasoning in another shallow bowl.
3. One at a time, dip the chicken pieces in the beaten egg and the Blackened seasoning, coating thoroughly.
4. Place the chicken pieces on the parchment and spritz with cooking spray.
5. Put the air fryer basket on sheet pan and place into oven. Select Air Fry and set time to 20 minutes. Flip the chicken and spritz it with cooking spray halfway through, or until the internal temperature reaches 165ºF (74ºC) and the chicken is no longer pink inside.
6. Let sit for 5 minutes before serving.

Turkey and Cranberry Quesadillas

Prep time: 7 minutes | Cook time: 6 minutes | Serves 4

6 low-sodium whole-wheat tortillas
⅓ cup shredded low-sodium low-fat Swiss cheese
¾ cup shredded cooked low-sodium turkey breast
2 tablespoons cranberry sauce
2 tablespoons dried cranberries
½ teaspoon dried basil
Olive oil spray, for spraying the tortillas

1. Preheat the air fryer oven to 400ºF (204ºC).
2. Put 3 tortillas on a work surface.
3. Evenly divide the Swiss cheese, turkey, cranberry sauce, and dried cranberries among the tortillas. Sprinkle with the basil and top with the remaining tortillas.
4. Spray the outsides of the tortillas with olive oil spray, then transfer to the air fryer basket.
5. Put the air fryer basket on sheet pan and place into oven. Select Air Fry and set time to 6 minutes, or until crisp and the cheese is melted.
6. Cut into quarters and serve.

Cajun Turkey

Prep time: 10 minutes | Cook time: 30 minutes | Serves 4

2 pounds (907 g) turkey thighs, skinless and boneless
1 red onion, sliced
2 bell peppers, sliced
1 habanero pepper, minced
1 carrot, sliced
1 tablespoon Cajun seasoning mix
1 tablespoon fish sauce
2 cups chicken broth
Nonstick cooking spray

1. Preheat the air fryer oven to 360ºF (182ºC).
2. Spritz the bottom and sides of a baking dish with nonstick cooking spray.
3. Arrange the turkey thighs in the baking dish. Add the onion, peppers, and carrot. Sprinkle with Cajun seasoning. Add the fish sauce and chicken broth.
4. Place the baking dish on wire rack and slide into oven. Select Bake and set time to 30 minutes, or until cooked through. Serve warm.

Crisp Paprika Chicken Drumsticks

Prep time: 5 minutes | Cook time: 25 minutes | Serves 2

2 teaspoons paprika	Pinch pepper
1 teaspoon packed brown sugar	4 (5-ounce / 142-g) chicken drumsticks, trimmed
1 teaspoon garlic powder	1 teaspoon vegetable oil
½ teaspoon dry mustard	1 scallion, green part only,
½ teaspoon salt	sliced thin on bias

1. Preheat the air fryer oven to 400ºF (204ºC).
2. Combine paprika, sugar, garlic powder, mustard, salt, and pepper in a bowl. Pat drumsticks dry with paper towels. Using metal skewer, poke 10 to 15 holes in skin of each drumstick. Rub with oil and sprinkle evenly with spice mixture.
3. Arrange the drumsticks in the air fryer basket, spaced evenly apart, alternating ends.
4. Put the air fryer basket on sheet pan and place into oven. Select Air Fry and set time to 25 minutes, or until chicken is crisp and registers 195ºF (91ºC). Flip the chicken halfway through cooking.
5. Transfer chicken to a serving platter, tent loosely with aluminum foil, and let rest for 5 minutes. Sprinkle with scallion and serve.

Orange and Honey Glazed Duck

Prep time: 5 minutes | Cook time: 15 minutes | Serves 2 to 3

1 pound (454 g) duck breasts (2 to 3 breasts)	¼ cup honey
Kosher salt and pepper, to taste	2 sprigs thyme, plus more for garnish
Juice and zest of 1 orange	2 firm tart apples, such as Fuji

1. Preheat the air fryer oven to 400ºF (204ºC).
2. Pat the duck breasts dry and, using a sharp knife, make 3 to 4 shallow, diagonal slashes in the skin. Turn the breasts and score the skin on the diagonal in the opposite direction to create a cross-hatch pattern. Season well with salt and pepper.
3. Place the duck breasts skin-side up in the air fryer basket.
4. Put the air fryer basket on sheet pan and place into oven. Select Air Fry and set time to 8 minutes.
5. Flip the duck breasts and continue cooking for 4 more minutes.
6. While the duck is cooking, prepare the sauce. Combine the orange juice and zest, honey, and thyme in a small saucepan. Bring to a boil, stirring to dissolve the honey, then reduce the heat and simmer until thickened. Core the apples and cut into quarters. Cut each quarter into 3 or 4 slices depending on the size.
7. After the duck has cooked on both sides, turn it and brush the skin with the orange-honey glaze. Air fry for 1 more minute. Remove the duck breasts to a cutting board and set aside to rest.
8. Toss the apple slices with the remaining orange-honey sauce in a medium bowl.
9. Arrange the apples in a single layer in the air fryer basket.
10. Put the air fryer basket on sheet pan and place into oven. Select Air Fry and set time to 10 minutes.
11. Slice the duck breasts on the bias and divide them and the apples among 2 or 3 plates.
12. Serve warm, garnished with additional thyme.

Turkey, Hummus, and Cheese Wraps

Prep time: 10 minutes | Cook time: 4 minutes | Serves 4

4 large whole wheat wraps	8 slices provolone cheese
½ cup hummus	1 cup fresh baby spinach,
16 thin slices deli turkey	or more to taste

1. Preheat the air fryer oven to 360ºF (182ºC).
2. To assemble, place 2 tablespoons of hummus on each wrap and spread to within about a half inch from edges. Top with 4 slices of turkey and 2 slices of provolone. Finish with ¼ cup of baby spinach, or pile on as much as you like.
3. Roll up each wrap. You don't need to fold or seal the ends.
4. Place the wraps in air fryer basket, seam-side down.
5. Put the air fryer basket on sheet pan and place into oven. Select Air Fry and set time to 4 minutes, or until the cheese is melted.
6. Serve warm.

Dill Chicken Strips

Prep time: 15 minutes | Cook time: 10 minutes | Serves 4

2 whole boneless, skinless chicken breasts, halved lengthwise
1 cup Italian dressing
3 cups finely crushed potato chips
1 tablespoon dried dill weed
1 tablespoon garlic powder
1 large egg, beaten
Cooking spray

1. In a large resealable bag, combine the chicken and Italian dressing. Seal the bag and refrigerate to marinate at least 1 hour.
2. In a shallow dish, stir together the potato chips, dill, and garlic powder. Place the beaten egg in a second shallow dish.
3. Remove the chicken from the marinade. Roll the chicken pieces in the egg and the potato chip mixture, coating thoroughly.
4. Preheat the air fryer oven to 325ºF (163ºC). Line the air fryer basket with parchment paper.
5. Place the coated chicken on the parchment and spritz with cooking spray.
6. Put the air fryer basket on sheet pan and place into oven. Select Air Fry and set time to 10 minutes, flipping the chicken and spritzing it with cooking spray halfway through, or until the outsides are crispy and the insides are no longer pink. Serve immediately.

Herbed Turkey Breast

Prep time: 20 minutes | Cook time: 45 minutes | Serves 6

1 tablespoon olive oil
Cooking spray
2 garlic cloves, minced
2 teaspoons Dijon mustard
1½ teaspoons rosemary
1½ teaspoons sage
1½ teaspoons thyme
1 teaspoon salt
½ teaspoon freshly ground black pepper
3 pounds (1.4 kg) turkey breast, thawed if frozen

1. Preheat the air fryer oven to 370ºF (188ºC). Spray the air fryer basket lightly with cooking spray.
2. In a small bowl, mix together the garlic, olive oil, Dijon mustard, rosemary, sage, thyme, salt, and pepper to make a paste. Smear the paste all over the turkey breast.
3. Place the turkey breast in the air fryer basket.
4. Put the air fryer basket on sheet pan and place into oven. Select Air Fry and set time to 20 minutes.
5. Flip turkey breast and baste it with any drippings. Air fry until the internal temperature of the meat reaches at least 170ºF (77ºC), 20 more minutes.
6. If desired, increase the temperature to 400ºF (204ºC), flip the turkey breast over one last time, and air fry for 5 minutes to get a crispy exterior.
7. Let the turkey rest for 10 minutes before slicing and serving.

Pecan-Crusted Turkey Cutlets

Prep time: 10 minutes | Cook time: 12 minutes | Serves 4

¾ cup panko bread crumbs
¼ teaspoon salt
¼ teaspoon pepper
¼ teaspoon dry mustard
¼ teaspoon poultry seasoning
½ cup pecans
¼ cup cornstarch
1 egg, beaten
1 pound (454 g) turkey cutlets, ½-inch thick
Salt and pepper, to taste
Cooking spray

1. Preheat the air fryer oven to 360ºF (182ºC).
2. Place the panko crumbs, salt, pepper, mustard, and poultry seasoning in a food processor. Process until crumbs are finely crushed. Add pecans and process just until nuts are finely chopped.
3. Place cornstarch in a shallow dish and beaten egg in another. Transfer coating mixture from food processor into a third shallow dish.
4. Sprinkle turkey cutlets with salt and pepper to taste.
5. Dip cutlets in cornstarch and shake off excess, then dip in beaten egg and finally roll in crumbs, pressing to coat well. Spray both sides with cooking spray.
6. Place the cutlets in air fryer basket in a single layer.
7. Put the air fryer basket on sheet pan and place into oven. Select Air Fry and set time to 12 minutes.
8. Serve warm.

Honey Rosemary Chicken

Prep time: 10 minutes | Cook time: 20 minutes | Serves 4

¼ cup balsamic vinegar
¼ cup honey
2 tablespoons olive oil
1 tablespoon dried rosemary leaves
1 teaspoon salt

½ teaspoon freshly ground black pepper
2 whole boneless, skinless chicken breasts (about 1 pound / 454 g each), halved
Cooking spray

1. In a large resealable bag, combine the vinegar, honey, olive oil, rosemary, salt, and pepper. Add the chicken pieces, seal the bag, and refrigerate to marinate for at least 2 hours.
2. Preheat the air fryer oven to 325ºF (163ºC). Line a sheet pan with parchment paper.
3. Remove the chicken from the marinade and place it on the parchment. Spritz with cooking spray.
4. Put the sheet pan on wire rack and slide into the oven. Select Bake and set time to 20 minutes, flipping the chicken and spraying it with cooking spray halfway through, or until the internal temperature reaches 165ºF (74ºC) and the chicken is no longer pink inside.
5. Let sit for 5 minutes before serving.

Mini Turkey Meatloaves with Carrot

Prep time: 6 minutes | Cook time: 22 minutes | Serves 4

⅓ cup minced onion
¼ cup grated carrot
2 garlic cloves, minced
2 tablespoons ground almonds

2 teaspoons olive oil
1 teaspoon dried marjoram
1 egg white
¾ pound (340 g) ground turkey breast

1. Preheat the air fryer oven to 400ºF (204ºC).
2. In a medium bowl, stir together the onion, carrot, garlic, almonds, olive oil, marjoram, and egg white.
3. Add the ground turkey. With your hands, gently but thoroughly mix until combined.
4. Double 16 foil muffin cup liners to make 8 cups. Divide the turkey mixture evenly among the liners. Place the cups in a sheet pan.
5. Put the sheet pan on wire rack and slide into the oven. Select Bake and set time to 22 minutes, or until the meatloaves reach an internal temperature of 165ºF (74ºC) on a meat thermometer. Serve immediately.

Turkey Hoisin Burgers

Prep time: 10 minutes | Cook time: 20 minutes | Serves 4

1 pound (454 g) lean ground turkey
¼ cup whole-wheat bread crumbs

¼ cup hoisin sauce
2 tablespoons soy sauce
4 whole-wheat buns
Olive oil spray

1. In a large bowl, mix together the turkey, bread crumbs, hoisin sauce, and soy sauce.
2. Form the mixture into 4 equal patties. Cover with plastic wrap and refrigerate the patties for 30 minutes.
3. Preheat the air fryer oven to 370ºF (188ºC). Spray the air fryer basket lightly with olive oil spray.
4. Place the patties in the air fryer basket in a single layer. Spray the patties lightly with olive oil spray.
5. Put the air fryer basket on sheet pan and place into oven. Select Air Fry and set time to 10 minutes. Flip the patties over, lightly spray with olive oil spray, and air fry for an additional 5 to 10 minutes, until golden brown.
6. Place the patties on buns and top with your choice of low-calorie burger toppings like sliced tomatoes, onions, and cabbage slaw. Serve immediately.

Chapter 5   Meats

Char Siu

Prep time: 8 hours 10 minutes | Cook time: 15 minutes | Serves 4

¼ cup honey
1 teaspoon Chinese five-spice powder
1 tablespoon Shaoxing wine (rice cooking wine)
1 tablespoon hoisin sauce
2 teaspoons minced garlic
2 teaspoons minced fresh
ginger
2 tablespoons soy sauce
1 tablespoon sugar
1 pound (454 g) fatty pork shoulder, cut into long, 1-inch-thick pieces
Cooking spray

1. Combine all the ingredients, except for the pork should, in a microwave-safe bowl. Stir to mix well. Microwave until the honey has dissolved. Stir periodically.
2. Pierce the pork pieces generously with a fork, then put the pork in a large bowl. Pour in half of the honey mixture. Set the remaining sauce aside until ready to serve.
3. Press the pork pieces into the mixture to coat and wrap the bowl in plastic and refrigerate to marinate for at least 8 hours.
4. Spritz the air fryer basket with cooking spray.
5. Discard the marinade and transfer the pork pieces in the basket.
6. Put the air fryer basket on sheet pan and place into oven. Select Air Fry, set temperature to 400ºF (205ºC) and set time to 15 minutes.
7. Flip the pork halfway through.
8. When cooking is complete, the pork should be well browned.
9. Meanwhile, microwave the remaining marinade on high for a minute or until it has a thick consistency. Stir periodically.
10. Remove the pork from the oven and allow to cool for 10 minutes before serving with the thickened marinade.

Gold Cutlets with Aloha Salsa

Prep time: 20 minutes | Cook time: 7 minutes | Serves 4

2 eggs
2 tablespoons milk
¼ cup all-purpose flour
¼ cup panko bread crumbs
4 teaspoons sesame seeds
1 pound (454 g) boneless,
Aloha Salsa:
1 cup fresh pineapple, chopped in small pieces
¼ cup red bell pepper, chopped
½ teaspoon ground cinnamon
1 teaspoon soy sauce
thin pork cutlets (½-inch thick)
¼ cup cornstarch
Salt and ground lemon pepper, to taste
Cooking spray

¼ cup red onion, finely chopped
⅛ teaspoon crushed red pepper
⅛ teaspoon ground black pepper

1. In a medium bowl, stir together all ingredients for salsa. Cover and refrigerate while cooking the pork.
2. Beat together eggs and milk in a large bowl. In another bowl, mix the flour, panko, and sesame seeds. Pour the cornstarch in a shallow dish.
3. Sprinkle pork cutlets with lemon pepper and salt. Dip pork cutlets in cornstarch, egg mixture, and then panko coating. Spritz both sides with cooking spray in air fryer basket.
4. Put the air fryer basket on sheet pan and place into oven. Select Air Fry, set the temperature to 400ºF (205ºC) and set the time to 7 minutes.
5. After 3 minutes, remove from the oven. Flip the cutlets with tongs. Return to the oven and continue cooking.
6. When cooking is complete, the pork should be crispy and golden brown on both sides.
7. Serve the fried cutlets with the Aloha salsa on the side.

Homemade Teriyaki Pork Ribs

Prep time: 5 minutes | Cook time: 30 minutes | Serves 4

¼ cup soy sauce
¼ cup honey
1 teaspoon garlic powder
1 teaspoon ground dried ginger

4 (8-ounce / 227-g) boneless country-style pork ribs
Cooking spray

1. Spritz the air fryer basket with cooking spray.
2. Make the teriyaki sauce: combine the soy sauce, honey, garlic powder, and ginger in a bowl. Stir to mix well.
3. Brush the ribs with half of the teriyaki sauce, then arrange the ribs in the pan. Spritz with cooking spray.
4. Put the air fryer basket on sheet pan and place into oven. Select Air Fry, set temperature to 350ºF (180ºC) and set time to 30 minutes.
5. After 15 minutes, remove from the oven. Flip the ribs and brush with remaining teriyaki sauce. Return to the oven and continue cooking.
6. When cooking is complete, the internal temperature of the ribs should reach at least 145ºF (63ºC).
7. Serve immediately.

Pork and Tricolor Vegetables Kebabs

Prep time: 1 hour 20 minutes | Cook time: 8 minutes | Serves 4

For the Pork:

1 pound (454 g) pork steak, cut in cubes
1 tablespoon white wine vinegar
3 tablespoons steak sauce
¼ cup soy sauce

1 teaspoon powdered chili
1 teaspoon red chili flakes
2 teaspoons smoked paprika
1 teaspoon garlic salt

For the Vegetable:

1 green squash, deseeded and cut in cubes
1 yellow squash, deseeded and cut in cubes
1 red pepper, cut in cubes

1 green pepper, cut in cubes
Salt and ground black pepper, to taste
Cooking spray

Special Equipment:

4 bamboo skewers, soaked in water for at least 30 minutes

1. Combine the ingredients for the pork in a large bowl. Press the pork to dunk in the marinade. Wrap the bowl in plastic and refrigerate for at least an hour.
2. Spritz the air fryer basket with cooking spray.
3. Remove the pork from the marinade and run the skewers through the pork and vegetables alternatively. Sprinkle with salt and pepper to taste.
4. Arrange the skewers in the basket and spritz with cooking spray.
5. Put the air fryer basket on sheet pan and place into oven. Select Air Fry, set temperature to 380ºF (193ºC) and set time to 8 minutes.
6. After 4 minutes, remove from the oven. Flip the skewers. Return to the oven and continue cooking.
7. When cooking is complete, the pork should be browned and the vegetables should be lightly charred and tender.
8. Serve immediately.

Citrus Carnitas

Prep time: 1 hour 10 minutes | Cook time: 25 minutes | Serves 6

2½ pounds (1.1 kg) boneless country-style pork ribs, cut into 2-inch pieces
3 tablespoons olive brine
1 tablespoon minced fresh oregano leaves
⅓ cup orange juice

1 teaspoon ground cumin
1 tablespoon minced garlic
1 teaspoon salt
1 teaspoon ground black pepper
Cooking spray

1. Combine all the ingredients in a large bowl. Toss to coat the pork ribs well. Wrap the bowl in plastic and refrigerate for at least an hour to marinate.
2. Spritz the air fryer basket with cooking spray.
3. Arrange the marinated pork ribs in the pan and spritz with cooking spray.
4. Put the air fryer basket on sheet pan and place into oven. Select Air Fry, set temperature to 400ºF (205ºC) and set time to 25 minutes.
5. Flip the ribs halfway through.
6. When cooking is complete, the ribs should be well browned.
7. Serve immediately.

Chapter 5: Meats | 61

Classic Walliser Schnitzel

Prep time: 5 minutes | Cook time: 14 minutes | Serves 2

½ cup pork rinds
½ tablespoon fresh parsley
½ teaspoon fennel seed
½ teaspoon mustard
⅓ tablespoon cider vinegar
1 teaspoon garlic salt
⅓ teaspoon ground black pepper
2 eggs
2 pork schnitzel, halved
Cooking spray

1. Spritz the air fryer basket with cooking spray.
2. Put the pork rinds, parsley, fennel seeds, and mustard in a food processor. Pour in the vinegar and sprinkle with salt and ground black pepper. Pulse until well combined and smooth.
3. Pour the pork rind mixture in a large bowl. Whisk the eggs in a separate bowl.
4. Dunk the pork schnitzel in the whisked eggs, then dunk in the pork rind mixture to coat well. Shake the excess off.
5. Arrange the schnitzel in the pan and spritz with cooking spray.
6. Put the air fryer basket on sheet pan and place into oven. Select Air Fry, set temperature to 350ºF (180ºC) and set time to 14 minutes.
7. After 7 minutes, remove from the oven. Flip the schnitzel. Return to the oven and continue cooking.
8. When cooking is complete, the schnitzel should be golden and crispy.
9. Serve immediately.

Lechon Kawali

Prep time: 10 minutes | Cook time: 30 minutes | Serves 4

1 pound (454 g) pork belly, cut into three thick chunks
6 garlic cloves
2 bay leaves
2 tablespoons soy sauce
1 teaspoon kosher salt
1 teaspoon ground black pepper
3 cups water
Cooking spray

1. Put all the ingredients in a pressure cooker, then put the lid on and cook on high for 15 minutes.
2. Natural release the pressure and release any remaining pressure, transfer the tender pork belly on a clean work surface. Allow to cool under room temperature until you can handle.
3. Generously Spritz the air fryer basket with cooking spray.
4. Cut each chunk into two slices, then put the pork slices in the pan.
5. Put the air fryer basket on sheet pan and place into oven. Select Air Fry, set temperature to 400ºF (205ºC) and set time to 15 minutes.
6. After 7 minutes, remove from the oven. Flip the pork. Return to the oven and continue cooking.
7. When cooking is complete, the pork fat should be crispy.
8. Serve immediately.

Macadamia Nuts Crusted Pork Rack

Prep time: 5 minutes | Cook time: 35 minutes | Serves 2

1 clove garlic, minced
2 tablespoons olive oil
1 pound (454 g) rack of pork
1 cup chopped macadamia nuts
1 tablespoon bread crumbs
1 tablespoon rosemary, chopped
1 egg
Salt and ground black pepper, to taste

1. Combine the garlic and olive oil in a small bowl. Stir to mix well.
2. On a clean work surface, rub the pork rack with the garlic oil and sprinkle with salt and black pepper on both sides.
3. Combine the macadamia nuts, bread crumbs, and rosemary in a shallow dish. Whisk the egg in a large bowl.
4. Dredge the pork in the egg, then roll the pork over the macadamia nut mixture to coat well. Shake the excess off.
5. Arrange the pork in the basket.
6. Put the air fryer basket on sheet pan and place into oven. Select Air Fry, set temperature to 350ºF (180ºC) and set time to 30 minutes.
7. After 30 minutes, remove from the oven. Flip the pork rack. Return to the oven and increase temperature to 390ºF (199ºC) and set time to 5 minutes. Keep cooking.
8. When cooking is complete, the pork should be browned.
9. Serve immediately.

Pork Meatballs with Red Chili

Prep time: 5 minutes | Cook time: 15 minutes | Serves 4

1 pound (454 g) ground pork
2 cloves garlic, finely minced
1 cup scallions, finely chopped
1½ tablespoons Worcestershire sauce
½ teaspoon freshly grated ginger root
1 teaspoon turmeric powder
1 tablespoon oyster sauce
1 small sliced red chili, for garnish
Cooking spray

1. Spritz the air fryer basket with cooking spray.
2. Combine all the ingredients, except for the red chili in a large bowl. Toss to mix well.
3. Shape the mixture into equally sized balls, then arrange them in the basket and spritz with cooking spray.
4. Put the air fryer basket on sheet pan and place into oven. Select Air Fry, set temperature to 350ºF (180ºC) and set time to 15 minutes.
5. After 7 minutes, remove from the oven. Flip the balls. Return to the oven and continue cooking.
6. When cooking is complete, the balls should be lightly browned.
7. Serve the pork meatballs with red chili on top.

Pork Chops with Carrots and Mushrooms

Prep time: 10 minutes | Cook time: 15 minutes | Serves 4

2 carrots, cut into sticks
1 cup mushrooms, sliced
2 garlic cloves, minced
2 tablespoons olive oil
1 pound (454 g) boneless pork chops
1 teaspoon dried oregano
1 teaspoon dried thyme
1 teaspoon cayenne pepper
Salt and ground black pepper, to taste
Cooking spray

1. In a mixing bowl, toss together the carrots, mushrooms, garlic, olive oil and salt until well combined.
2. Add the pork chops to a different bowl and season with oregano, thyme, cayenne pepper, salt and black pepper.

3. Lower the vegetable mixture in the greased basket. Place the seasoned pork chops on top.
4. Put the air fryer basket on sheet pan and place into oven. Select Air Fry, set temperature to 360ºF (182ºC) and set time to 15 minutes.
5. After 7 minutes, remove from the oven. Flip the pork and stir the vegetables. Return to the oven and continue cooking.
6. When cooking is complete, the pork chops should be browned and the vegetables should be tender.
7. Transfer the pork chops to the serving dishes and let cool for 5 minutes. Serve warm with vegetable on the side.

Calf's Liver Golden Strips

Prep time: 15 minutes | Cook time: 4 to 5 minutes | Serves 4

1 pound (454 g) sliced calf's liver, cut into about ½-inch-wide strips
Salt and ground black pepper, to taste
2 eggs
2 tablespoons milk
½ cup whole wheat flour
1½ cups panko bread crumbs
½ cup plain bread crumbs
½ teaspoon salt
¼ teaspoon ground black pepper
Cooking spray

1. Sprinkle the liver strips with salt and pepper.
2. Beat together the egg and milk in a bowl. Place wheat flour in a shallow dish. In a second shallow dish, mix panko, plain bread crumbs, ½ teaspoon salt, and ¼ teaspoon pepper.
3. Dip liver strips in flour, egg wash, and then bread crumbs, pressing in coating slightly to make crumbs stick.
4. Spritz the air fryer basket with cooking spray. Place strips in a single layer in the basket.
5. Put the air fryer basket on sheet pan and place into oven. Select Air Fry, set the temperature to 400ºF (205ºC) and set the time to 4 minutes.
6. After 2 minutes, remove from the oven. Flip the strips with tongs. Return to the oven and continue cooking.
7. When cooking is complete, the liver strips should be crispy and golden.
8. Serve immediately.

Chapter 5: Meats | 63

Beef and Spinach Meatloaves

Prep time: 15 minutes | Cook time: 45 minutes | Serves 2

1 large egg, beaten
1 cup frozen spinach
⅓ cup almond meal
¼ cup chopped onion
¼ cup plain Greek milk
¼ teaspoon salt
¼ teaspoon dried sage
2 teaspoons olive oil, divided
Freshly ground black

pepper, to taste
½ pound (227 g) extra-lean ground beef
¼ cup tomato paste
1 tablespoon granulated stevia
¼ teaspoon Worcestershire sauce
Cooking spray

1. Coat a shallow sheet pan with cooking spray.
2. In a large bowl, combine the beaten egg, spinach, almond meal, onion, milk, salt, sage, 1 teaspoon of olive oil, and pepper.
3. Crumble the beef over the spinach mixture. Mix well to combine. Divide the meat mixture in half. Shape each half into a loaf. Place the loaves in the prepared pan.
4. In a small bowl, whisk together the tomato paste, stevia, Worcestershire sauce, and remaining 1 teaspoon of olive oil. Spoon half of the sauce over each meatloaf.
5. Place the sheet pan on wire rack and slide into oven. Select Bake, set the temperature to 350°F (180°C) and set the time to 40 minutes.
6. When cooking is complete, an instant-read thermometer inserted in the center of the meatloaves should read at least 165°F (74°C).
7. Serve immediately.

Dijon Pork Tenderloin

Prep time: 15 minutes | Cook time: 15 minutes | Serves 4

3 tablespoons Dijon mustard
3 tablespoons honey
1 teaspoon dried rosemary
1 tablespoon olive oil

1 pound (454 g) pork tenderloin, rinsed and drained
Salt and freshly ground black pepper, to taste

1. In a small bowl, combine the Dijon mustard, honey, and rosemary. Stir to combine.
2. Rub the pork tenderloin with salt and pepper on all sides on a clean work surface.
3. Heat the olive oil in an oven-safe skillet over high heat. Sear the pork loin on all sides in the skillet for 6 minutes or until golden brown. Flip the pork halfway through.
4. Remove from the heat and spread honey-mustard mixture evenly to coat the pork loin.
5. Place the sausages in the sheet pan. Place the sheet pan on wire rack and slide into oven. Select Bake, set temperature to 425°F (220°C), and set time to 15 minutes.
6. When cooking is complete, an instant-read thermometer inserted in the pork should register at least 145°F (63°C).
7. Remove from the oven and allow to rest for 3 minutes. Slice the pork into ½-inch slices and serve.

Italian Sausages and Red Grapes

Prep time: 10 minutes | Cook time: 20 minutes | Serves 6

2 pounds (905 g) seedless red grapes
3 shallots, sliced
2 teaspoons fresh thyme
2 tablespoons olive oil
½ teaspoon kosher salt

Freshly ground black pepper, to taste
6 links (about 1½ pounds / 680 g) hot Italian sausage
3 tablespoons balsamic vinegar

1. Place the grapes in a large bowl. Add the shallots, thyme, olive oil, salt, and pepper. Gently toss. Place the grapes in the sheet pan. Arrange the sausage links evenly in the pan.
2. Place the sheet pan on wire rack and slide into oven. Select Air Roast, set temperature to 375°F (190°C), and set time to 20 minutes.
3. After 10 minutes, remove the pan. Turn over the sausages and sprinkle the vinegar over the sausages and grapes. Gently toss the grapes and move them to one side of the pan. Return the pan to the oven and continue cooking.
4. When cooking is complete, the grapes should be very soft and the sausages browned. Serve immediately.

Mushroom and Sausage Calzones

Prep time: 10 minutes | Cook time: 24 minutes | Serves 4

2 links Italian sausages (about ½ pound / 227 g)
1 pound (454 g) pizza dough, thawed
3 tablespoons olive oil, divided
¼ cup Marinara sauce
½ cup roasted mushrooms
1 cup shredded Mozzarella cheese

1. Place the sausages in the sheet pan.
2. Place the sheet pan on wire rack and slide into oven. Select Air Roast, set temperature to 375ºF (190ºC), and set time to 12 minutes.
3. After 6 minutes, remove from the oven and turn over the sausages. Return to the oven and continue cooking.
4. While the sausages cook, divide the pizza dough into 4 equal pieces. One at a time, place a piece of dough onto a square of parchment paper 9 inches in diameter. Brush the dough on both sides with ¾ teaspoon of olive oil, then top the dough with another piece of parchment. Press the dough into a 7-inch circle. Remove the top piece of parchment and set aside. Repeat with the remaining pieces of dough.
5. When cooking is complete, remove from the oven. Place the sausages on a cutting board. Let them cool for several minutes, then slice into ¼-inch rounds and cut each round into 4 pieces.
6. One at a time, spread a tablespoon of marinara sauce over half of a dough circle, leaving a ½-inch border at the edges. Cover with a quarter of the sausage pieces and add a quarter of the mushrooms. Sprinkle with ¼ cup of cheese. Pull the other side of the dough over the filling and pinch the edges together to seal. Transfer from the parchment to the sheet pan. Repeat with the other rounds of dough, sauce, sausage, mushrooms, and cheese.
7. Brush the tops of the calzones with 1 tablespoon of olive oil.
8. Select Roast, set temperature to 450ºF (235ºC), and set time to 12 minutes.
9. After 6 minutes, remove from the oven. The calzones should be golden brown. Turn over the calzones and brush the tops with the remaining olive oil. Return the pan to the oven and continue cooking.
10. When cooking is complete, the crust should be a deep golden brown on both sides. Remove from the oven. The center should be molten; let cool for several minutes before serving.

Sriracha Beef and Broccoli

Prep time: 10 minutes | Cook time: 15 minutes | Serves 4

12 ounces (340 g) broccoli, cut into florets (about 4 cups)
1 pound (454 g) flat iron steak, cut into thin strips
½ teaspoon kosher salt
¾ cup soy sauce
1 teaspoon Sriracha sauce
3 tablespoons freshly squeezed orange juice
1 teaspoon cornstarch
1 medium onion, thinly sliced

1. Line the sheet pan with aluminum foil. Place the broccoli on top and sprinkle with 3 tablespoons of water. Seal the broccoli in the foil in a single layer.
2. Place the sheet pan on wire rack and slide into oven. Select Air Roast, set temperature to 375ºF (190ºC), and set time to 6 minutes.
3. While the broccoli steams, sprinkle the steak with the salt. In a small bowl, whisk together the soy sauce, Sriracha, orange juice, and cornstarch. Place the onion and beef in a large bowl.
4. When cooking is complete, remove from the oven. Open the packet of broccoli and use tongs to transfer the broccoli to the bowl with the beef and onion, discarding the foil and remaining water. Pour the sauce over the beef and vegetables and toss to coat. Place the mixture in the sheet pan.
5. Select Roast, set temperature to 375ºF (190ºC), and set time to 9 minutes.
6. After about 4 minutes, remove from the oven and gently toss the ingredients. Return to the oven and continue cooking.
7. When cooking is complete, the sauce should be thickened, the vegetables tender, and the beef barely pink in the center. Serve warm.

Chapter 5: Meats | 65

Worcestershire Ribeye Steaks

Prep time: 35 minutes | Cook time: 10 to 12 minutes | Serves 2 to 4

2 (8-ounce / 227-g) boneless ribeye steaks
4 teaspoons Worcestershire sauce
½ teaspoon garlic powder
Salt and ground black pepper, to taste
4 teaspoons olive oil

1. Brush the steaks with Worcestershire sauce on both sides. Sprinkle with garlic powder and coarsely ground black pepper. Drizzle the steaks with olive oil. Allow steaks to marinate for 30 minutes.
2. Transfer the steaks into the basket.
3. Put the air fryer basket on sheet pan and place into oven. Select Air Roast, set the temperature to 400°F (205°C) and set time to 4 minutes.
4. After 2 minutes, remove from the oven. Flip the steaks. Return to the oven and continue cooking.
5. When cooking is complete, the steaks should be well browned.
6. Remove the steaks from the basket and let sit for 5 minutes. Salt and serve.

Ravioli with Beef-Marinara Sauce

Prep time: 10 minutes | Cook time: 10 minutes | Serves 4

1 (20-ounce / 567-g) package frozen cheese ravioli
1 teaspoon kosher salt
1¼ cups water
6 ounces (170 g) cooked ground beef
2½ cups Marinara sauce
¼ cup grated Parmesan cheese, for garnish

1. Place the ravioli in an even layer in the sheet pan. Stir the salt into the water until dissolved and pour it over the ravioli.
2. Place the sheet pan on wire rack and slide into oven. Select Bake, set temperature to 450°F (235°C), and set time to 10 minutes.
3. While the ravioli is cooking, mix the ground beef into the marinara sauce in a medium bowl.
4. After 6 minutes, remove the pan from the oven. Blot off any remaining water, or drain the ravioli and return them to the pan. Pour the meat sauce over the ravioli. Return the pan to the oven and continue cooking.

5. When cooking is complete, the ravioli should be tender and sauce heated through. Gently stir the ingredients. Serve the ravioli with the Parmesan cheese, if desired.

Spicy Pork Lettuce Wraps

Prep time: 10 minutes | Cook time: 12 minutes | Serves 4

1 (1-pound / 454-g) medium pork tenderloin, silver skin and external fat trimmed
⅔ cup soy sauce, divided
1 teaspoon cornstarch
1 medium jalapeño, deseeded and minced
1 can diced water chestnuts
½ large red bell pepper, deseeded and chopped
2 scallions, chopped, white and green parts separated
1 head butter lettuce
½ cup roasted, chopped almonds
¼ cup coarsely chopped cilantro

1. Cut the tenderloin into ¼-inch slices and place them in the sheet pan. Baste with about 3 tablespoons of soy sauce. Stir the cornstarch into the remaining sauce and set aside.
2. Place the sheet pan on wire rack and slide into oven. Select Air Roast, set temperature to 375°F (190°C), and set time to 12 minutes.
3. After 5 minutes, remove from the oven. Place the pork slices on a cutting board. Place the jalapeño, water chestnuts, red pepper, and the white parts of the scallions in the sheet pan and pour the remaining sauce over. Stir to coat the vegetables with the sauce. Return the pan to the oven and continue cooking.
4. While the vegetables cook, chop the pork into small pieces. Separate the lettuce leaves, discarding any tough outer leaves and setting aside the small inner leaves for another use. You'll want 12 to 18 leaves, depending on size and your appetites.
5. After 5 minutes, remove from the oven. Add the pork to the vegetables, stirring to combine. Return the pan to the oven and continue cooking for the remaining 2 minutes until the pork is warmed back up and the sauce has reduced slightly.
6. When cooking is complete, remove from the oven. Place the pork and vegetables in a medium serving bowl and stir in half the green parts of the scallions. To serve, spoon some pork and vegetables into each of the lettuce leaves. Top with the remaining scallion greens and garnish with the nuts and cilantro.

Sirloin Steak and Pepper Fajitas

Prep time: 10 minutes | Cook time: 15 minutes | Serves 4

8 (6-inch) flour tortillas
1 pound (454 g) top sirloin steak, sliced ¼-inch thick
1 red bell pepper, deseeded and sliced ½-inch thick
1 green bell pepper, deseeded and sliced ½-inch thick
1 jalapeño, deseeded and
sliced thin
1 medium onion, sliced ½-inch thick
2 tablespoons vegetable oil
2 tablespoons Mexican seasoning
1 teaspoon kosher salt
2 tablespoons salsa
1 small avocado, sliced

1. Line the sheet pan with aluminum foil. Place the tortillas on the foil in two stacks and wrap in the foil.
2. Place the sheet pan on wire rack and slide into oven. Select Air Roast, set temperature to 325°F (163°C), and set time to 6 minutes.
3. After 3 minutes, remove from the oven and flip the packet of tortillas over. Return to the oven and continue cooking.
4. While the tortillas warm, place the steak, bell peppers, jalapeño, and onion in a large bowl and drizzle the oil over. Sprinkle with the Mexican seasoning and salt, and toss to coat.
5. When cooking is complete, remove from the oven and place the packet of tortillas on top of the oven to keep warm. Place the beef and peppers mixture in the sheet pan, spreading out into a single layer as much as possible.
6. Select Roast, set temperature to 375°F (190°C), and set time to 9 minutes.
7. After about 5 minutes, remove from the oven and stir the ingredients. Return to the oven and continue cooking.
8. When cooking is complete, the vegetables will be soft and browned in places, and the beef will be browned on the outside and barely pink inside. Remove from the oven. Unwrap the tortillas and spoon the fajita mixture into the tortillas. Serve with salsa and avocado slices.

Pork with Butternut Squash and Apples

Prep time: 15 minutes | Cook time: 13 minutes | Serves 4

4 boneless pork loin chops, ¾- to 1-inch thick
1 teaspoon kosher salt, divided
2 tablespoons Dijon mustard
2 tablespoons brown sugar
1 pound (454 g) butternut squash, cut into 1-inch cubes
1 large apple, peeled and cut into 12 to 16 wedges
1 medium onion, thinly sliced
½ teaspoon dried thyme
¼ teaspoon freshly ground black pepper
1 tablespoon unsalted butter, melted
½ cup chicken stock

1. Sprinkle the pork chops on both sides with ½ teaspoon of kosher salt. In a small bowl, whisk together the mustard and brown sugar. Baste about half of the mixture on one side of the pork chops. Place the chops, basted-side up, in the sheet pan.
2. Place the squash in a large bowl. Add the apple, onion, thyme, remaining kosher salt, pepper, and butter and toss to coat. Arrange the squash-fruit mixture around the chops on the pan. Pour the chicken stock over the mixture, avoiding the chops.
3. Place the sheet pan on wire rack and slide into oven. Select Air Roast, set temperature to 350°F (180°C), and set time to 13 minutes.
4. After about 7 minutes, remove from the oven. Gently toss the squash mixture and turn over the chops. Baste the chops with the remaining mustard mixture. Return the pan to the oven and continue cooking.
5. When cooking is complete, the pork chops should register at least 145°F (63°C) in the center on a meat thermometer, and the squash and apples should be tender. If necessary, continue cooking for up to 3 minutes more.
6. Remove from the oven. Spoon the squash and apples onto four plates, and place a pork chop on top. Serve immediately.

Chapter 5: Meats | 67

Pork Chop Roast

Prep time: 5 minutes | Cook time: 20 minutes | Serves 2

2 (10-ounce / 284-g) bone-in, center cut pork chops, 1-inch thick
2 teaspoons Worcestershire sauce
Salt and ground black pepper, to taste
Cooking spray

1. Rub the Worcestershire sauce on both sides of pork chops.
2. Season with salt and pepper to taste.
3. Spritz the air fryer basket with cooking spray and place the chops in the basket side by side.
4. Put the air fryer basket on sheet pan and place into oven. Select Air Roast, set the temperature to 350°F (180°C) and set the time to 20 minutes.
5. After 10 minutes, remove from the oven. Flip the pork chops with tongs. Return to the oven and continue cooking.
6. When cooking is complete, the pork should be well browned on both sides.
7. Let rest for 5 minutes before serving.

Fast Lamb Satay

Prep time: 5 minutes | Cook time: 8 minutes | Serves 2

¼ teaspoon cumin
1 teaspoon ginger
½ teaspoons nutmeg
Salt and ground black
pepper, to taste
2 boneless lamb steaks
Cooking spray

1. Combine the cumin, ginger, nutmeg, salt and pepper in a bowl.
2. Cube the lamb steaks and massage the spice mixture into each one.
3. Leave to marinate for 10 minutes, then transfer onto metal skewers.
4. Preheat the air fryer oven to 400°F (204°C).
5. Put the skewers in the air fryer basket and spritz with cooking spray.
6. Put the air fryer basket on sheet pan and place into oven. Select Air Fry and set time to 8 minutes.
7. Serve hot.

Miso Marinated Steak

Prep time: 5 minutes | Cook time: 12 minutes | Serves 4

¾ pound (340 g) flank steak
1½ tablespoons sake
1 tablespoon brown miso
paste
1 teaspoon honey
2 cloves garlic, pressed
1 tablespoon olive oil

1. Put all the ingredients in a Ziploc bag. Shake to cover the steak well with the seasonings and refrigerate for at least 1 hour.
2. Preheat the air fryer oven to 400°F (204°C).
3. Coat all sides of the steak with cooking spray, then put the steak in the air fryer basket.
4. Put the air fryer basket on sheet pan and place into oven. Select Air Fry and set time to 12 minutes, turning the steak twice during the cooking time. Serve immediately.

Spaghetti Squash Lasagna

Prep time: 5 minutes | Cook time: 1 hour 15 minutes | Serves 6

2 large spaghetti squash, cooked (about 2¾ pounds / 1.2 kg)
4 pounds (1.8 kg) ground beef
1 (2½-pound / 1.1-kg) large jar Marinara sauce
25 slices Mozzarella cheese
30 ounces whole-milk ricotta cheese

1. Preheat the air fryer oven to 375°F (191°C).
2. Slice the spaghetti squash and place it face down inside a baking dish. Fill with water until covered.
3. Place the baking dish on wire rack and slide into oven. Select Bake and set time to 45 minutes, or until skin is soft.
4. Sear the ground beef in a skillet over medium-high heat for 5 minutes or until browned, then add the marinara sauce and heat until warm. Set aside.
5. Scrape the flesh off the cooked squash to resemble strands of spaghetti.
6. Layer the lasagna in a large greased pan in alternating layers of spaghetti squash, beef sauce, Mozzarella, ricotta. Repeat until all the ingredients have been used.
7. Place the pan on wire rack and slide into oven. Select Bake and set time to 30 minutes.
8. Serve warm.

Air Fried London Broil

Prep time: 15 minutes | Cook time: 25 minutes | Serves 8

2 pounds (907 g) London broil
3 large garlic cloves, minced
3 tablespoons balsamic vinegar
3 tablespoons whole-grain mustard
2 tablespoons olive oil
Sea salt and ground black pepper, to taste
½ teaspoons dried hot red pepper flakes

1. Wash and dry the London broil. Score its sides with a knife.
2. Mix the remaining ingredients. Rub this mixture into the broil, coating it well. Allow to marinate for a minimum of 3 hours.
3. Preheat the air fryer oven to 400ºF (204ºC).
4. Put the broil in the air fryer basket. Put the air fryer basket on sheet pan and place into oven. Select Air Fry and set time to 15 minutes.
5. Turn it over and air fry for an additional 10 minutes. Serve warm.

Pepperoni and Bell Pepper Pockets

Prep time: 5 minutes | Cook time: 8 minutes | Serves 4

4 bread slices, 1-inch thick
Olive oil, for misting
24 slices pepperoni
1 ounce (28 g) roasted red peppers, drained and patted dry
1 ounce (28 g) Pepper Jack cheese, cut into 4 slices

1. Preheat the air fryer oven to 360ºF (182ºC).
2. Spray both sides of bread slices with olive oil.
3. Stand slices upright and cut a deep slit in the top to create a pocket (almost to the bottom crust, but not all the way through).
4. Stuff each bread pocket with 6 slices of pepperoni, a large strip of roasted red pepper, and a slice of cheese.
5. Put bread pockets in the air fryer basket, standing up.
6. Put the air fryer basket on sheet pan and place into oven. Select Air Fry and set time to 8 minutes, or until filling is heated through and bread is lightly browned.
7. Serve hot.

Air Fried Lamb Ribs

Prep time: 5 minutes | Cook time: 18 minutes | Serves 4

2 tablespoons mustard
1 pound (454 g) lamb ribs
1 teaspoon rosemary, chopped
Salt and ground black pepper, to taste
¼ cup mint leaves, chopped
1 cup Greek yogurt

1. Preheat the air fryer oven to 350ºF (177ºC).
2. Use a brush to apply the mustard to the lamb ribs, and season with rosemary, salt, and pepper. Put them in the air fryer basket.
3. Put the air fryer basket on sheet pan and place into oven. Select Air Fry and set time to 18 minutes.
4. Meanwhile, combine the mint leaves and yogurt in a bowl.
5. Remove the lamb ribs from the oven when cooked and serve with the mint yogurt.

Classic Spring Rolls

Prep time: 10 minutes | Cook time: 8 minutes | Serves 20

⅓ cup noodles
1 cup ground beef
1 teaspoon soy sauce
1 cup fresh mix vegetables
3 garlic cloves, minced
1 small onion, diced
1 tablespoon sesame oil
1 packet spring roll sheets
2 tablespoons cold water

1. Cook the noodle in enough hot water to soften them up, drain them and snip them to make them shorter.
2. In a frying pan over medium heat, cook the beef, soy sauce, mixed vegetables, garlic, and onion in sesame oil until the beef is cooked through. Take the pan off the heat and throw in the noodles. Mix well to incorporate everything.
3. Unroll a spring roll sheet and lay it flat. Scatter the filling diagonally across it and roll it up, brushing the edges lightly with water to act as an adhesive. Repeat until you have used up all the sheets and the filling.
4. Preheat the air fryer oven to 350ºF (177ºC).
5. Coat each spring roll with a light brushing of oil and transfer to the air fryer basket.
6. Put the air fryer basket on sheet pan and place into oven. Select Air Fry and set time to 8 minutes.
7. Serve hot.

Chapter 5: Meats | 69

Sumptuous Pizza Tortilla Rolls

Prep time: 10 minutes | Cook time: 15 minutes | Serves 4

1 teaspoon butter
½ medium onion, slivered
½ red or green bell pepper, julienned
4 ounces (113 g) fresh white mushrooms, chopped
½ cup pizza sauce
8 flour tortillas
8 thin slices deli ham
24 pepperoni slices
1 cup shredded Mozzarella cheese
Cooking spray

1. Preheat the air fryer oven to 390ºF (199ºC).
2. Put butter, onions, bell pepper, and mushrooms in a sheet pan.
3. Put the sheet pan on wire rack and slide into the oven. Select Bake and set time to 3 minutes.
4. Stir and bake for 3 to 4 minutes longer until just crisp and tender. Remove the pan and set aside.
5. To assemble rolls, spread about 2 teaspoons of pizza sauce on one half of each tortilla. Top with a slice of ham and 3 slices of pepperoni. Divide sautéed vegetables among tortillas and top with cheese.
6. Roll up tortillas, secure with toothpicks if needed, and spray with oil. Put the rolls in the air fryer basket.
7. Put the air fryer basket on sheet pan and place into oven. Select Air Fry and set time to 4 minutes.
8. Flip and air fry for 4 minutes, until heated through and lightly browned.
9. Serve immediately.

Lollipop Lamb Chops

Prep time: 15 minutes | Cook time: 7 minutes | Serves 4

½ small clove garlic
¼ cup packed fresh parsley
¾ cup packed fresh mint
½ teaspoon lemon juice
¼ cup grated Parmesan cheese
⅓ cup shelled pistachios
¼ teaspoon salt
1 tablespoon dried thyme
½ cup olive oil
8 lamb chops (1 rack)
2 tablespoons vegetable oil
Salt and freshly ground black pepper, to taste
1 tablespoon dried rosemary, chopped

1. Make the pesto by combining the garlic, parsley and mint in a food processor and process until finely chopped. Add the lemon juice, Parmesan cheese, pistachios and salt. Process until all the ingredients have turned into a paste. With the processor running, slowly pour the olive oil in. Scrape the sides of the processor with a spatula and process for another 30 seconds.
2. Preheat the air fryer oven to 400ºF (204ºC).
3. Rub both sides of the lamb chops with vegetable oil and season with salt, pepper, rosemary and thyme, pressing the herbs into the meat gently with the fingers. Transfer the lamb chops to the air fryer basket.
4. Put the air fryer basket on sheet pan and place into oven. Select Air Fry and set time to 5 minutes.
5. Flip the chops over and air fry for an additional 2 minutes.
6. Serve the lamb chops with mint pesto drizzled on top.

Orange Pork Tenderloin

Prep time: 15 minutes | Cook time: 23 minutes | Serves 3 to 4

2 tablespoons brown sugar
2 teaspoons cornstarch
2 teaspoons Dijon mustard
½ cup orange juice
½ teaspoon soy sauce
2 teaspoons grated fresh ginger
¼ cup white wine
Zest of 1 orange
1 pound (454 g) pork tenderloin
Salt and freshly ground black pepper, to taste
Oranges, halved, for garnish
Fresh parsley, for garnish

1. Combine the brown sugar, cornstarch, Dijon mustard, orange juice, soy sauce, ginger, white wine and orange zest in a small saucepan and bring the mixture to a boil on the stovetop. Lower the heat and simmer while you air fry the pork tenderloin or until the sauce has thickened.
2. Preheat the air fryer oven to 370ºF (188ºC).
3. Season all sides of the pork tenderloin with salt and freshly ground black pepper. Transfer the tenderloin to the air fryer basket.
4. Put the air fryer basket on sheet pan and place into oven. Select Air Fry and set time to 23 minutes, or until the internal temperature reaches 145ºF (63ºC). Flip the tenderloin over halfway through the cooking process and baste with the sauce.
5. Transfer the tenderloin to a cutting board and let it rest for 5 minutes. Slice the pork at a slight angle and serve immediately with orange halves and fresh parsley.

Teriyaki Pork and Mushroom Rolls

Prep time: 10 minutes | Cook time: 8 minutes | Serves 6

4 tablespoons brown sugar
4 tablespoons mirin
4 tablespoons soy sauce
1 teaspoon almond flour
2-inch ginger, chopped

6 (4-ounce / 113-g) pork belly slices
6 ounces (170 g) Enoki mushrooms

1. Mix the brown sugar, mirin, soy sauce, almond flour, and ginger together until brown sugar dissolves.
2. Take pork belly slices and wrap around a bundle of mushrooms. Brush each roll with teriyaki sauce. Chill for half an hour.
3. Preheat the air fryer oven to 350°F (177°C).
4. Add the marinated pork rolls to the air fryer basket. Put the air fryer basket on sheet pan and place into oven. Select Air Fry and set time to 8 minutes. Flip the rolls halfway through the cooking time.
5. Serve immediately.

Lamb Meatballs

Prep time: 20 minutes | Cook time: 8 minutes | Serves 4

Meatballs:
½ small onion, finely diced
1 clove garlic, minced
1 pound (454 g) ground lamb
2 tablespoons fresh parsley, finely chopped (plus more for garnish)
2 teaspoons fresh oregano,

finely chopped
2 tablespoons milk
1 egg yolk
Salt and freshly ground black pepper, to taste
½ cup crumbled feta cheese, for garnish

Tomato Sauce:
2 tablespoons butter
1 clove garlic, smashed
Pinch crushed red pepper flakes
¼ teaspoon ground

cinnamon
1 (28-ounce / 794-g) can crushed tomatoes
Salt, to taste
Olive oil, for greasing

1. Combine all ingredients for the meatballs in a large bowl and mix just until everything is combined. Shape the mixture into 1½-inch balls or shape the meat

between two spoons to make quenelles.
2. Preheat the air fryer oven to 400°F (204°C).
3. Make the tomato sauce: Put the butter, garlic and red pepper flakes in a sauté pan and heat over medium heat on the stovetop. Let the garlic sizzle a little, but before the butter browns, add the cinnamon and tomatoes. Bring to a simmer and simmer for 15 minutes. Season with salt.
4. Grease the air fryer basket with olive oil and transfer the meatballs to the air fryer basket in a single layer.
5. Put the air fryer basket on sheet pan and place into oven. Select Air Fry and set time to 8 minutes, giving the basket a shake once during the cooking process.
6. To serve, spoon a pool of the tomato sauce onto plates and add the meatballs. Sprinkle the feta cheese on top and garnish with more fresh parsley.

Beef and Vegetable Cubes

Prep time: 15 minutes | Cook time: 17 minutes | Serves 4

2 tablespoons olive oil
1 tablespoon apple cider vinegar
1 teaspoon fine sea salt
½ teaspoons ground black pepper
1 teaspoon shallot powder
¾ teaspoon smoked cayenne pepper
½ teaspoons garlic powder

¼ teaspoon ground cumin
1 pound (454 g) top round steak, cut into cubes
4 ounces (113 g) broccoli, cut into florets
4 ounces (113 g) mushrooms, sliced
1 teaspoon dried basil
1 teaspoon celery seeds

1. Massage the olive oil, vinegar, salt, black pepper, shallot powder, cayenne pepper, garlic powder, and cumin into the cubed steak, ensuring to coat each piece evenly.
2. Allow to marinate for a minimum of 3 hours.
3. Preheat the air fryer oven to 365°F (185°C).
4. Put the beef cubes in the air fryer basket. Put the air fryer basket on sheet pan and place into oven. Select Air Fry and set time to 12 minutes.
5. When the steak is cooked through, place it in a bowl.
6. Wipe the grease from the basket and pour in the vegetables. Season them with basil and celery seeds.
7. Increase the temperature to 400°F (204°C) and air fry for 5 to 6 minutes. When the vegetables are hot, serve them with the steak.

Chapter 5: Meats | 71

Pork with Aloha Salsa

Prep time: 20 minutes | Cook time: 8 minutes | Serves 4

2 eggs
2 tablespoons milk
¼ cup flour
¼ cup panko bread crumbs
4 teaspoons sesame seeds
1 pound (454 g) boneless,
Aloha Salsa:
1 cup fresh pineapple, chopped in small pieces
¼ cup red onion, finely chopped
¼ cup green or red bell pepper, chopped
½ teaspoon ground

thin pork cutlets (⅜- to ½-inch thick)
Lemon pepper and salt, to taste
¼ cup cornstarch
Cooking spray

cinnamon
1 teaspoon low-sodium soy sauce
⅛ teaspoon crushed red pepper
⅛ teaspoon ground black pepper

1. In a medium bowl, stir together all ingredients for salsa. Cover and refrigerate while cooking the pork.
2. Preheat the air fryer oven to 390°F (199°C).
3. Beat the eggs and milk in a shallow dish.
4. In another shallow dish, mix the flour, panko, and sesame seeds.
5. Sprinkle pork cutlets with lemon pepper and salt.
6. Dip pork cutlets in cornstarch, egg mixture, and then panko coating. Spray both sides with cooking spray and transfer to the air fryer basket.
7. Put the air fryer basket on sheet pan and place into oven. Select Air Fry and set time to 3 minutes.
8. Turn cutlets over, spraying both sides, and continue air frying for 5 minutes or until well done.
9. Serve fried cutlets with salsa on the side.

Cheesy Beef Meatballs

Prep time: 5 minutes | Cook time: 18 minutes | Serves 6

1 pound (454 g) ground beef
½ cup grated Parmesan cheese

1 tablespoon minced garlic
½ cup Mozzarella cheese
1 teaspoon freshly ground pepper

1. Preheat the air fryer oven to 400°F (204°C).
2. In a bowl, mix all the ingredients together. Roll the meat mixture into 5 generous meatballs. Arrange them in the air fryer basket.
3. Put the air fryer basket on sheet pan and place into oven. Select Air Fry and set time to 18 minutes.
4. Serve immediately.

Mongolian Flank Steak

Prep time: 20 minutes | Cook time: 15 minutes | Serves 4

1½ pounds (680 g) flank steak, thinly sliced on the bias into ¼-inch strips
Marinade:
2 tablespoons soy sauce
1 clove garlic, smashed
Sauce:
1 tablespoon vegetable oil
2 cloves garlic, minced
1 tablespoon finely grated fresh ginger
3 dried red chili peppers
¾ cup soy sauce

Pinch crushed red pepper flakes

¾ cup chicken stock
5 to 6 tablespoons brown sugar
½ cup cornstarch, divided
1 bunch scallions, sliced into 2-inch pieces

1. Marinate the beef in the soy sauce, garlic and red pepper flakes for one hour.
2. In the meantime, make the sauce. Heat a small saucepan over medium heat on the stovetop. Add the oil, garlic, ginger and dried chili peppers and sauté for just a minute or two. Add the soy sauce, chicken stock and brown sugar and continue to simmer for a few minutes. Dissolve 3 tablespoons of cornstarch in 3 tablespoons of water and stir this into the saucepan. Stir the sauce over medium heat until it thickens. Set this aside.
3. Preheat the air fryer oven to 400°F (204°C).
4. Remove the beef from the marinade and transfer it to a zipper sealable plastic bag with the remaining cornstarch. Shake it around to completely coat the beef and transfer the coated strips of beef to a baking sheet or plate, shaking off any excess cornstarch. Spray the strips with vegetable oil on all sides and transfer them to the air fryer basket.
5. Put the air fryer basket on sheet pan and place into oven. Select Air Fry and set time to 15 minutes, shaking the basket to toss and rotate the beef strips throughout the cooking process. Add the scallions for the last 4 minutes of the cooking.
6. Transfer the hot beef strips and scallions to a bowl and toss with the sauce, coating all the beef strips with the sauce. Serve warm.

Mushroom and Beef Meatloaf

Prep time: 10 minutes | Cook time: 25 minutes | Serves 4

1 pound (454 g) ground beef
1 egg, beaten
1 mushrooms, sliced
1 tablespoon thyme
1 small onion, chopped
3 tablespoons bread crumbs
Ground black pepper, to taste

1. Preheat the air fryer oven to 400°F (204°C).
2. Put all the ingredients into a large bowl and combine entirely. Transfer the meatloaf mixture into a loaf pan.
3. Place the pan on wire rack and slide into oven. Select Bake and set time to 25 minutes.
4. Cool for 5 minutes before slicing and serving.

Provolone Stuffed Beef and Pork Meatballs

Prep time: 15 minutes | Cook time: 12 minutes | Serves 4 to 6

1 tablespoon olive oil
1 small onion, finely chopped
1 to 2 cloves garlic, minced
¾ pound (340 g) ground beef
¾ pound (340 g) ground pork
¾ cup bread crumbs
¼ cup grated Parmesan cheese
¼ cup finely chopped fresh parsley
½ teaspoon dried oregano
1½ teaspoons salt
Freshly ground black pepper, to taste
2 eggs, lightly beaten
5 ounces (142 g) sharp or aged provolone cheese, cut into 1-inch cubes

1. Preheat a skillet over medium-high heat. Add the oil and cook the onion and garlic until tender, but not browned.
2. Transfer the onion and garlic to a large bowl and add the beef, pork, bread crumbs, Parmesan cheese, parsley, oregano, salt, pepper and eggs. Mix well until all the ingredients are combined. Divide the mixture into 12 evenly sized balls. Make one meatball at a time, by pressing a hole in the meatball mixture with the finger and pushing a piece of provolone cheese into the hole. Mold the meat back into a ball, enclosing the cheese.
3. Preheat the air fryer oven to 380°F (193°C).

4. Transfer the meatballs to the air fryer basket.
5. Put the air fryer basket on sheet pan and place into oven. Select Air Fry and set time to 12 minutes, shaking the basket and turning the meatballs twice during the cooking process.
6. Serve warm.

Pulled Pork

Prep time: 5 minutes | Cook time: 24 minutes | Serves 1

2 tablespoons barbecue dry rub
1 pound (454 g) pork
tenderloin
⅓ cup heavy cream
1 teaspoon butter, melted

1. Preheat the air fryer oven to 370°F (188°C).
2. Massage the dry rub into the tenderloin, coating it well. Transfer to the air fryer basket.
3. Put the air fryer basket on sheet pan and place into oven. Select Air Fry and set time to 20 minutes.
4. When done, shred with two forks. Toss with the heavy cream and butter.
5. Return to the oven and air fry for a further 4 minutes.
6. Serve warm.

Potato and Prosciutto Salad

Prep time: 10 minutes | Cook time: 7 minutes | Serves 8

Salad:
4 pounds (1.8 kg) potatoes, boiled and cubed
15 slices prosciutto, diced
2 cups shredded Cheddar cheese
Dressing:
15 ounces (425 g) sour cream
2 tablespoons mayonnaise
1 teaspoon salt
1 teaspoon black pepper
1 teaspoon dried basil

1. Preheat the air fryer oven to 350°F (177°C).
2. Put the potatoes, prosciutto, and Cheddar in a baking dish.
3. Place the baking dish on wire rack and slide into oven. Select Bake and set time to 7 minutes.
4. In a separate bowl, mix the sour cream, mayonnaise, salt, pepper, and basil using a whisk.
5. Coat the salad with the dressing and serve.

Chapter 5: Meats | 73

Pork and Pinto Bean Gorditas

Prep time: 20 minutes | Cook time: 21 minutes | Serves 4

1 pound (454 g) lean ground pork
2 tablespoons chili powder
2 tablespoons ground cumin
1 teaspoon dried oregano
2 teaspoons paprika
1 teaspoon garlic powder
½ cup water
1 (15-ounce / 425-g) can pinto beans, drained and rinsed
½ cup taco sauce
Salt and freshly ground black pepper, to taste
2 cups grated Cheddar cheese
5 (12-inch) flour tortillas
4 (8-inch) crispy corn tortilla shells
4 cups shredded lettuce
1 tomato, diced
⅓ cup sliced black olives
Sour cream, for serving
Tomato salsa, for serving
Cooking spray

1. Preheat the air fryer oven to 400ºF (204ºC). Spritz the air fryer basket with cooking spray.
2. Put the ground pork in the air fryer basket. Put the air fryer basket on sheet pan and place into oven. Select Air Fry and set time to 10 minutes, stirring a few times to gently break up the meat.
3. Combine the chili powder, cumin, oregano, paprika, garlic powder and water in a small bowl. Stir the spice mixture into the browned pork. Stir in the beans and taco sauce and air fry for an additional minute. Transfer the pork mixture to a bowl. Season with salt and freshly ground black pepper.
4. Sprinkle ½ cup of the grated cheese in the center of the flour tortillas, leaving a 2-inch border around the edge free of cheese and filling. Divide the pork mixture among the four tortillas, placing it on top of the cheese. Put a crunchy corn tortilla on top of the pork and top with shredded lettuce, diced tomatoes, and black olives. Cut the remaining flour tortilla into 4 quarters. These quarters of tortilla will serve as the bottom of the gordita. Put one quarter tortilla on top of each gordita and fold the edges of the bottom flour tortilla up over the sides, enclosing the filling. While holding the seams down, brush the bottom of the gordita with olive oil and place the seam side down on the countertop while you finish the remaining three gorditas.
5. Preheat the air fryer oven to 380ºF (193ºC).
6. Transfer the gorditas carefully to the air fryer basket, seam-side down. Brush or spray the top tortilla with oil.
7. Put the air fryer basket on sheet pan and place into oven. Select Air Fry and set time to 5 minutes.
8. Carefully turn the gorditas over and air fry for an additional 4 to 5 minutes until both sides are browned.
9. Serve warm with sour cream and salsa.

Beef Schnitzel

Prep time: 5 minutes | Cook time: 12 minutes | Serves 1

½ cup friendly bread crumbs
2 tablespoons olive oil
Pepper and salt, to taste
1 egg, beaten
1 thin beef schnitzel

1. Preheat the air fryer oven to 350ºF (177ºC).
2. In a shallow dish, combine the bread crumbs, oil, pepper, and salt.
3. In a second shallow dish, place the beaten egg.
4. Dredge the schnitzel in the egg before rolling it in the bread crumbs.
5. Put the coated schnitzel in the air fryer basket. Put the air fryer basket on sheet pan and place into oven. Select Air Fry and set time to 12 minutes. Flip the schnitzel halfway through.
6. Serve immediately.

Barbecue Pork Ribs

Prep time: 5 minutes | Cook time: 30 minutes | Serves 4

1 tablespoon barbecue dry rub
1 teaspoon mustard
1 tablespoon apple cider
vinegar
1 teaspoon sesame oil
1 pound (454 g) pork ribs, chopped

1. Combine the dry rub, mustard, apple cider vinegar, and sesame oil, then coat the ribs with this mixture. Refrigerate the ribs for 20 minutes.
2. Preheat the air fryer oven to 360ºF (182ºC).
3. When the ribs are ready, place them in the air fryer basket.
4. Put the air fryer basket on sheet pan and place into oven. Select Air Fry and set time to 15 minutes.
5. Flip them and air fry on the other side for a further 15 minutes.
6. Serve immediately.

Citrus Pork Loin Roast

Prep time: 10 minutes | Cook time: 45 minutes | Serves 8

1 tablespoon lime juice
1 tablespoon orange marmalade
1 teaspoon coarse brown mustard
1 teaspoon curry powder
1 teaspoon dried lemongrass
2 pound (907 g) boneless pork loin roast
Salt and ground black pepper, to taste
Cooking spray

1. Preheat the air fryer oven to 360ºF (182ºC).
2. Mix the lime juice, marmalade, mustard, curry powder, and lemongrass.
3. Rub mixture all over the surface of the pork loin. Season with salt and pepper.
4. Spray the air fryer basket with cooking spray and place pork roast diagonally in the basket.
5. Put the air fryer basket on sheet pan and place into oven. Select Air Fry and set time to 45 minutes, or until the internal temperature reaches at least 145ºF (63ºC).
6. Wrap roast in foil and let rest for 10 minutes before slicing and serving.

Beef Steak Fingers

Prep time: 5 minutes | Cook time: 8 minutes | Serves 4

4 small beef cube steaks
Salt and ground black pepper, to taste
½ cup flour
Cooking spray

1. Preheat the air fryer oven to 390ºF (199ºC).
2. Cut cube steaks into 1-inch-wide strips. Sprinkle lightly with salt and pepper to taste. Roll in flour to coat all sides.
3. Spritz the air fryer basket with cooking spray.
4. Put steak strips in air fryer basket in a single layer. Spritz top of steak strips with cooking spray.
5. Put the air fryer basket on sheet pan and place into oven. Select Air Fry and set time to 4 minutes.
6. Turn strips over and spritz with cooking spray. Air fry for 4 more minutes and test with fork for doneness. Steak fingers should be crispy outside with no red juices inside.
7. Serve immediately.

Char Siew

Prep time: 10 minutes | Cook time: 20 minutes | Serves 4 to 6

1 strip of pork shoulder butt with a good amount of fat marbling
Olive oil, for brushing the pan
Marinade:
1 teaspoon sesame oil
4 tablespoons raw honey
1 teaspoon low-sodium dark soy sauce
1 teaspoon light soy sauce
1 tablespoon rose wine
2 tablespoons Hoisin sauce

1. Combine all the marinade ingredients together in a Ziploc bag. Put pork in bag, making sure all sections of pork strip are engulfed in the marinade. Chill for 3 to 24 hours.
2. Take out the strip 30 minutes before preheating the air fryer to 350ºF (177ºC).
3. Put foil on a sheet pan and brush with olive oil. Put marinated pork strip onto prepared pan.
4. Place the pan on wire rack and slide into oven. Select Bake and set time to 20 minutes. Glaze with marinade every 5 to 10 minutes.
5. Remove strip and leave to cool a few minutes before slicing and serving.

Vietnamese Pork Chops

Prep time: 15 minutes | Cook time: 12 minutes | Serves 2

1 tablechops

1. Combine shallot, garlic, fish sauce, lemongrass, soy sauce, brown sugar, olive oil, and pepper in a bowl. Stir to mix well.
2. Put the pork chops in the bowl. Toss to coat well. Place the bowl in the refrigerator to marinate for 2 hours.
3. Preheat the air fryer oven to 400ºF (204ºC).
4. Remove the pork chops from the bowl and discard the marinade. Transfer the chops into the air fryer basket.
5. Put the air fryer basket on sheet pan and place into oven. Select Air Fry and set time to 12 minutes, or until lightly browned. Flip the pork chops halfway through the cooking time.
6. Remove the pork chops from the basket and serve hot.

Rosemary Ribeye Steaks

Prep time: 10 minutes | Cook time: 15 minutes | Serves 2

¼ cup butter
1 clove garlic, minced
Salt and ground black pepper, to taste

1½ tablespoons balsamic vinegar
¼ cup rosemary, chopped
2 ribeye steaks

1. Melt the butter in a skillet over medium heat. Add the garlic and fry until fragrant.
2. Remove the skillet from the heat and add the salt, pepper, and vinegar. Allow it to cool.
3. Add the rosemary, then pour the mixture into a Ziploc bag.
4. Put the ribeye steaks in the bag and shake well, coating the meat well. Refrigerate for an hour, then allow to sit for a further 20 minutes.
5. Preheat the air fryer oven to 400°F (204°C).
6. Put the steaks in the air fryer basket. Put the air fryer basket on sheet pan and place into oven. Select Air Fry and set time to 15 minutes.
7. Serve immediately.

Smoked Beef

Prep time: 10 minutes | Cook time: 45 minutes | Serves 8

2 pounds (907 g) roast beef, at room temperature
2 tablespoons extra-virgin olive oil
1 teaspoon sea salt flakes
1 teaspoon ground black

pepper
1 teaspoon smoked paprika
Few dashes of liquid smoke
2 jalapeño peppers, thinly sliced

1. Preheat the air fryer oven to 330°F (166°C).
2. With kitchen towels, pat the beef dry.
3. Massage the extra-virgin olive oil, salt, black pepper, and paprika into the meat. Cover with liquid smoke, then place in a sheet pan.
4. Put the sheet pan on wire rack and slide into the oven. Select Bake and set time to 30 minutes.
5. Flip the roast over and allow to bake for another 15 minutes.
6. When cooked through, serve topped with sliced jalapeños.

Sweet and Sour Pork

Prep time: 20 minutes | Cook time: 14 minutes | Serves 2 to 4

⅓ cup all-purpose flour
⅓ cup cornstarch
2 teaspoons Chinese five-spice powder
1 teaspoon salt
Freshly ground black pepper, to taste
1 egg
2 tablespoons milk
¾ pound (340 g) boneless pork, cut into 1-inch cubes
Vegetable or canola oil
1½ cups large chunks of

red and green peppers
½ cup ketchup
2 tablespoons rice wine vinegar or apple cider vinegar
2 tablespoons brown sugar
¼ cup orange juice
1 tablespoon soy sauce
1 clove garlic, minced
1 cup cubed pineapple
Chopped scallions, for garnish

1. Set up a dredging station with two bowls. Combine the flour, cornstarch, Chinese five-spice powder, salt and pepper in one large bowl. Whisk the egg and milk together in a second bowl. Dredge the pork cubes in the flour mixture first, then dip them into the egg and then back into the flour to coat on all sides. Spray the coated pork cubes with vegetable or canola oil.
2. Preheat the air fryer oven to 400°F (204°C).
3. Toss the pepper chunks with a little oil, then transfer to the air fryer basket.
4. Put the air fryer basket on sheet pan and place into oven. Select Air Fry and set time to 5 minutes, shaking the basket halfway through the cooking time.
5. While the peppers are cooking, start making the sauce. Combine the ketchup, rice wine vinegar, brown sugar, orange juice, soy sauce, and garlic in a medium saucepan and bring the mixture to a boil on the stovetop. Reduce the heat and simmer for 5 minutes. When the peppers have finished air frying, add them to the saucepan along with the pineapple chunks. Simmer the peppers and pineapple in the sauce for an additional 2 minutes. Set aside and keep warm.
6. Add the dredged pork cubes to the air fryer basket and air fry for 6 minutes, shaking the basket to turn the cubes over for the last minute of the cooking process.
7. When ready to serve, toss the cooked pork with the pineapple, peppers and sauce. Serve garnished with chopped scallions.

Skirt Steak Fajitas

Prep time: 15 minutes | Cook time: 30 minutes | Serves 4

2 tablespoons olive oil
¼ cup lime juice
1 clove garlic, minced
½ teaspoon ground cumin
½ teaspoon hot sauce
½ teaspoon salt
2 tablespoons chopped fresh cilantro
1 pound (454 g) skirt steak
1 onion, sliced
1 teaspoon chili powder
1 red pepper, sliced
1 green pepper, sliced
Salt and freshly ground black pepper, to taste
8 flour tortillas
Toppings:
Shredded lettuce
Crumbled Queso Fresco (or grated Cheddar cheese)
Sliced black olives
Diced tomatoes
Sour cream
Guacamole

1. Combine the olive oil, lime juice, garlic, cumin, hot sauce, salt and cilantro in a shallow dish. Add the skirt steak and turn it over several times to coat all sides. Pierce the steak with a needle-style meat tenderizer or paring knife. Marinate the steak in the refrigerator for at least 3 hours, or overnight. When you are ready to cook, remove the steak from the refrigerator and let it sit at room temperature for 30 minutes.
2. Preheat the air fryer oven to 400ºF (204ºC).
3. Toss the onion slices with the chili powder and a little olive oil and transfer them to the air fryer basket.
4. Put the air fryer basket on sheet pan and place into oven. Select Air Fry and set time to 5 minutes.
5. Add the red and green peppers to the air fryer basket with the onions, season with salt and pepper and air fry for 8 more minutes, until the onions and peppers are soft. Transfer the vegetables to a dish and cover with aluminum foil to keep warm.
6. Put the skirt steak in the air fryer basket and pour the marinade over the top. Air fry at 400ºF (204ºC) for 12 minutes. Flip the steak over and air fry for an additional 5 minutes. Transfer the cooked steak to a cutting board and let the steak rest for a few minutes. If the peppers and onions need to be heated, return them to the oven for just 1 to 2 minutes.
7. Thinly slice the steak at an angle, cutting against the grain of the steak. Serve the steak with the onions and peppers, the warm tortillas and the fajita toppings on the side.

Swedish Beef Meatballs

Prep time: 10 minutes | Cook time: 12 minutes | Serves 8

1 pound (454 g) ground beef
1 egg, beaten
2 carrots, shredded
2 bread slices, crumbled
1 small onion, minced
½ teaspoons garlic salt
Pepper and salt, to taste
1 cup tomato sauce
2 cups pasta sauce

1. Preheat the air fryer oven to 400ºF (204ºC).
2. In a bowl, combine the ground beef, egg, carrots, crumbled bread, onion, garlic salt, pepper and salt.
3. Divide the mixture into equal amounts and shape each one into a small meatball.
4. Put them in the air fryer basket. Put the air fryer basket on sheet pan and place into oven. Select Air Fry and set time to 7 minutes.
5. Transfer the meatballs to a baking dish and top with the tomato sauce and pasta sauce.
6. Reduce the temperature to 320ºF (160ºC). Place the baking dish on wire rack and slide into oven. Select Bake and set time to 5 minutes.
7. Serve hot.

Chapter 5: Meats | 77

Chapter 6   Appetizers and Snacks

Kale Chips with Sesame

Prep time: 15 minutes | Cook time: 8 minutes | Serves 5

8 cups deribbed kale leaves, torn into 2-inch pieces
1½ tablespoons olive oil
¾ teaspoon chili powder
¼ teaspoon garlic powder
½ teaspoon paprika
2 teaspoons sesame seeds

1. In a large bowl, toss the kale with the olive oil, chili powder, garlic powder, paprika, and sesame seeds until well coated.
2. Transfer the kale to the air fryer basket.
3. Put the air fryer basket on sheet pan and place into oven. Select Air Fry, set temperature to 350ºF (180ºC), and set time to 8 minutes.
4. Flip the kale twice during cooking.
5. When cooking is complete, the kale should be crispy. Remove from the oven and serve warm.

Carrot Chips

Prep time: 15 minutes | Cook time: 10 minutes | Serves 4

4 to 5 medium carrots, trimmed and thinly sliced
1 tablespoon olive oil, plus
more for greasing
1 teaspoon seasoned salt

1. Toss the carrot slices with 1 tablespoon of olive oil and salt in a medium bowl until thoroughly coated.
2. Grease the air fryer basket with the olive oil. Place the carrot slices in the greased basket.
3. Put the air fryer basket on sheet pan and place into oven. Select Air Fry, set temperature to 390ºF (199ºC), and set time to 10 minutes.
4. Stir the carrot slices halfway through the cooking time.
5. When cooking is complete, the chips should be crisp-tender. Remove from the oven and allow to cool for 5 minutes before serving.

Cinnamon Apple Wedges

Prep time: 10 minutes | Cook time: 12 minutes | Serves 4

2 medium apples, cored and sliced into ¼-inch wedges
1 teaspoon canola oil
2 teaspoons peeled and
grated fresh ginger
½ teaspoon ground cinnamon
½ cup low-fat Greek vanilla yogurt, for serving

1. In a large bowl, toss the apple wedges with the canola oil, ginger, and cinnamon until evenly coated. Put the apple wedges in the air fryer basket.
2. Put the air fryer basket on sheet pan and place into oven. Select Air Fry, set temperature to 360ºF (182ºC), and set time to 12 minutes.
3. When cooking is complete, the apple wedges should be crisp-tender. Remove the apple wedges from the oven and serve drizzled with the yogurt.

Spiced Apple Chips

Prep time: 10 minutes | Cook time: 10 minutes | Serves 4

4 medium apples (any type will work), cored and thinly sliced
¼ teaspoon nutmeg
¼ teaspoon cinnamon
Cooking spray

1. Place the apple slices in a large bowl and sprinkle the spices on top. Toss to coat.
2. Put the apple slices in the air fryer basket in a single layer and spray them with cooking spray.
3. Put the air fryer basket on sheet pan and place into oven. Select Air Fry, set temperature to 360ºF (182ºC), and set time to 10 minutes.
4. Stir the apple slices halfway through.
5. When cooking is complete, the apple chips should be crispy. Transfer the apple chips to a paper towel-lined plate and rest for 5 minutes before serving.

Corn and Black Bean Salsa

Prep time: 10 minutes | Cook time: 10 minutes | Serves 4

½ (15-ounce / 425-g) can corn, drained and rinsed
½ (15-ounce / 425-g) can black beans, drained and rinsed
¼ cup chunky salsa
2 ounces (57 g) reduced-fat cream cheese, softened
¼ cup shredded reduced-fat Cheddar cheese
½ teaspoon paprika
½ teaspoon ground cumin
Salt and freshly ground black pepper, to taste

1. Combine the corn, black beans, salsa, cream cheese, Cheddar cheese, paprika, and cumin in a medium bowl. Sprinkle with salt and pepper and stir until well blended.
2. Pour the mixture into the sheet pan.
3. Put the pan on wire rack and slide into oven. Select Air Fry, set temperature to 325ºF (163ºC), and set time to 10 minutes.
4. When cooking is complete, the mixture should be heated through. Rest for 5 minutes and serve warm.

Sweet and Salty Snack Mix

Prep time: 5 minutes | Cook time: 10 minutes | Makes about 10 cups

3 tablespoons butter, melted
½ cup honey
1 teaspoon salt
2 cups granola
2 cups sesame sticks
2 cups crispy corn puff cereal
2 cups mini pretzel crisps
1 cup cashews
1 cup pepitas
1 cup dried cherries

1. In a small mixing bowl, mix together the butter, honey, and salt until well incorporated.
2. In a large bowl, combine the granola, sesame sticks, corn puff cereal and pretzel crisps, cashews, and pepitas. Drizzle with the butter mixture and toss until evenly coated. Transfer the snack mix to the air fryer basket.
3. Put the air fryer basket on sheet pan and place into oven. Select Air Fry, set temperature to 370ºF (188ºC), and set time to 10 minutes.
4. Stir the snack mix halfway through the cooking time.
5. When cooking is complete, they should be lightly toasted. Remove from the oven and allow to cool completely. Scatter with the dried cherries and mix well. Serve immediately.

Veggie Salmon Nachos

Prep time: 10 minutes | Cook time: 10 minutes | Serves 6

, chopped

1. Preheat the air fryer oven to 360ºF (182ºC).
2. In a sheet pan, layer the tortilla chips. Top with the salmon, black beans, red bell pepper, carrot, jalapeño, and Swiss cheese.
3. Put the sheet pan on wire rack and slide into the oven. Select Bake and set time to 10 minutes, or until the cheese is melted and starts to brown.
4. Top with the tomato and serve.

Avocado Chips

Prep time: 15 minutes | Cook time: 10 minutes | Serves 4

1 egg
1 tablespoon lime juice
⅛ teaspoon hot sauce
2 tablespoons flour
¾ cup panko bread crumbs
¼ cup cornmeal
¼ teaspoon salt
1 large avocado, pitted, peeled, and cut into ½-inch slices
Cooking spray

1. Whisk together the egg, lime juice, and hot sauce in a small bowl.
2. On a sheet of wax paper, place the flour. In a separate sheet of wax paper, combine the bread crumbs, cornmeal, and salt.
3. Dredge the avocado slices one at a time in the flour, then in the egg mixture, finally roll them in the bread crumb mixture to coat well.
4. Place the breaded avocado slices in the air fryer basket and mist them with cooking spray.
5. Put the air fryer basket on sheet pan and place into oven. Select Air Fry, set temperature to 390ºF (199ºC), and set time to 10 minutes.
6. When cooking is complete, the slices should be nicely browned and crispy. Transfer the avocado slices to a plate and serve.

Tangy Fried Pickle Spears

Prep time: 5 minutes | Cook time: 15 minutes | Serves 6

2 jars sweet and sour pickle spears, patted dry
2 medium-sized eggs
⅓ cup milk
1 teaspoon garlic powder
1 teaspoon sea salt
½ teaspoon shallot powder
⅓ teaspoon chili powder
⅓ cup all-purpose flour
Cooking spray

1. Spritz the air fryer basket with cooking spray.
2. In a bowl, beat together the eggs with milk. In another bowl, combine garlic powder, sea salt, shallot powder, chili powder and all-purpose flour until well blended.
3. One by one, roll the pickle spears in the powder mixture, then dredge them in the egg mixture. Dip them in the powder mixture a second time for additional coating.
4. Place the coated pickles in the basket.
5. Put the air fryer basket on sheet pan and place into oven. Select Air Fry, set temperature to 385ºF (196ºC), and set time to 15 minutes.
6. Stir the pickles halfway through the cooking time.
7. When cooking is complete, they should be golden and crispy. Transfer to a plate and let cool for 5 minutes before serving.

Bruschetta with Tomato and Basil

Prep time: 5 minutes | Cook time: 3 minutes | Serves 6

4 tomatoes, diced
⅓ cup shredded fresh basil
¼ cup shredded Parmesan cheese
1 tablespoon balsamic vinegar
1 tablespoon minced garlic
1 teaspoon olive oil
1 teaspoon salt
1 teaspoon freshly ground black pepper
1 loaf French bread, cut into 1-inch-thick slices
Cooking spray

1. Mix together the tomatoes and basil in a medium bowl. Add the cheese, vinegar, garlic, olive oil, salt, and pepper and stir until well incorporated. Set aside.
2. Spritz the sheet pan with cooking spray and lay the bread slices in the pan in a single layer. Spray the slices with cooking spray.
3. Place the sheet pan on wire rack and slide into oven. Select Bake, set temperature to 250ºF (121ºC), and set time to 3 minutes.
4. When cooking is complete, remove from the oven to a plate. Top each slice with a generous spoonful of the tomato mixture and serve.

Italian Rice Balls

Prep time: 20 minutes | Cook time: 10 minutes | Makes 8 rice balls

1½ cups cooked sticky rice
½ teaspoon Italian seasoning blend
¾ teaspoon salt, divided
8 black olives, pitted
1 ounce (28 g) Mozzarella cheese, cut into tiny pieces
(small enough to stuff into olives)
2 eggs
⅓ cup Italian bread crumbs
¾ cup panko bread crumbs
Cooking spray

1. Stuff each black olive with a piece of Mozzarella cheese.
2. In a bowl, combine the cooked sticky rice, Italian seasoning blend, and ½ teaspoon of salt and stir to mix well. Form the rice mixture into a log with your hands and divide it into 8 equal portions. Mold each portion around a black olive and roll into a ball.
3. Transfer to the freezer to chill for 10 to 15 minutes until firm.
4. In a shallow dish, place the Italian bread crumbs. In a separate shallow dish, whisk the eggs. In a third shallow dish, combine the panko bread crumbs and remaining salt.
5. One by one, roll the rice balls in the Italian bread crumbs, then dip in the whisked eggs, finally coat them with the panko bread crumbs.
6. Arrange the rice balls in the air fryer basket and spritz both sides with cooking spray.
7. Put the air fryer basket on sheet pan and place into oven. Select Air Fry, set temperature to 390ºF (199ºC), and set time to 10 minutes.
8. Flip the balls halfway through the cooking time.
9. When cooking is complete, the rice balls should be golden brown. Remove from the oven and serve warm.

Crispy Cod Fingers

Prep time: 5 minutes | Cook time: 12 minutes | Serves 4

2 eggs
2 tablespoons milk
2 cups flour
1 cup cornmeal
1 teaspoon seafood seasoning

Salt and black pepper, to taste
1 cup bread crumbs
1 pound (454 g) cod fillets, cut into 1-inch strips

1. Beat the eggs with the milk in a shallow bowl. In another shallow bowl, combine the flour, cornmeal, seafood seasoning, salt, and pepper. On a plate, place the bread crumbs.
2. Dredge the cod strips, one at a time, in the flour mixture, then in the egg mixture, finally roll in the bread crumb to coat evenly.
3. Transfer the cod strips to the air fryer basket.
4. Put the air fryer basket on sheet pan and place into oven. Select Air Fry, set temperature to 400°F (205°C), and set time to 12 minutes.
5. When cooking is complete, the cod strips should be crispy. Remove from the oven to a paper towel-lined plate and serve warm.

Mushroom and Spinach Calzones

Prep time: 15 minutes | Cook time: 26 to 27 minutes | Serves 4

2 tablespoons olive oil
1 onion, chopped
2 garlic cloves, minced
¼ cup chopped mushrooms
1 pound (454 g) spinach, chopped
1 tablespoon Italian seasoning
½ teaspoon oregano

Salt and black pepper, to taste
1½ cups marinara sauce
1 cup ricotta cheese, crumbled
1 (13-ounce / 369-g) pizza crust
Cooking spray

Make the Filling:
1. Heat the olive oil in a pan over medium heat until shimmering.
2. Add the onion, garlic, and mushrooms and sauté for 4

minutes, or until softened.
3. Stir in the spinach and sauté for 2 to 3 minutes, or until the spinach is wilted. Sprinkle with the Italian seasoning, oregano, salt, and pepper and mix well.
4. Add the marinara sauce and cook for about 5 minutes, stirring occasionally, or until the sauce is thickened.
5. Remove the pan from the heat and stir in the ricotta cheese. Set aside.
Make the Calzones:
6. Spritz the air fryer basket with cooking spray. Set aside.
7. Roll the pizza crust out with a rolling pin on a lightly floured work surface, then cut it into 4 rectangles.
8. Spoon ¼ of the filling into each rectangle and fold in half. Crimp the edges with a fork to seal. Mist them with cooking spray. Transfer the calzones to the basket.
9. Put the air fryer basket on sheet pan and place into oven. Select Air Fry, set temperature to 375°F (190°C), and set time to 15 minutes.
10. Flip the calzones halfway through the cooking time.
11. When cooking is complete, the calzones should be golden brown and crisp. Transfer the calzones to a paper towel-lined plate and serve.

Lemony Endive in Curried Yogurt

Prep time: 5 minutes | Cook time: 10 minutes | Serves 6

6 heads endive
½ cup plain and fat-free yogurt
3 tablespoons lemon juice

1 teaspoon garlic powder
½ teaspoon curry powder
Salt and ground black pepper, to taste

1. Wash the endives, and slice them in half lengthwise.
2. In a bowl, mix together the yogurt, lemon juice, garlic powder, curry powder, salt and pepper.
3. Brush the endive halves with the marinade, coating them completely. Allow to sit for at least 30 minutes or up to 24 hours.
4. Preheat the air fryer oven to 320°F (160°C).
5. Put the endives in the air fryer basket.
6. Put the air fryer basket on sheet pan and place into oven. Select Air Fry and set time to 10 minutes.
7. Serve hot.

Peppery Chicken Meatballs

Prep time: 5 minutes | Cook time: 18 minutes | Makes 16 meatballs

2 teaspoons olive oil
¼ cup minced onion
¼ cup minced red bell pepper
2 vanilla wafers, crushed

1 egg white
½ teaspoon dried thyme
½ pound (227 g) ground chicken breast

1. Preheat the air fryer oven to 370ºF (188ºC).
2. In a mixing bowl, combine the olive oil, onion, and red bell pepper. Transfer to the air fryer basket.
3. Put the air fryer basket on sheet pan and place into oven. Select Air Fry and set time to 5 minutes, or until the vegetables are tender.
4. In a medium bowl, mix the cooked vegetables, crushed wafers, egg white, and thyme until well combined
5. Mix in the chicken, gently but thoroughly, until everything is combined.
6. Form the mixture into 16 meatballs and place them in the air fryer basket.
7. Put the air fryer basket on sheet pan and place into oven. Select Air Fry and set time to 13 minutes, or until the meatballs reach an internal temperature of 165ºF (74ºC) on a meat thermometer.
8. Serve immediately.

Air Fried Chicken Wings

Prep time: 1 hour 20 minutes | Cook time: 18 minutes | Serves 4 2 pounds (907 g) chicken wings

Cooking spray
Marinade:
1 cup buttermilk
½ teaspoon salt
Coating:
1 cup flour
1 cup panko bread crumbs
2 tablespoons poultry

½ teaspoon black pepper

seasoning
2 teaspoons salt

1. Whisk together all the ingredients for the marinade in a large bowl.
2. Add the chicken wings to the marinade and toss well.

Transfer to the refrigerator to marinate for at least an hour.
3. Spritz the air fryer basket with cooking spray. Set aside.
4. Thoroughly combine all the ingredients for the coating in a shallow bowl.
5. Remove the chicken wings from the marinade and shake off any excess. Roll them in the coating mixture.
6. Place the chicken wings in the basket in a single layer. Mist the wings with cooking spray.
7. Put the air fryer basket on sheet pan and place into oven. Select Air Fry, set temperature to 360ºF (182ºC), and set time to 18 minutes.
8. Flip the wings halfway through the cooking time.
9. When cooking is complete, the wings should be crisp and golden brown on the outside. Remove from the oven to a plate and serve hot.

Cripsy Artichoke Bites

Prep time: 10 minutes | Cook time: 8 minutes | Serves 4

14 whole artichoke hearts packed in water
½ cup all-purpose flour
1 egg

⅓ cup panko bread crumbs
1 teaspoon Italian seasoning
Cooking spray

1. Drain the artichoke hearts and dry thoroughly with paper towels.
2. Place the flour on a plate. Beat the egg in a shallow bowl until frothy. Thoroughly combine the bread crumbs and Italian seasoning in a separate shallow bowl.
3. Dredge the artichoke hearts in the flour, then in the beaten egg, and finally roll in the bread crumb mixture until evenly coated.
4. Place the artichoke hearts in the air fryer basket and mist them with cooking spray.
5. Put the air fryer basket on sheet pan and place into oven. Select Air Fry, set temperature to 375ºF (190ºC), and set time to 8 minutes.
6. Flip the artichoke hearts halfway through the cooking time.
7. When cooking is complete, the artichoke hearts should start to brown and the edges should be crispy. Remove from the oven and let the artichoke hearts sit for 5 minutes before serving.

Crispy Spiced Chickpeas

Prep time: 5 minutes | Cook time: 12 minutes | Makes 1½ cups

1 can (15-ounce / 425-g) chickpeas, rinsed and dried with paper towels	¼ teaspoon mustard powder
1 tablespoon olive oil	¼ teaspoon sweet paprika
½ teaspoon dried rosemary	¼ teaspoon cayenne pepper
½ teaspoon dried parsley	Kosher salt and freshly ground black pepper, to
½ teaspoon dried chives	taste

1. Preheat the air fryer oven to 350°F (177°C).
2. In a large bowl, combine all the ingredients, except for the kosher salt and black pepper, and toss until the chickpeas are evenly coated in the herbs and spices.
3. Transfer the chickpeas and seasonings to the air fryer basket.
4. Put the air fryer basket on sheet pan and place into oven. Select Air Fry and set time to 12 minutes, or until browned and crisp. Shake the basket halfway through the cooking time.
5. Transfer the crispy chickpeas to a bowl, sprinkle with kosher salt and black pepper, and serve warm.

Honey Sriracha Chicken Wings

Prep time: 5 minutes | Cook time: 15 minutes | Serves 4

1 tablespoon Sriracha hot sauce	½ teaspoon kosher salt
1 tablespoon honey	16 chicken wings and drumettes
1 garlic clove, minced	Cooking spray

1. Preheat the air fryer oven to 360°F (182°C).
2. In a large bowl, whisk together the Sriracha hot sauce, honey, minced garlic, and kosher salt, then add the chicken and toss to coat.
3. Spray the air fryer basket with cooking spray, then place the wings in the basket.
4. Put the air fryer basket on sheet pan and place into oven. Select Air Fry and set time to 15 minutes, flipping halfway through.
5. Remove the wings and allow to cool on a wire rack for 10 minutes before serving.

Tortilla Chips

Prep time: 5 minutes | Cook time: 3 minutes | Serves 2

8 corn tortillas	Salt, to taste
1 tablespoon olive oil	

1. Preheat the air fryer oven to 390°F (199°C).
2. Slice the corn tortillas into triangles. Coat with a light brushing of olive oil.
3. Put the tortilla pieces in the air fryer basket. Put the air fryer basket on sheet pan and place into oven. Select Air Fry and set time to 3 minutes.
4. Season with salt before serving.

Spicy Chicken Wings

Prep time: 5 minutes | Cook time: 20 minutes | Serves 2 to 4

1¼ pounds (567 g) chicken wings, separated into flats and drumettes	Kosher salt and freshly ground black pepper, to taste
1 teaspoon baking powder	1 tablespoon unsalted
1 teaspoon cayenne pepper	butter, melted
¼ teaspoon garlic powder	
For serving:	
Blue cheese dressing	Carrot sticks
Celery	

1. Place the chicken wings on a large plate, then sprinkle evenly with the baking powder, cayenne, and garlic powder. Toss the wings with your hands, making sure the baking powder and seasonings fully coat them, until evenly incorporated. Let the wings stand in the refrigerator for 1 hour or up to overnight.
2. Preheat the air fryer oven to 400°F (204°C).
3. Season the wings with salt and black pepper, then transfer to the air fryer basket.
4. Put the air fryer basket on sheet pan and place into oven. Select Air Fry and set time to 20 minutes, or until the wings are crisp and golden brown.
5. Transfer the wings to a bowl and toss with the butter while they're hot.
6. Arrange the wings on a platter and serve warm with the blue cheese dressing, celery and carrot sticks.

Herbed Pita Chips

Prep time: 5 minutes | Cook time: 5 to 6 minutes | Serves 4

¼ teaspoon dried basil
¼ teaspoon marjoram
¼ teaspoon ground oregano
¼ teaspoon garlic powder
¼ teaspoon ground thyme
¼ teaspoon salt
2 whole 6-inch pitas, whole grain or white
Cooking spray

1. Preheat the air fryer oven to 330°F (166°C).
2. Mix all the seasonings together.
3. Cut each pita half into 4 wedges. Break apart wedges at the fold.
4. Mist one side of pita wedges with oil. Sprinkle with half of seasoning mix.
5. Turn pita wedges over, mist the other side with oil, and sprinkle with remaining seasonings. Place the pita wedges in a sheet pan.
6. Put the sheet pan on wire rack and slide into the oven. Select Bake and set time to 4 minutes. Shake the pan halfway through the cooking time.
7. If needed, bake for 1 or 2 more minutes until crisp. Serve hot.

Sweet Bacon Tater Tots

Prep time: 5 minutes | Cook time: 17 minutes | Serves 4

24 frozen tater tots
6 slices cooked bacon
2 tablespoons maple syrup
1 cup shredded Cheddar cheese

1. Preheat the air fryer oven to 400°F (204°C).
2. Put the tater tots in the air fryer basket.
3. Put the air fryer basket on sheet pan and place into oven. Select Air Fry and set time to 10 minutes. Shake the basket halfway through the cooking time.
4. Meanwhile, cut the bacon into 1-inch pieces.
5. Remove the tater tots from the air fryer basket and put into a sheet pan. Top with the bacon and drizzle with the maple syrup.
6. Return to the oven and air fry for an additional 5 minutes, or until the tots and bacon are crisp.
7. Top with the cheese and air fry for 2 minutes, or until the cheese is melted.
8. Serve hot.

Veggie Shrimp Toast

Prep time: 15 minutes | Cook time: 6 minutes | Serves 4

8 large raw shrimp, peeled and finely chopped
1 egg white
2 garlic cloves, minced
3 tablespoons minced red bell pepper
1 medium celery stalk, minced
2 tablespoons cornstarch
¼ teaspoon Chinese five-spice powder
3 slices firm thin-sliced no-sodium whole-wheat bread

1. Preheat the air fryer oven to 350°F (177°C).
2. In a small bowl, stir together the shrimp, egg white, garlic, red bell pepper, celery, cornstarch, and five-spice powder. Top each slice of bread with one-third of the shrimp mixture, spreading it evenly to the edges. With a sharp knife, cut each slice of bread into 4 strips.
3. Place the shrimp toasts in the air fryer basket in a single layer.
4. Put the air fryer basket on sheet pan and place into oven. Select Air Fry and set time to 6 minutes, or until crisp and golden brown.
5. Serve hot.

Mozzarella Arancini

Prep time: 5 minutes | Cook time: 10 minutes | Makes 16 arancini

2 cups cooked rice, cooled
2 eggs, beaten
1½ cups panko bread crumbs, divided
½ cup grated Parmesan
cheese
2 tablespoons minced fresh basil
16 ¾-inch cubes Mozzarella cheese
2 tablespoons olive oil

1. Preheat the air fryer oven to 400°F (204°C).
2. In a medium bowl, combine the rice, eggs, ½ cup of the bread crumbs, Parmesan cheese, and basil. Form this mixture into 16 1½-inch balls.
3. Poke a hole in each of the balls with your finger and insert a Mozzarella cube. Form the rice mixture firmly around the cheese.
4. On a shallow plate, combine the remaining 1 cup of the bread crumbs with the olive oil and mix well. Roll the rice balls in the bread crumbs to coat. Put in the air fryer basket.
5. Put the air fryer basket on sheet pan and place into oven. Select Air Fry and set time to 10 minutes, or until golden brown.
6. Serve hot.

Lemony Pear Chips

Prep time: 15 minutes | Cook time: 11 to 13 minutes | Serves 4

2 firm Bosc pears, cut crosswise into ⅛-inch-thick slices
1 tablespoon freshly squeezed lemon juice
½ teaspoon ground cinnamon
⅛ teaspoon ground cardamom

1. Preheat the air fryer oven to 380°F (193°C).
2. Separate the smaller stem-end pear rounds from the larger rounds with seeds. Remove the core and seeds from the larger slices. Sprinkle all slices with lemon juice, cinnamon, and cardamom.
3. Put the smaller chips into the air fryer basket.
4. Put the air fryer basket on sheet pan and place into oven. Select Air Fry and set time to 5 minutes, or until light golden brown. Shake the basket once during cooking. Remove from the oven.
5. Repeat with the larger slices, air frying for 6 to 8 minutes, or until light golden brown, shaking the basket once during cooking.
6. Remove the chips from the oven. Cool and serve or store in an airtight container at room temperature up for to 2 days.

Lemony Chicken Drumsticks

Prep time: 5 minutes | Cook time: 30 minutes | Serves 2

2 teaspoons freshly ground coarse black pepper
1 teaspoon baking powder
½ teaspoon garlic powder
4 chicken drumsticks (4 ounces / 113 g each)
Kosher salt, to taste
1 lemon

1. In a small bowl, stir together the pepper, baking powder, and garlic powder. Place the drumsticks on a plate and sprinkle evenly with the baking powder mixture, turning the drumsticks so they're well coated. Let the drumsticks stand in the refrigerator for at least 1 hour or up to overnight.
2. Preheat the air fryer oven to 375°F (191°C).
3. Sprinkle the drumsticks with salt, then transfer them to the air fryer basket.
4. Put the air fryer basket on sheet pan and place into oven. Select Air Fry and set time to 30 minutes, or until cooked through and crisp on the outside.
5. Transfer the drumsticks to a serving platter and finely grate the zest of the lemon over them while they're hot. Cut the lemon into wedges and serve with the warm drumsticks.

Pigs in a Blanket

Prep time: 5 minutes | Cook time: 14 minutes | Serves 4 to 6

24 cocktail smoked sausages
6 slices deli-sliced Cheddar cheese, each cut into 8
rectangular pieces
1 (8-ounce / 227-g) tube refrigerated crescent roll dough

1. Preheat the air fryer oven to 350°F (177°C).
2. Unroll the crescent roll dough into one large sheet. If your crescent roll dough has perforated seams, pinch or roll all the perforated seams together. Cut the large sheet of dough into 4 rectangles. Then cut each rectangle into 6 pieces by making one slice lengthwise in the middle and 2 slices horizontally. You should have 24 pieces of dough.
3. Make a deep slit lengthwise down the center of the cocktail sausage. Stuff two pieces of cheese into the slit in the sausage. Roll one piece of crescent dough around the stuffed cocktail sausage, leaving the ends of the sausage exposed. Pinch the seam together. Repeat with the remaining sausages.
4. Put the sausages seam-side down in the basket. Put the air fryer basket on sheet pan and place into oven. Select Air Fry and set time to 7 minutes.
5. Serve hot.

Chapter 6: Appetizers and Snacks | 85

Poutine with Waffle Fries

Prep time: 10 minutes | Cook time: 17 minutes | Serves 4

2 cups frozen waffle cut fries
2 teaspoons olive oil
1 red bell pepper, chopped
2 green onions, sliced
1 cup shredded Swiss cheese
½ cup bottled chicken gravy

1. Preheat the air fryer oven to 380ºF (193ºC).
2. Toss the waffle fries with the olive oil and place in the air fryer basket.
3. Put the air fryer basket on sheet pan and place into oven. Select Air Fry and set time to 12 minutes, or until the fries are crisp and light golden brown. Shake the basket halfway through the cooking time.
4. When done, transfer the fries to a sheet pan and top with the pepper, green onions, and cheese.
5. Return to the oven and air fry for 3 minutes, or until the vegetables are crisp and tender.
6. Remove the pan from the oven and drizzle the gravy over the fries. Air fry for 2 minutes more, or until the gravy is hot.
7. Serve immediately.

Tortellini with Spicy Dipping Sauce

Prep time: 5 minutes | Cook time: 10 minutes | Serves 4

¾ cup mayonnaise
2 tablespoons mustard
1 egg
½ cup flour
½ teaspoon dried oregano
1½ cups bread crumbs
2 tablespoons olive oil
2 cups frozen cheese tortellini

1. Preheat the air fryer oven to 380ºF (193ºC).
2. In a small bowl, combine the mayonnaise and mustard and mix well. Set aside.
3. In a shallow bowl, beat the egg. In a separate bowl, combine the flour and oregano. In another bowl, combine the bread crumbs and olive oil, and mix well.
4. Drop the tortellini, a few at a time, into the egg, then into the flour, then into the egg again, and then into the bread crumbs to coat. Put them into the air fryer basket.
5. Put the air fryer basket on sheet pan and place into oven. Select Air Fry and set time to 10 minutes. Shake the basket halfway through the cooking time, or until the tortellini are crisp and golden brown on the outside.
6. Serve with the mayonnaise mixture.

Chapter 7   Desserts

Crispy Pineapple Rings

Prep time: 5 minutes | Cook time: 7 minutes | Serves 6

1 cup rice milk
⅔ cup flour
½ cup water
¼ cup unsweetened flaked coconut
4 tablespoons sugar
½ teaspoon baking soda
½ teaspoon baking powder
½ teaspoon vanilla essence
½ teaspoon ground cinnamon
¼ teaspoon ground anise star
Pinch of kosher salt
1 medium pineapple, peeled and sliced

1. In a large bowl, stir together all the ingredients except the pineapple.
2. Dip each pineapple slice into the batter until evenly coated.
3. Arrange the pineapple slices in the air fryer basket.
4. Put the air fryer basket on sheet pan and place into oven. Select Air Fry, set temperature to 380ºF (193ºC), and set time to 7 minutes.
5. When cooking is complete, the pineapple rings should be golden brown.
6. Remove from the oven to a plate and cool for 5 minutes before serving.

Pineapple Sticks

Prep time: 5 minutes | Cook time: 10 minutes | Serves 4

½ fresh pineapple, cut into sticks
¼ cup desiccated coconut

1. Preheat the air fryer oven to 400ºF (204ºC).
2. Coat the pineapple sticks in the desiccated coconut and put each one in the air fryer basket.
3. Put the air fryer basket on sheet pan and place into oven. Select Air Fry and set time to 10 minutes.
4. Serve immediately

Coconut Pineapple Sticks

Prep time: 10 minutes | Cook time: 10 minutes | Serves 4

½ fresh pineapple, cut into sticks
¼ cup desiccated coconut

1. Place the desiccated coconut on a plate and roll the pineapple sticks in the coconut until well coated.
2. Lay the pineapple sticks in the air fryer basket.
3. Put the air fryer basket on sheet pan and place into oven. Select Air Fry, set temperature to 400ºF (205ºC), and set time to 10 minutes.
4. When cooking is complete, the pineapple sticks should be crisp-tender.
5. Serve warm.

Baked Peaches and Blueberries

Prep time: 10 minutes | Cook time: 10 minutes | Serves 6

3 peaches, peeled, halved, and pitted
2 tablespoons packed brown sugar
1 cup plain Greek yogurt
¼ teaspoon ground cinnamon
1 teaspoon pure vanilla extract
1 cup fresh blueberries

1. Place the peaches in the sheet pan, cut-side up. Top with a generous sprinkle of brown sugar.
2. Place the sheet pan on wire rack and slide into oven. Select Bake, set temperature to 380ºF (193ºC), and set time to 10 minutes.
3. Meanwhile, whisk together the yogurt, cinnamon, and vanilla in a small bowl until smooth.
4. When cooking is complete, the peaches should be lightly browned and caramelized.
5. Remove the peaches from the oven to a plate. Serve topped with the yogurt mixture and fresh blueberries.

Black and White Brownies

Prep time: 10 minutes | Cook time: 20 minutes | Makes 1 dozen brownies

1 egg
¼ cup brown sugar
2 tablespoons white sugar
2 tablespoons safflower oil
1 teaspoon vanilla
⅓ cup all-purpose flour
¼ cup cocoa powder
¼ cup white chocolate chips
Nonstick cooking spray

1. Spritz the sheet pan with nonstick cooking spray.
2. Whisk together the egg, brown sugar, and white sugar in a medium bowl. Mix in the safflower oil and vanilla and stir to combine.
3. Add the flour and cocoa powder and stir just until incorporated. Fold in the white chocolate chips.
4. Scrape the batter into the prepared sheet pan.
5. Place the sheet pan on wire rack and slide into oven. Select Bake, set temperature to 340ºF (171ºC), and set time to 20 minutes.
6. When done, the brownie should spring back when touched lightly with your fingers.
7. Transfer to a wire rack and let cool for 30 minutes before slicing to serve.

Chocolate Cheesecake

Prep time: 5 minutes | Cook time: 18 minutes | Serves 6

Crust:
½ cup butter, melted
½ cup coconut flour
2 tablespoons stevia
Cooking spray
Topping:
4 ounces (113 g) unsweetened baker's chocolate
1 cup mascarpone cheese,
at room temperature
1 teaspoon vanilla extract
2 drops peppermint extract

1. Lightly coat the sheet pan with cooking spray.
2. In a mixing bowl, whisk together the butter, flour, and stevia until well combined. Transfer the mixture to the prepared sheet pan.
3. Place the sheet pan on wire rack and slide into oven. Select Bake, set temperature to 350ºF (180ºC), and set time to 18 minutes.

4. When done, a toothpick inserted in the center should come out clean.
5. Remove the crust from the oven to a wire rack to cool.
6. Once cooled completely, place it in the freezer for 20 minutes.
7. When ready, combine all the ingredients for the topping in a small bowl and stir to incorporate.
8. Spread this topping over the crust and let it sit for another 15 minutes in the freezer.
9. Serve chilled.

Apple Fritters

Prep time: 30 minutes | Cook time: 7 minutes | Serves 6

1 cup chopped, peeled Granny Smith apple
½ cup granulated sugar
1 teaspoon ground cinnamon
1 cup all-purpose flour
1 teaspoon baking powder
1 teaspoon salt
2 tablespoons milk
2 tablespoons butter, melted
1 large egg, beaten
Cooking spray
¼ cup confectioners' sugar (optional)

1. Mix together the apple, granulated sugar, and cinnamon in a small bowl. Allow to sit for 30 minutes.
2. Combine the flour, baking powder, and salt in a medium bowl. Add the milk, butter, and egg and stir to incorporate.
3. Pour the apple mixture into the bowl of flour mixture and stir with a spatula until a dough forms.
4. Make the fritters: On a clean work surface, divide the dough into 12 equal portions and shape into 1-inch balls. Flatten them into patties with your hands.
5. Line the sheet pan with parchment paper and spray it with cooking spray.
6. Transfer the apple fritters onto the parchment paper, evenly spaced but not too close together. Spray the fritters with cooking spray.
7. Place the sheet pan on wire rack and slide into oven. Select Bake, set temperature to 350ºF (180ºC), and set time to 7 minutes.
8. Flip the fritters halfway through the cooking time.
9. When cooking is complete, the fritters should be lightly browned.
10. Remove from the oven to a plate and serve with the confectioners' sugar sprinkled on top, if desired.

Blackberry and Peach Cobbler

Prep time: 10 minutes | Cook time: 20 minutes | Serves 4

Filling:

1 (6-ounce / 170-g) package blackberries

1½ cups chopped peaches, cut into ½-inch thick slices

2 teaspoons arrowroot or cornstarch

2 tablespoons coconut sugar

1 teaspoon lemon juice

Topping:

2 tablespoons sunflower oil

1 tablespoon maple syrup

1 teaspoon vanilla

3 tablespoons coconut sugar

½ cup rolled oats

⅓ cup whole-wheat pastry flour

1 teaspoon cinnamon

¼ teaspoon nutmeg

⅛ teaspoon sea salt

Make the Filling:

1. Combine the blackberries, peaches, arrowroot, coconut sugar, and lemon juice in the sheet pan.
2. Using a rubber spatula, stir until well incorporated. Set aside.

Make the Topping:

3. Combine the oil, maple syrup, and vanilla in a mixing bowl and stir well. Whisk in the remaining ingredients. Spread this mixture evenly over the filling.
4. Place the sheet pan on wire rack and slide into oven. Select Bake, set temperature to 320°F (160°C), and set time to 20 minutes.
5. When cooked, the topping should be crispy and golden brown. Serve warm

Peanut Butter-Chocolate Bread Pudding

Prep time: 10 minutes | Cook time: 10 minutes | Serves 8

1 egg

1 egg yolk

¾ cup chocolate milk

3 tablespoons brown sugar

3 tablespoons peanut butter

2 tablespoons cocoa

powder

1 teaspoon vanilla

5 slices firm white bread, cubed

Nonstick cooking spray

1. Spritz the sheet pan with nonstick cooking spray.

2. Whisk together the egg, egg yolk, chocolate milk, brown sugar, peanut butter, cocoa powder, and vanilla until well combined.
3. Fold in the bread cubes and stir to mix well. Allow the bread soak for 10 minutes.
4. When ready, transfer the egg mixture to the prepared sheet pan.
5. Place the sheet pan on wire rack and slide into oven. Select Bake, set temperature to 330°F (166°C), and set time to 10 minutes.
6. When done, the pudding should be just firm to the touch.
7. Serve at room temperature.

Ricotta Lemon Poppy Seed Cake

Prep time: 15 minutes | Cook time: 55 minutes | Serves 4

Unsalted butter, at room temperature

1 cup almond flour

½ cup sugar

3 large eggs

¼ cup heavy cream

¼ cup full-fat ricotta cheese

¼ cup coconut oil, melted

2 tablespoons poppy seeds

1 teaspoon baking powder

1 teaspoon pure lemon extract

Grated zest and juice of 1 lemon, plus more zest for garnish

1. Preheat the air fryer oven to 325°F (163°C).
2. Generously butter a round sheet pan. Line the bottom of the pan with parchment paper cut to fit.
3. In a large bowl, combine the almond flour, sugar, eggs, cream, ricotta, coconut oil, poppy seeds, baking powder, lemon extract, lemon zest, and lemon juice. Beat with a hand mixer on medium speed until well blended and fluffy.
4. Pour the batter into the prepared pan. Cover the pan tightly with aluminum foil.
5. Put the sheet pan on wire rack and slide into the oven. Select Bake and set time to 45 minutes.
6. Remove the foil and bake for 10 to 15 minutes more until a knife (do not use a toothpick) inserted into the center of the cake comes out clean.
7. Let the cake cool in the pan on a wire rack for 10 minutes. Remove the cake from pan and let it cool on the rack for 15 minutes before slicing.
8. Top with additional lemon zest, slice and serve.

Chapter 7: Desserts | 89

Coconut Chip Mixed Berry Crisp

Prep time: 5 minutes | Cook time: 20 minutes | Serves 6

1 tablespoon butter, melted
12 ounces (340 g) mixed berries
⅓ cup granulated Swerve
1 teaspoon pure vanilla extract
½ teaspoon ground cinnamon
¼ teaspoon ground cloves
¼ teaspoon grated nutmeg
½ cup coconut chips, for garnish

1. Coat the sheet pan with melted butter.
2. Put the remaining ingredients except the coconut chips in the prepared sheet pan.
3. Place the sheet pan on wire rack and slide into oven. Select Bake, set temperature to 330°F (166°C), and set time to 20 minutes.
4. When cooking is complete, remove from the oven. Serve garnished with the coconut chips.

Summer Berry Crisp

Prep time: 10 minutes | Cook time: 12 minutes | Serves 4

½ cup fresh blueberries
½ cup chopped fresh strawberries
⅓ cup frozen raspberries, thawed
1 tablespoon honey
1 tablespoon freshly
squeezed lemon juice
⅔ cup whole-wheat pastry flour
3 tablespoons packed brown sugar
2 tablespoons unsalted butter, melted

1. Place the blueberries, strawberries, and raspberries in the sheet pan and drizzle the honey and lemon juice over the top.
2. Combine the pastry flour and brown sugar in a small mixing bowl.
3. Add the butter and whisk until the mixture is crumbly. Scatter the flour mixture on top of the fruit.
4. Place the sheet pan on wire rack and slide into oven. Select Bake, set temperature to 380°F (193°C), and set time to 12 minutes.
5. When cooking is complete, the fruit should be bubbly and the topping should be golden brown.
6. Remove from the oven and serve on a plate.

Lemony Blackberry Crisp

Prep time: 5 minutes | Cook time: 15 minutes | Serves 1

2 tablespoons lemon juice
⅓ cup powdered erythritol
¼ teaspoon xantham gum
2 cup blackberries
1 cup crunchy granola

1. Preheat the air fryer oven to 350°F (177°C).
2. In a bowl, combine the lemon juice, erythritol, xantham gum, and blackberries. Transfer to a round baking dish and cover with aluminum foil.
3. Place the baking dish on wire rack and slide into oven. Select Bake and set time to 12 minutes.
4. Remove the dish from the oven, give the blackberries a stir, and top with the granola.
5. Return the dish to the oven and bake at 320°F (160°C) for an additional 3 minutes.
6. Let rest for 5 to 10 minutes before serving.

Oatmeal and Carrot Cookie Cups

Prep time: 10 minutes | Cook time: 8 minutes | Makes 16 cups

3 tablespoons unsalted butter, at room temperature
¼ cup packed brown sugar
1 tablespoon honey
1 egg white
½ teaspoon vanilla extract
⅓ cup finely grated carrot
½ cup quick-cooking oatmeal
⅓ cup whole-wheat pastry flour
½ teaspoon baking soda
¼ cup dried cherries

1. Preheat the air fryer oven to 350°F (177°C)
2. In a medium bowl, beat the butter, brown sugar, and honey until well combined.
3. Add the egg white, vanilla, and carrot. Beat to combine.
4. Stir in the oatmeal, pastry flour, and baking soda.
5. Stir in the dried cherries.
6. Double up 32 mini muffin foil cups to make 16 cups. Fill each with about 4 teaspoons of dough. Put the cups in a sheet pan.
7. Put the sheet pan on wire rack and slide into the oven. Select Bake and set time to 8 minutes, or until light golden brown and just set.
8. Serve warm.

Pumpkin Pudding and Vanilla Wafers

Prep time: 10 minutes | Cook time: 15 minutes | Serves 4

1 cup canned no-salt-added pumpkin purée (not pumpkin pie filling)
¼ cup packed brown sugar
3 tablespoons all-purpose flour
1 egg, whisked
2 tablespoons milk
1 tablespoon unsalted butter, melted
1 teaspoon pure vanilla extract
4 low-fat vanilla wafers, crumbled
Cooking spray

1. Coat the sheet pan with cooking spray. Set aside.
2. Mix the pumpkin purée, brown sugar, flour, whisked egg, milk, melted butter, and vanilla in a medium bowl and whisk to combine. Transfer the mixture to the sheet pan.
3. Place the sheet pan on wire rack and slide into oven. Select Bake, set temperature to 350ºF (180ºC), and set time to 15 minutes.
4. When cooking is complete, the pudding should be set.
5. Remove the pudding from the oven to a wire rack to cool.
6. Divide the pudding into four bowls and serve with the vanilla wafers sprinkled on top.

Glazed Apples

Prep time: 5 minutes | Cook time: 10 minutes | Serves 4

4 small apples, cored and cut in half
2 tablespoons salted butter or coconut oil, melted
2 tablespoons sugar
1 teaspoon apple pie spice
Ice cream, heavy cream, or whipped cream, for serving

1. Preheat the air fryer oven to 350ºF (177ºC).
2. Put the apples in a large bowl. Drizzle with the melted butter and sprinkle with the sugar and apple pie spice. Use the hands to toss, ensuring the apples are evenly coated. Put the apples in the air fryer basket.
3. Put the air fryer basket on sheet pan and place into oven. Select Air Fry and set time to 10 minutes. Pierce the apples with a fork to ensure they are tender.
4. Serve with ice cream, or top with a splash of heavy cream or a spoonful of whipped cream.

Cinnamon S'mores

Prep time: 5 minutes | Cook time: 3 minutes | Makes 12 s'mores

12 whole cinnamon graham crackers, halved
2 (1.55-ounce / 44-g)
chocolate bars, cut into 12 pieces
12 marshmallows

1. Arrange 12 graham cracker squares in the sheet pan in a single layer.
2. Top each square with a piece of chocolate.
3. Place the sheet pan on wire rack and slide into oven. Select Bake, set temperature to 350ºF (180ºC), and set time to 3 minutes.
4. Bake for 2 minutes. Remove the pan and place a marshmallow on each piece of melted chocolate. Bake for another 1 minute.
5. Remove from the oven to a serving plate.
6. Serve topped with the remaining graham cracker squares

Oatmeal Raisin Bars

Prep time: 15 minutes | Cook time: 15 minutes | Serves 8

⅓ cup all-purpose flour
¼ teaspoon kosher salt
¼ teaspoon baking powder
¼ teaspoon ground cinnamon
¼ cup light brown sugar, lightly packed
¼ cup granulated sugar
½ cup canola oil
1 large egg
1 teaspoon vanilla extract
1⅓ cups quick-cooking oats
⅓ cup raisins

1. Preheat the air fryer oven to 360ºF (182ºC).
2. In a large bowl, combine the all-purpose flour, kosher salt, baking powder, ground cinnamon, light brown sugar, granulated sugar, canola oil, egg, vanilla extract, quick-cooking oats, and raisins.
3. Spray a sheet pan with nonstick cooking spray, then pour the oat mixture into the pan and press down to evenly distribute.
4. Put the sheet pan on wire rack and slide into the oven. Select Bake and set time to 15 minutes, or until golden brown.
5. Remove from the oven and allow to cool in the pan on a wire rack for 20 minutes before slicing and serving.

Chapter 7: Desserts | 91

Jelly Doughnuts

Prep time: 5 minutes | Cook time: 5 minutes | Serves 8

1 (16.3-ounce / 462-g) package large refrigerator biscuits
Cooking spray

1¼ cups good-quality raspberry jam
Confectioners' sugar, for dusting

1. Preheat the air fryer oven to 350°F (177°C).
2. Separate biscuits into 8 rounds. Spray both sides of rounds lightly with oil.
3. Spray the air fryer basket with oil and place the rounds in the basket.
4. Put the air fryer basket on sheet pan and place into oven. Select Air Fry and set time to 5 minutes, or until golden brown.
5. Transfer to a wire rack and let cool.
6. Fill a pastry bag, fitted with small plain tip, with raspberry jam; use tip to poke a small hole in the side of each doughnut, then fill the centers with the jam. Dust doughnuts with confectioners' sugar. Serve immediately.

Lemony Apple Butter

Prep time: 10 minutes | Cook time: 1 hour | Makes 1¼ cups

Cooking spray
2 cups unsweetened applesauce
⅔ cup packed light brown sugar
3 tablespoons fresh lemon

juice
½ teaspoon kosher salt
¼ teaspoon ground cinnamon
⅛ teaspoon ground allspice

1. Preheat the air fryer oven to 340°F (171°C).
2. Spray a metal cake pan with cooking spray. Whisk together all the ingredients in a bowl until smooth, then pour into the greased pan.
3. Place the pan on wire rack and slide into oven. Select Bake and set time to 60 minutes, or until the apple mixture is caramelized, reduced to a thick purée, and fragrant.
4. Remove the pan from the oven, stir to combine the caramelized bits at the edge with the rest, then let cool completely to thicken.
5. Serve immediately.

Pumpkin Pudding

Prep time: 10 minutes | Cook time: 15 minutes | Serves 4

3 cups pumpkin purée
3 tablespoons honey
1 tablespoon ginger
1 tablespoon cinnamon
1 teaspoon clove

1 teaspoon nutmeg
1 cup full-fat cream
2 eggs
1 cup sugar

1. Preheat the air fryer oven to 390°F (199°C).
2. In a bowl, stir all the ingredients together to combine. Scrape the mixture into a greased baking dish.
3. Place the baking dish on wire rack and slide into oven. Select Bake and set time to 15 minutes.
4. Serve warm.

Chocolate Pecan Pie

Prep time: 20 minutes | Cook time: 25 minutes | Serves 8

1 (9-inch) unbaked pie crust
Filling:

2 large eggs
⅓ cup butter, melted
1 cup sugar
½ cup all-purpose flour

1 cup milk chocolate chips
1½ cups coarsely chopped pecans
2 tablespoons bourbon

1. Whisk the eggs and melted butter in a large bowl until creamy.
2. Add the sugar and flour and stir to incorporate. Mix in the milk chocolate chips, pecans, and bourbon and stir until well combined.
3. Use a fork to prick holes in the bottom and sides of the pie crust. Pour the prepared filling into the pie crust. Place the pie crust in the sheet pan.
4. Place the sheet pan on wire rack and slide into oven. Select Bake, set temperature to 350°F (180°C), and set time to 25 minutes.
5. When cooking is complete, a toothpick inserted in the center should come out clean.
6. Allow the pie cool for 10 minutes in the pan before serving.

Caramelized Fruit Kebabs

Prep time: 10 minutes | Cook time: 4 minutes | Serves 4

2 peaches, peeled, pitted, and thickly sliced	1 tablespoon honey
3 plums, halved and pitted	½ teaspoon ground cinnamon
3 nectarines, halved and pitted	¼ teaspoon ground allspice
	Pinch cayenne pepper
Special Equipment:	8 metal skewers

1. Thread, alternating peaches, plums, and nectarines onto the metal skewers.
2. Thoroughly combine the honey, cinnamon, allspice, and cayenne in a small bowl. Brush generously the glaze over the fruit skewers.
3. Transfer the fruit skewers to the air fryer basket.
4. Put the air fryer basket on sheet pan and place into oven. Select Air Fry, set temperature to 400°F (205°C), and set time to 4 minutes.
5. When cooking is complete, the fruit should be caramelized.
6. Remove the fruit skewers from the oven and let rest for 5 minutes before serving.

Berry Crumble

Prep time: 5 minutes | Cook time: 35 minutes | Serves 6

2 ounces (57 g) unsweetened mixed berries	1 teaspoon xanthan gum
½ cup granulated Swerve	½ teaspoon ground cinnamon
2 tablespoons golden flaxseed meal	¼ teaspoon ground star anise
Topping:	
½ stick butter, cut into small pieces	⅓ cup unsweetened coconut, finely shredded
1 cup powdered Swerve	½ teaspoon baking powder
⅔ cup almond flour	Cooking spray

1. Coat 6 ramekins with cooking spray.

2. In a mixing dish, stir together the mixed berries, granulated Swerve, flaxseed meal, xanthan gum, cinnamon, star anise. Divide the berry mixture evenly among the prepared ramekins.
3. Combine the remaining ingredients in a separate mixing dish and stir well. Scatter the topping over the berry mixture.
4. Put the ramekins on wire rack and slide into oven. Select Bake, set temperature to 330°F (166°C), and set time to 35 minutes.
5. When done, the topping should be golden brown.
6. Serve warm.

Spice Cookies

Prep time: 15 minutes | Cook time: 12 minutes | Serves 4

4 tablespoons (½ stick) unsalted butter, at room temperature	2 teaspoons ground ginger
2 tablespoons agave nectar	1 teaspoon ground cinnamon
1 large egg	½ teaspoon freshly grated nutmeg
2 tablespoons water	1 teaspoon baking soda
2½ cups almond flour	¼ teaspoon kosher salt
½ cup sugar	

1. Preheat the air fryer oven to 325°F (163°C).
2. Line the bottom of a sheet pan with parchment paper.
3. In a large bowl using a hand mixer, beat together the butter, agave, egg, and water on medium speed until fluffy.
4. Add the almond flour, sugar, ginger, cinnamon, nutmeg, baking soda, and salt. Beat on low speed until well combined.
5. Roll the dough into 2-tablespoon balls and arrange them on the parchment paper in the pan. (They don't really spread too much, but try to leave a little room between them).
6. Put the sheet pan on wire rack and slide into the oven. Select Bake and set time to 12 minutes, or until the tops of cookies are lightly browned.
7. Transfer to a wire rack and let cool completely. Serve immediately

Chapter 7: Desserts | 93

Breaded Bananas with Chocolate Sauce

Prep time: 10 minutes | Cook time: 7 minutes | Serves 6

¼ cup cornstarch
¼ cup plain bread crumbs
1 large egg, beaten
3 bananas, halved

crosswise
Cooking spray
Chocolate sauce, for serving

1. Place the cornstarch, bread crumbs, and egg in three separate bowls.
2. Roll the bananas in the cornstarch, then in the beaten egg, and finally in the bread crumbs to coat well.
3. Spritz the air fryer basket with cooking spray.
4. Arrange the banana halves in the basket and mist them with cooking spray.
5. Put the air fryer basket on sheet pan and place into oven. Select Air Fry, set temperature to 350ºF (180ºC), and set time to 7 minutes.
6. After about 5 minutes, flip the bananas and continue to air fry for another 2 minutes.
7. When cooking is complete, remove the bananas from the oven to a serving plate. Serve with the chocolate sauce drizzled over the top.

Pineapple Galette

Prep time: 10 minutes | Cook time: 40 minutes | Serves 2

¼ medium-size pineapple, peeled, cored, and cut crosswise into ¼-inch-thick slices
2 tablespoons dark rum
1 teaspoon vanilla extract
½ teaspoon kosher salt
Finely grated zest of ½ lime

1 store-bought sheet puff pastry, cut into an 8-inch round
3 tablespoons granulated sugar
2 tablespoons unsalted butter, cubed and chilled
Coconut ice cream, for serving

1. Preheat the air fryer oven to 310ºF (154ºC).
2. In a small bowl, combine the pineapple slices, rum,

vanilla, salt, and lime zest and let stand for at least 10 minutes to allow the pineapple to soak in the rum.
3. Meanwhile, press the puff pastry round into the bottom and up the sides of a round metal cake pan and use the tines of a fork to dock the bottom and sides.
4. Arrange the pineapple slices on the bottom of the pastry in more or less a single layer, then sprinkle with the sugar and dot with the butter. Drizzle with the leftover juices from the bowl.
5. Place the pan on wire rack and slide into oven. Select Bake and set time to 40 minutes, or until the pastry is puffed and golden brown and the pineapple is lightly caramelized on top.
6. Transfer the pan to a wire rack to cool for 15 minutes. Unmold the galette from the pan and serve warm with coconut ice cream.

Orange Cake

Prep time: 10 minutes | Cook time: 23 minutes | Serves 8

Nonstick baking spray with flour
1¼ cups all-purpose flour
⅓ cup yellow cornmeal
¾ cup white sugar
1 teaspoon baking soda

¼ cup safflower oil
1¼ cups orange juice, divided
1 teaspoon vanilla
¼ cup powdered sugar

1. Preheat the air fryer oven to 350ºF (177ºC).
2. Spray a sheet pan with nonstick spray and set aside.
3. In a medium bowl, combine the flour, cornmeal, sugar, baking soda, safflower oil, 1 cup of the orange juice, and vanilla, and mix well.
4. Pour the batter into the sheet pan. Put the sheet pan on wire rack and slide into the oven. Select Bake and set time to 23 minutes, or until a toothpick inserted in the center of the cake comes out clean.
5. Remove the cake from the oven and place on a cooling rack. Using a toothpick, make about 20 holes in the cake.
6. In a small bowl, combine remaining ¼ cup of orange juice and the powdered sugar and stir well. Drizzle this mixture over the hot cake slowly so the cake absorbs it.
7. When cooled completely, cut into wedges and serve.

Fudgy Chocolate Brownies

Prep time: 5 minutes | Cook time: 21 minutes | Serves 8

1 stick butter, melted

1 cup Swerve

2 eggs

1 cup coconut flour

½ cup unsweetened cocoa powder

2 tablespoons flaxseed meal

1 teaspoon baking powder

1 teaspoon vanilla essence

A pinch of salt

A pinch of ground cardamom

Cooking spray

1. Spray the sheet pan with cooking spray.
2. Beat together the melted butter and Swerve in a large mixing dish until fluffy. Whisk in the eggs.
3. Add the coconut flour, cocoa powder, flaxseed meal, baking powder, vanilla essence, salt, and cardamom and stir with a spatula until well incorporated. Spread the mixture evenly into the prepared sheet pan.
4. Place the sheet pan on wire rack and slide into oven. Select Bake, set temperature to 350ºF (180ºC), and set time to 21 minutes.
5. When cooking is complete, a toothpick inserted in the center should come out clean.
6. Remove from the oven and place on a wire rack to cool completely. Cut into squares and serve immediately.

Rich Chocolate Cookie

Prep time: 10 minutes | Cook time: 9 minutes | Serves 4

Nonstick baking spray with flour

3 tablespoons softened butter

⅓ cup plus 1 tablespoon brown sugar

1 egg yolk

½ cup flour

2 tablespoons ground white chocolate

¼ teaspoon baking soda

½ teaspoon vanilla

¾ cup chocolate chips

1. Preheat the air fryer oven to 350ºF (177ºC).
2. In a medium bowl, beat the butter and brown sugar

together until fluffy. Stir in the egg yolk.

3. Add the flour, white chocolate, baking soda, and vanilla, and mix well. Stir in the chocolate chips.
4. Line a sheet pan with parchment paper. Spray the parchment paper with nonstick baking spray with flour.
5. Spread the batter into the prepared pan, leaving a ½-inch border on all sides.
6. Put the sheet pan on wire rack and slide into the oven. Select Bake and set time to 9 minutes, or until the cookie is light brown and just barely set.
7. Remove the pan from the oven and let cool for 10 minutes. Remove the cookie from the pan, remove the parchment paper, and let cool on a wire rack.
8. Serve immediately.

Pear and Apple Crisp

Prep time: 10 minutes | Cook time: 20 minutes | Serves 6

½ pound (227 g) apples, cored and chopped

½ pound (227 g) pears, cored and chopped

1 cup flour

1 cup sugar

1 tablespoon butter

1 teaspoon ground cinnamon

¼ teaspoon ground cloves

1 teaspoon vanilla extract

¼ cup chopped walnuts

Whipped cream, for serving

1. Preheat the air fryer oven to 340ºF (171ºC).
2. Lightly grease a baking dish and place the apples and pears inside.
3. Combine the rest of the ingredients, except the walnuts and whipped cream, until a coarse, crumbly texture is achieved.
4. Pour the mixture over the fruits and spread it evenly. Top with the chopped walnuts.
5. Place the baking dish on wire rack and slide into oven. Select Bake and set time to 20 minutes, or until the top turns golden brown.
6. Serve at room temperature with whipped cream.

Pecan and Cherry Stuffed Apples

Prep time: 10 minutes | Cook time: 22 minutes | Serves 4

4 apples (about 1¼ pounds / 567 g)
¼ cup chopped pecans
⅓ cup dried tart cherries
1 tablespoon melted butter
3 tablespoons brown sugar
¼ teaspoon allspice
Pinch salt
Ice cream, for serving

1. Cut off top ½ inch from each apple; reserve tops. With a melon baller, core through stem ends without breaking through the bottom. (Do not trim bases.)
2. Preheat the air fryer oven to 350°F (177°C).
3. Combine pecans, cherries, butter, brown sugar, allspice, and a pinch of salt. Stuff mixture into the hollow centers of the apples. Cover with apple tops. Arrange the stuffed apples in the air fryer basket.
4. Put the air fryer basket on sheet pan and place into oven. Select Air Fry and set time to 22 minutes, or just until tender.
5. Serve warm with ice cream.

Pineapple and Chocolate Cake

Prep time: 10 minutes | Cook time: 38 minutes | Serves 4

2 cups flour
4 ounces (113 g) butter, melted
¼ cup sugar
½ pound (227 g) pineapple, chopped
½ cup pineapple juice
1 ounce (28 g) dark chocolate, grated
1 large egg
2 tablespoons skimmed milk

1. Preheat the air fryer oven to 370°F (188°C).
2. Grease a cake tin with a little oil or butter.
3. In a bowl, combine the butter and flour to create a crumbly consistency.
4. Add the sugar, chopped pineapple, juice, and grated dark chocolate and mix well.
5. In a separate bowl, combine the egg and milk. Add this mixture to the flour mixture and stir well until a soft dough forms. Pour the mixture into the cake tin.
6. Place the cake tin on wore rack and slide into oven. Select Bake and set time to 38 minutes.
7. Cool for 5 minutes before serving.

Apple Turnovers

Prep time: 10 minutes | Cook time: 10 minutes | Serves 4

1 apple, peeled, quartered, and thinly sliced
½ teaspoons pumpkin pie spice
Juice of ½ lemon
1 tablespoon granulated sugar
Pinch of kosher salt
6 sheets phyllo dough
Nonstick cooking spray

1. Preheat the air fryer oven to 330°F (166°C).
2. In a medium bowl, combine the apple, pumpkin pie spice, lemon juice, granulated sugar, and kosher salt.
3. Cut the phyllo dough sheets into 4 equal pieces and place individual tablespoons of apple filling in the center of each piece, then fold in both sides and roll from front to back.
4. Spray the air fryer basket with nonstick cooking spray, then place the turnovers in the basket.
5. Put the air fryer basket on sheet pan and place into oven. Select Air Fry and set time to 10 minutes, or until golden brown.
6. Remove the turnovers and allow to cool on a wire rack for 10 minutes before serving.

Chapter 8   Casseroles, Frittatas, and Quiches

Greek Frittata

Prep time: 7 minutes | Cook time: 8 minutes | Serves 2

1 cup chopped mushrooms
2 cups spinach, chopped
4 eggs, lightly beaten
3 ounces (85 g) feta cheese, crumbled
2 tablespoons heavy cream
A handful of fresh parsley, chopped
Salt and ground black pepper, to taste
Cooking spray

1. Spritz the sheet pan with cooking spray.
2. Whisk together all the ingredients in a large bowl. Stir to mix well.
3. Pour the mixture in the prepared sheet pan.
4. Place the sheet pan on wire rack and slide into oven. Select Bake, set temperature to 350ºF (180ºC) and set time to 8 minutes.
5. Stir the mixture halfway through.
6. When cooking is complete, the eggs should be set.
7. Serve immediately.

Sumptuous Beef and Bean Chili Casserole

Prep time: 15 minutes | Cook time: 31 minutes | Serves 4

1 tablespoon olive oil
½ cup finely chopped bell pepper
½ cup chopped celery
1 onion, chopped
2 garlic cloves, minced
1 pound (454 g) ground beef
1 can diced tomatoes
½ teaspoon parsley
½ tablespoon chili powder
1 teaspoon chopped cilantro
1½ cups vegetable broth
1 (8-ounce / 227-g) can cannellini beans
Salt and ground black pepper, to taste

1. Heat the olive oil in a nonstick skillet over medium heat until shimmering.
2. Add the bell pepper, celery, onion, and garlic to the skillet and sauté for 5 minutes or until the onion is translucent.
3. Add the ground beef and sauté for an additional 6 minutes or until lightly browned.
4. Mix in the tomatoes, parsley, chili powder, cilantro and vegetable broth, then cook for 10 more minutes. Stir constantly.
5. Pour them in the sheet pan, then mix in the beans and sprinkle with salt and ground black pepper.
6. Place the sheet pan on wire rack and slide into oven. Select Bake, set temperature to 350ºF (180ºC) and set time to 10 minutes.
7. When cooking is complete, the vegetables should be tender and the beef should be well browned.
8. Remove from the oven and serve immediately.

Herbed Cheddar Frittata

Prep time: 10 minutes | Cook time: 20 minutes | Serves 4

½ cup shredded Cheddar cheese
½ cup half-and-half
4 large eggs
2 tablespoons chopped scallion greens
2 tablespoons chopped fresh parsley
½ teaspoon kosher salt
½ teaspoon ground black pepper
Cooking spray

1. Spritz the sheet pan with cooking spray.
2. Whisk together all the ingredients in a large bowl, then pour the mixture into the prepared sheet pan.
3. Place the sheet pan on wire rack and slide into oven. Select Bake, set temperature to 300ºF (150ºC) and set time to 20 minutes.
4. Stir the mixture halfway through.
5. When cooking is complete, the eggs should be set.
6. Serve immediately.

Spinach and Chickpea Casserole

Prep time: 10 minutes | Cook time: 21 to 22 minutes | Serves 4

2 tablespoons olive oil
2 garlic cloves, minced
1 tablespoon ginger, minced
1 onion, chopped
1 chili pepper, minced
Salt and ground black
pepper, to taste
1 pound (454 g) spinach
1 can coconut milk
½ cup dried tomatoes, chopped
1 (14-ounce / 397-g) can chickpeas, drained

1. Heat the olive oil in a saucepan over medium heat. Sauté the garlic and ginger in the olive oil for 1 minute, or until fragrant.
2. Add the onion, chili pepper, salt and pepper to the saucepan. Sauté for 3 minutes.
3. Mix in the spinach and sauté for 3 to 4 minutes or until the vegetables become soft. Remove from heat.
4. Pour the vegetable mixture into the sheet pan. Stir in coconut milk, dried tomatoes and chickpeas until well blended.
5. Place the sheet pan on wire rack and slide into oven. Select Bake, set temperature to 370ºF (188ºC) and set time to 15 minutes.
6. When cooking is complete, transfer the casserole to a serving dish. Let cool for 5 minutes before serving.

Chicken Divan

Prep time: 5 minutes | Cook time: 24 minutes | Serves 4

4 chicken breasts
Salt and ground black pepper, to taste
1 head broccoli, cut into florets
½ cup cream of mushroom
soup
1 cup shredded Cheddar cheese
½ cup croutons
Cooking spray

1. Spritz the air fryer basket with cooking spray.
2. Put the chicken breasts in the basket and sprinkle with salt and ground black pepper.
3. Put the air fryer basket on sheet pan and place into oven. Select Air Fry, set temperature to 390ºF (199ºC) and set time to 14 minutes.
4. Flip the breasts halfway through the cooking time.
5. When cooking is complete, the breasts should be well browned and tender.
6. Remove the breasts from the oven and allow to cool for a few minutes on a plate, then cut the breasts into bite-size pieces.
7. Combine the chicken, broccoli, mushroom soup, and Cheddar cheese in a large bowl. Stir to mix well.
8. Spritz the sheet pan with cooking spray. Pour the chicken mixture into the pan. Spread the croutons over the mixture.
9. Place the sheet pan on wire rack and slide into oven. Select Bake, set time to 10 minutes.
10. When cooking is complete, the croutons should be lightly browned and the mixture should be set.
11. Remove from the oven and serve immediately.

Creamy Pork Gratin

Prep time: 15 minutes | Cook time: 21 minutes | Serves 4

2 tablespoons olive oil
2 pounds (907 g) pork tenderloin, cut into serving-size pieces
1 teaspoon dried marjoram
¼ teaspoon chili powder
1 teaspoon coarse sea salt
½ teaspoon freshly ground black pepper
1 cup Ricotta cheese
1½ cups chicken broth
1 tablespoon mustard
Cooking spray

1. Spritz the sheet pan with cooking spray.
2. Heat the olive oil in a nonstick skillet over medium-high heat until shimmering.
3. Add the pork and sauté for 6 minutes or until lightly browned.
4. Transfer the pork to the prepared sheet pan and sprinkle with marjoram, chili powder, salt, and ground black pepper.
5. Combine the remaining ingredients in a large bowl. Stir to mix well. Pour the mixture over the pork in the pan.
6. Place the sheet pan on wire rack and slide into oven. Select Bake, set temperature to 350ºF (180ºC) and set time to 15 minutes.
7. Stir the mixture halfway through.
8. When cooking is complete, the mixture should be frothy and the cheese should be melted.
9. Serve immediately.

Chorizo, Corn, and Potato Frittata

Prep time: 8 minutes | Cook time: 12 minutes | Serves 4

2 tablespoons olive oil
1 chorizo, sliced
4 eggs
½ cup corn
1 large potato, boiled and cubed

1 tablespoon chopped parsley
½ cup feta cheese, crumbled
Salt and ground black pepper, to taste

1. Heat the olive oil in a nonstick skillet over medium heat until shimmering.
2. Add the chorizo and cook for 4 minutes or until golden brown.
3. Whisk the eggs in a bowl, then sprinkle with salt and ground black pepper.
4. Mix the remaining ingredients in the egg mixture, then pour the chorizo and its fat into the sheet pan. Pour in the egg mixture.
5. Place the sheet pan on wire rack and slide into oven. Select Bake, set temperature to 330ºF (166ºC) and set time to 8 minutes.
6. Stir the mixture halfway through.
7. When cooking is complete, the eggs should be set.
8. Serve immediately.

Goat Cheese and Asparagus Frittata

Prep time: 5 minutes | Cook time: 25 minutes | Serves 2 to 4

1 cup asparagus spears, cut into 1-inch pieces
1 teaspoon vegetable oil
1 tablespoon milk
6 eggs, beaten
2 ounces (57 g) goat

cheese, crumbled
1 tablespoon minced chives, optional
Kosher salt and pepper, to taste

1. Add the asparagus spears to a small bowl and drizzle with the vegetable oil. Toss until well coated and transfer to the air fryer basket.
2. Put the air fryer basket on sheet pan and place into oven. Select Air Fry, set temperature to 400ºF (205ºC) and set time to 5 minutes.

3. Flip the asparagus halfway through.
4. When cooking is complete, the asparagus should be tender and slightly wilted.
5. Remove from the oven to the sheet pan.
6. Stir together the milk and eggs in a medium bowl. Pour the mixture over the asparagus in the pan. Sprinkle with the goat cheese and the chives (if using) over the eggs. Season with salt and pepper.
7. Place the sheet pan on wire rack and slide into oven. Select Bake, set temperature to 320ºF (160ºC) and set time to 20 minutes.
8. When cooking is complete, the top should be golden and the eggs should be set.
9. Transfer to a serving dish. Slice and serve.

Sumptuous Vegetable Frittata

Prep time: 15 minutes | Cook time: 20 minutes | Serves 2

4 eggs
⅓ cup milk
2 teaspoons olive oil
1 large zucchini, sliced
2 asparagus, sliced thinly
⅓ cup sliced mushrooms
1 cup baby spinach

1 small red onion, sliced
⅓ cup crumbled feta cheese
⅓ cup grated Cheddar cheese
¼ cup chopped chives
Salt and ground black pepper, to taste

1. Line the sheet pan with parchment paper.
2. Whisk together the eggs, milk, salt, and ground black pepper in a large bowl. Set aside.
3. Heat the olive oil in a nonstick skillet over medium heat until shimmering.
4. Add the zucchini, asparagus, mushrooms, spinach, and onion to the skillet and sauté for 5 minutes or until tender.
5. Pour the sautéed vegetables into the prepared sheet pan, then spread the egg mixture over and scatter with cheeses.
6. Place the sheet pan on wire rack and slide into oven. Select Bake, set temperature to 380ºF (193ºC) and set time to 15 minutes.
7. Stir the mixture halfway through.
8. When cooking is complete, the egg should be set and the edges should be lightly browned.
9. Remove the frittata from the oven and sprinkle with chives before serving.

Chapter 8: Casseroles, Frittatas, and Quiches | 99

Kale Frittata

Prep time: 5 minutes | Cook time: 11 minutes | Serves 2

1 cup kale, chopped
1 teaspoon olive oil
4 large eggs, beaten
Kosher salt, to taste

2 tablespoons water
3 tablespoons crumbled feta
Cooking spray

1. Spritz the sheet pan with cooking spray.
2. Add the kale to the sheet pan and drizzle with olive oil.
3. Place the sheet pan on wire rack and slide into oven. Select Air Broil, set temperature to 360°F (182°C) and set time to 3 minutes.
4. Stir the kale halfway through.
5. When cooking is complete, the kale should be wilted.
6. Meanwhile, combine the eggs with salt and water in a large bowl. Stir to mix well.
7. Make the frittata: When broiling is complete, pour the eggs into the sheet pan and spread with feta cheese.
8. Place the sheet pan on wire rack and slide into oven. Select Bake, set temperature to 300°F (150°C) and set time to 8 minutes.
9. When cooking is complete, the eggs should be set and the cheese should be melted.
10. Remove from the oven and serve the frittata immediately.

Shrimp Spinach Frittata

Prep time: 6 minutes | Cook time: 14 minutes | Serves 4

4 whole eggs
1 teaspoon dried basil
½ cup shrimp, cooked and chopped
½ cup baby spinach

½ cup rice, cooked
½ cup Monterey Jack cheese, grated
Salt, to taste
Cooking spray

1. Spritz the sheet pan with cooking spray.
2. Whisk the eggs with basil and salt in a large bowl until bubbly, then mix in the shrimp, spinach, rice, and cheese.
3. Pour the mixture into the sheet pan.
4. Place the sheet pan on wire rack and slide into oven. Select Bake, set temperature to 360°F (182°C) and set

time to 14 minutes.
5. Stir the mixture halfway through.
6. When cooking is complete, the eggs should be set and the frittata should be golden brown.
7. Slice to serve.

Keto Cheese Quiche

Prep time: 20 minutes | Cook time: 1 hour | Serves 8

Crust:
1¼ cups blanched almond flour
1 large egg, beaten
Filling:
4 ounces (113 g) cream cheese
1 cup shredded Swiss cheese
⅓ cup minced leeks
4 large eggs, beaten
½ cup chicken broth

1¼ cups grated Parmesan cheese
¼ teaspoon fine sea salt

⅛ teaspoon cayenne pepper
¾ teaspoon fine sea salt
1 tablespoon unsalted butter, melted
Chopped green onions, for garnish
Cooking spray

1. Spritz the sheet pan with cooking spray.
2. Combine the flour, egg, Parmesan, and salt in a large bowl. Stir to mix until a satiny and firm dough forms.
3. Arrange the dough between two grease parchment papers, then roll the dough into a 1/16-inch thick circle.
4. Make the crust: Transfer the dough into the prepared pan and press to coat the bottom.
5. Place the sheet pan on wire rack and slide into oven. Select Bake, set temperature to 325°F (163°C) and set time to 12 minutes.
6. When cooking is complete, the edges of the crust should be lightly browned.
7. Meanwhile, combine the ingredient for the filling, except for the green onions in a large bowl.
8. Pour the filling over the cooked crust and cover the edges of the crust with aluminum foil.
9. Place the sheet pan on wire rack and slide into oven. Select Bake, set time to 15 minutes.
10. When cooking is complete, reduce the heat to 300°F (150°C) and set time to 30 minutes.
11. When cooking is complete, a toothpick inserted in the center should come out clean.
12. Remove from the oven and allow to cool for 10 minutes before serving.

Mediterranean Quiche

Prep time: 10 minutes | Cook time: 30 minutes | Serves 4

4 eggs
¼ cup chopped Kalamata olives
½ cup chopped tomatoes
¼ cup chopped onion
½ cup milk
1 cup crumbled feta cheese
½ tablespoon chopped oregano
½ tablespoon chopped basil
Salt and ground black pepper, to taste
Cooking spray

1. Spritz the sheet pan with cooking spray.
2. Whisk the eggs with remaining ingredients in a large bowl. Stir to mix well.
3. Pour the mixture into the prepared sheet pan.
4. Place the sheet pan on wire rack and slide into oven. Select Bake, set temperature to 340°F (171°C) and set time to 30 minutes.
5. When cooking is complete, the eggs should be set and a toothpick inserted in the center should come out clean.
6. Serve immediately.

Smoked Trout and Crème Fraiche Frittata

Prep time: 8 minutes | Cook time: 17 minutes | Serves 4

2 tablespoons olive oil
1 onion, sliced
1 egg, beaten
½ tablespoon horseradish sauce
6 tablespoons crème fraiche
1 cup diced smoked trout
2 tablespoons chopped fresh dill
Cooking spray

1. Spritz the sheet pan with cooking spray.
2. Heat the olive oil in a nonstick skillet over medium heat until shimmering.
3. Add the onion and sauté for 3 minutes or until translucent.
4. Combine the egg, horseradish sauce, and crème fraiche in a large bowl. Stir to mix well, then mix in the sautéed onion, smoked trout, and dill.
5. Pour the mixture in the prepared sheet pan.
6. Place the sheet pan on wire rack and slide into oven. Select Bake, set temperature to 350°F (180°C) and set time to 14 minutes.

7. Stir the mixture halfway through.
8. When cooking is complete, the egg should be set and the edges should be lightly browned.
9. Serve immediately.

Mini Quiche Cups

Prep time: 15 minutes | Cook time: 14 minutes | Makes 10 quiche cups

4 ounces (113 g) ground pork sausage
3 eggs
¾ cup milk
Cooking spray
4 ounces (113 g) sharp Cheddar cheese, grated

Special Equipment:
20 foil muffin cups

1. Preheat the air fryer oven to 390°F (199°C). Spritz the air fryer basket with cooking spray.
2. Divide sausage into 3 portions and shape each into a thin patty.
3. Put the patties in the air fryer basket. Put the air fryer basket on sheet pan and place into oven. Select Air Fry and set time to 6 minutes.
4. While sausage is cooking, prepare the egg mixture. Combine the eggs and milk in a large bowl and whisk until well blended. Set aside.
5. When sausage has cooked fully, remove patties from the basket, drain well, and use a fork to crumble the meat into small pieces.
6. Double the foil cups into 10 sets. Remove paper liners from the top muffin cups and spray the foil cups lightly with cooking spray.
7. Divide crumbled sausage among the 10 muffin cup sets.
8. Top each with grated cheese, divided evenly among the cups. Put the cups in a sheet pan.
9. Pour egg mixture into each cup, filling until each cup is at least ⅔ full.
10. Put the sheet pan on wire rack and slide into the oven. Select Bake and set time to 8 minutes. A knife inserted into the center shouldn't have any raw egg on it when removed.
11. Serve warm.

Broccoli, Carrot, and Tomato Quiche

Prep time: 6 minutes | Cook time: 14 minutes | Serves 4

4 eggs
1 teaspoon dried thyme
1 cup whole milk
1 steamed carrots, diced
2 cups steamed broccoli florets
2 medium tomatoes, diced
¼ cup crumbled feta cheese
1 cup grated Cheddar cheese
1 teaspoon chopped parsley
Salt and ground black pepper, to taste
Cooking spray

1. Spritz the sheet pan with cooking spray.
2. Whisk together the eggs, thyme, salt, and ground black pepper in a bowl and fold in the milk while mixing.
3. Put the carrots, broccoli, and tomatoes in the prepared sheet pan, then spread with feta cheese and ½ cup Cheddar cheese. Pour the egg mixture over, then scatter with remaining Cheddar on top.
4. Place the sheet pan on wire rack and slide into oven. Select Bake, set temperature to 350ºF (180ºC) and set time to 14 minutes.
5. When cooking is complete, the egg should be set and the quiche should be puffed.
6. Remove the quiche from the oven and top with chopped parsley, then slice to serve.

Vegetable Frittata

Prep time: 15 minutes | Cook time: 21 minutes | Serves 2

4 eggs
¼ cup milk
Sea salt and ground black pepper, to taste
1 zucchini, sliced
½ bunch asparagus, sliced
½ cup mushrooms, sliced
½ cup spinach, shredded
½ cup red onion, sliced
½ tablespoon olive oil
5 tablespoons feta cheese, crumbled
4 tablespoons Cheddar cheese, grated
¼ bunch chives, minced

1. In a bowl, mix the eggs, milk, salt and pepper.
2. Over a medium heat, sauté the vegetables for 6 minutes with the olive oil in a nonstick pan.
3. Put some parchment paper in the bottom of a baking tin. Pour in the vegetables, followed by the egg mixture.

Top with the feta and grated Cheddar.
4. Preheat the air fryer oven to 320ºF (160ºC).
5. Place the baking tin on wire rack and slide into oven. Select Bake and set time to 15 minutes.
6. Remove the frittata and leave to cool for 5 minutes.
7. Top with the minced chives and serve.

Mac and Cheese

Prep time: 10 minutes | Cook time: 10 minutes | Serves 2

1 cup cooked macaroni
1 cup grated Cheddar cheese
½ cup warm milk
Salt and ground black pepper, to taste
1 tablespoon grated Parmesan cheese

1. Preheat the air fryer oven to 350ºF (177ºC).
2. In a baking dish, mix all the ingredients, except for Parmesan.
3. Place the baking dish on wire rack and slide into oven. Select Bake and set time to 10 minutes.
4. Add the Parmesan cheese on top and serve.

Cheesy Bacon Quiche

Prep time: 15 minutes | Cook time: 20 minutes | Serves 4

1 tablespoon olive oil
1 shortcrust pastry
3 tablespoons Greek yogurt
½ cup grated Cheddar cheese
3 ounces (85 g) chopped bacon
4 eggs, beaten
¼ teaspoon garlic powder
Pinch of black pepper
¼ teaspoon onion powder
¼ teaspoon sea salt
Flour, for sprinkling

1. Preheat the air fryer oven to 330ºF (166ºC).
2. Take 8 ramekins and grease with olive oil. Coat with a sprinkling of flour, tapping to remove any excess.
3. Cut the shortcrust pastry in 8 and place each piece at the bottom of each ramekin.
4. Put all the other ingredients in a bowl and combine well. Spoon equal amounts of the filling into each piece of pastry.
5. Place the ramekins on wire rack and slide into oven. Select Bake and set time to 20 minutes.
6. Serve warm.

Shrimp Quiche

Prep time: 15 minutes | Cook time: 20 minutes | Serves 2

2 teaspoons vegetable oil

4 large eggs

½ cup half-and-half

4 ounces (113 g) raw shrimp, chopped

1 cup shredded Parmesan or Swiss cheese

¼ cup chopped scallions

1 teaspoon sweet smoked paprika

1 teaspoon herbes de Provence

1 teaspoon black pepper

½ to 1 teaspoon kosher salt

1. Preheat the air fryer oven to 300°F (149°C). Generously grease a sheet pan with vegetable oil.

2. In a large bowl, beat together the eggs and half-and-half. Add the shrimp, ¾ cup of the cheese, the scallions, paprika, herbes de Provence, pepper, and salt. Stir with a fork to thoroughly combine. Pour the egg mixture into the prepared pan.

3. Put the sheet pan on wire rack and slide into the oven. Select Bake and set time to 20 minutes.

4. After 17 minutes, sprinkle the remaining ¼ cup cheese on top and bake for the remaining 3 minutes, or until the cheese has melted, the eggs are set, and a toothpick inserted into the center comes out clean.

5. Serve the quiche warm.

Chapter 9 Wraps and Sandwiches

Chicken and Yogurt Taquitos

Prep time: 15 minutes | Cook time: 12 minutes | Serves 4

1 cup cooked chicken, shredded
¼ cup Greek yogurt
¼ cup salsa
1 cup shredded Mozzarella cheese
Salt and ground black pepper, to taste
4 flour tortillas
Cooking spray

1. Spritz the air fryer basket with cooking spray.
2. Combine all the ingredients, except for the tortillas, in a large bowl. Stir to mix well.
3. Make the taquitos: Unfold the tortillas on a clean work surface, then scoop up 2 tablespoons of the chicken mixture in the middle of each tortilla. Roll the tortillas up to wrap the filling.
4. Arrange the taquitos in the basket and spritz with cooking spray.
5. Put the air fryer basket on sheet pan and place into oven. Select Air Fry, set temperature to 380ºF (193ºC) and set time to 12 minutes.
6. Flip the taquitos halfway through the cooking time.
7. When cooked, the taquitos should be golden brown and the cheese should be melted.
8. Serve immediately.

Pork Momos

Prep time: 20 minutes | Cook time: 20 minutes | Serves 4

2 tablespoons olive oil
1 pound (454 g) ground pork
1 shredded carrot
1 onion, chopped
1 teaspoon soy sauce
16 wonton wrappers
Salt and ground black pepper, to taste
Cooking spray

1. Heat the olive oil in a nonstick skillet over medium heat until shimmering.
2. Add the ground pork, carrot, onion, soy sauce, salt, and ground black pepper and sauté for 10 minutes or until the pork is well browned and carrots are tender.
3. Unfold the wrappers on a clean work surface, then divide the cooked pork and vegetables on the wrappers. Fold the edges around the filling to form momos. Nip the top to seal the momos.
4. Arrange the momos in the air fryer basket and spritz with cooking spray.
5. Put the air fryer basket on sheet pan and place into oven. Select Air Fry, set temperature to 320ºF (160ºC) and set time to 10 minutes.
6. When cooking is complete, the wrappers will be lightly browned.
7. Serve immediately.

Thai Pork Sliders

Prep time: 10 minutes | Cook time: 14 minutes | Makes 6 sliders

1 pound (454 g) ground pork
1 tablespoon Thai curry paste
1½ tablespoons fish sauce
¼ cup thinly sliced scallions, white and green parts
2 tablespoons minced peeled fresh ginger
1 tablespoon light brown sugar
1 teaspoon ground black pepper
6 slider buns, split open lengthwise, warmed
Cooking spray

1. Spritz the air fryer basket with cooking spray.
2. Combine all the ingredients, except for the buns in a large bowl. Stir to mix well.
3. Divide and shape the mixture into six balls, then bash the balls into six 3-inch-diameter patties.
4. Arrange the patties in the basket and spritz with cooking spray.
5. Put the air fryer basket on sheet pan and place into oven. Select Air Fry, set temperature to 375ºF (190ºC) and set time to 14 minutes.
6. Flip the patties halfway through the cooking time.
7. When cooked, the patties should be well browned.
8. Assemble the buns with patties to make the sliders and serve immediately.

Crispy Crab and Cream Cheese Wontons

Prep time: 10 minutes | Cook time: 10 minutes | Serves 6 to 8

24 wonton wrappers, thawed if frozen
Filling:
5 ounces (142 g) lump crabmeat, drained and patted dry
4 ounces (113 g) cream cheese, at room temperature
2 scallions, sliced

Cooking spray

1½ teaspoons toasted sesame oil
1 teaspoon Worcestershire sauce
Kosher salt and ground black pepper, to taste

1. Spritz the air fryer basket with cooking spray.
2. In a medium-size bowl, place all the ingredients for the filling and stir until well mixed. Prepare a small bowl of water alongside.
3. On a clean work surface, lay the wonton wrappers. Scoop 1 teaspoon of the filling in the center of each wrapper. Wet the edges with a touch of water. Fold each wonton wrapper diagonally in half over the filling to form a triangle.
4. Arrange the wontons in the pan. Spritz the wontons with cooking spray.
5. Put the air fryer basket on sheet pan and place into oven. Select Air Fry, set temperature to 350ºF (180ºC) and set time to 10 minutes.
6. Flip the wontons halfway through the cooking time.
7. When cooking is complete, the wontons will be crispy and golden brown.
8. Serve immediately.

Crispy Chicken Egg Rolls

Prep time: 10 minutes | Cook time: 23 to 24 minutes | Serves 4

1 pound (454 g) ground chicken
2 teaspoons olive oil
2 garlic cloves, minced
1 teaspoon grated fresh ginger
2 cups white cabbage,

shredded
1 onion, chopped
¼ cup soy sauce
8 egg roll wrappers
1 egg, beaten
Cooking spray

1. Spritz the air fryer basket with cooking spray.
2. Heat olive oil in a saucepan over medium heat. Sauté the garlic and ginger in the olive oil for 1 minute, or until fragrant. Add the ground chicken to the saucepan. Sauté for 5 minutes, or until the chicken is cooked through. Add the cabbage, onion and soy sauce and sauté for 5 to 6 minutes, or until the vegetables become soft. Remove the saucepan from the heat.
3. Unfold the egg roll wrappers on a clean work surface. Divide the chicken mixture among the wrappers and brush the edges of the wrappers with the beaten egg. Tightly roll up the egg rolls, enclosing the filling. Arrange the rolls in the pan.
4. Put the air fryer basket on sheet pan and place into oven. Select Air Fry, set temperature to 370ºF (188ºC) and set time to 12 minutes.
5. Flip the rolls halfway through the cooking time.
6. When cooked, the rolls will be crispy and golden brown.
7. Transfer to a platter and let cool for 5 minutes before serving.

Bacon and Bell Pepper Sandwich

Prep time: 10 minutes | Cook time: 6 minutes | Serves 4

⅓ cup spicy barbecue sauce
2 tablespoons honey
8 slices cooked bacon, cut into thirds
1 red bell pepper, sliced

1 yellow bell pepper, sliced
3 pita pockets, cut in half
1¼ cups torn butter lettuce leaves
2 tomatoes, sliced

1. Preheat the air fryer oven to 350ºF (177ºC).
2. In a small bowl, combine the barbecue sauce and the honey. Brush this mixture lightly onto the bacon slices and the red and yellow pepper slices.
3. Put the peppers into the air fryer basket. Put the air fryer basket on sheet pan and place into oven. Select Air Fry and set time to 4 minutes. Shake the basket, add the bacon, and air fry for 2 minutes, or until the bacon is browned and the peppers are tender.
4. Fill the pita halves with the bacon, peppers, any remaining barbecue sauce, lettuce, and tomatoes, and serve immediately.

Chapter 9: Wraps and Sandwiches | 105

Sweet Potato and Black Bean Burritos

Prep time: 15 minutes | Cook time: 30 minutes | Makes 6 burritos

2 sweet potatoes, peeled and cut into a small dice
1 tablespoon vegetable oil
Kosher salt and ground black pepper, to taste
6 large flour tortillas
1 (16-ounce / 454-g) can refried black beans, divided
1½ cups baby spinach, divided
6 eggs, scrambled
¾ cup grated Cheddar cheese, divided
¼ cup salsa
¼ cup sour cream
Cooking spray

1. Put the sweet potatoes in a large bowl, then drizzle with vegetable oil and sprinkle with salt and black pepper. Toss to coat well.
2. Place the potatoes in the air fryer basket.
3. Put the air fryer basket on sheet pan and place into oven. Select Air Fry, set temperature to 400°F (205°C) and set time to 10 minutes.
4. Flip the potatoes halfway through the cooking time.
5. When done, the potatoes should be lightly browned. Remove the potatoes from the oven.
6. Unfold the tortillas on a clean work surface. Divide the black beans, spinach, air fried sweet potatoes, scrambled eggs, and cheese on top of the tortillas.
7. Fold the long side of the tortillas over the filling, then fold in the shorter side to wrap the filling to make the burritos.
8. Wrap the burritos in the aluminum foil and put in the pan.
9. Put the air fryer basket on sheet pan and place into oven. Select Air Fry, set temperature to 350°F (180°C) and set time to 20 minutes.
10. Flip the burritos halfway through the cooking time.
11. Remove the burritos from the oven and spread with sour cream and salsa. Serve immediately.

Air Fried Cream Cheese Wontons

Prep time: 5 minutes | Cook time: 6 minutes | Serves 4

2 ounces (57 g) cream cheese, softened
1 tablespoon sugar
16 square wonton wrappers
Cooking spray

1. Spritz the air fryer basket with cooking spray.
2. In a mixing bowl, stir together the cream cheese and sugar until well mixed. Prepare a small bowl of water alongside.
3. On a clean work surface, lay the wonton wrappers. Scoop ¼ teaspoon of cream cheese in the center of each wonton wrapper. Dab the water over the wrapper edges. Fold each wonton wrapper diagonally in half over the filling to form a triangle.
4. Arrange the wontons in the pan. Spritz the wontons with cooking spray.
5. Put the air fryer basket on sheet pan and place into oven. Select Air Fry, set temperature to 350°F (180°C) and set time to 6 minutes.
6. Flip the wontons halfway through the cooking time.
7. When cooking is complete, the wontons will be golden brown and crispy.
8. Divide the wontons among four plates. Let rest for 5 minutes before serving.

Cheesy Chicken Sandwich

Prep time: 10 minutes | Cook time: 7 minutes | Serves 1

⅓ cup chicken, cooked and shredded
2 Mozzarella slices
1 hamburger bun
¼ cup shredded cabbage
1 teaspoon mayonnaise
2 teaspoons butter, melted
1 teaspoon olive oil
½ teaspoon balsamic vinegar
¼ teaspoon smoked paprika
¼ teaspoon black pepper
¼ teaspoon garlic powder
Pinch of salt

1. Preheat the air fryer oven to 370°F (188°C).
2. Brush some butter onto the outside of the hamburger bun.
3. In a bowl, coat the chicken with the garlic powder, salt, pepper, and paprika.
4. In a separate bowl, stir together the mayonnaise, olive oil, cabbage, and balsamic vinegar to make coleslaw.
5. Slice the bun in two. Start building the sandwich, starting with the chicken, followed by the Mozzarella, the coleslaw, and finally the top bun. Transfer the sandwich to a sheet pan.
6. Put the sheet pan on wire rack and slide into the oven. Select Bake and set time to 7 minutes.
7. Serve immediately.

106 | Chapter 9: Wraps and Sandwiches

Lamb and Feta Hamburgers

Prep time: 15 minutes | Cook time: 16 minutes | Makes 4 burgers

1½ pounds (680 g) ground lamb
¼ cup crumbled feta
1½ teaspoons tomato paste
1½ teaspoons minced garlic
1 teaspoon ground dried ginger
1 teaspoon ground coriander
¼ teaspoon salt
¼ teaspoon cayenne pepper
4 kaiser rolls or hamburger buns, split open lengthwise, warmed
Cooking spray

1. Spritz the air fryer basket with cooking spray.
2. Combine all the ingredients, except for the buns, in a large bowl. Coarsely stir to mix well.
3. Shape the mixture into four balls, then pound the balls into four 5-inch diameter patties.
4. Arrange the patties in the pan and spritz with cooking spray.
5. Put the air fryer basket on sheet pan and place into oven. Select Air Fry, set temperature to 375ºF (190ºC) and set time to 16 minutes.
6. Flip the patties halfway through the cooking time.
7. When cooking is complete, the patties should be well browned.
8. Assemble the buns with patties to make the burgers and serve immediately.

Cabbage and Pork Gyoza

Prep time: 10 minutes | Cook time: 10 minutes | Makes 48 gyozas

1 pound (454 g) ground pork
1 head Napa cabbage (about 1 pound / 454 g), sliced thinly and minced
½ cup minced scallions
1 teaspoon minced fresh chives
1 teaspoon soy sauce
1 teaspoon minced fresh ginger
1 tablespoon minced garlic
1 teaspoon granulated sugar
2 teaspoons kosher salt
48 to 50 wonton or dumpling wrappers
Cooking spray

1. Spritz the air fryer basket with cooking spray. Set aside.
2. Make the filling: Combine all the ingredients, except for the wrappers in a large bowl. Stir to mix well.
3. Unfold a wrapper on a clean work surface, then dab the edges with a little water. Scoop up 2 teaspoons of the filling mixture in the center.
4. Make the gyoza: Fold the wrapper over to filling and press the edges to seal. Pleat the edges if desired. Repeat with remaining wrappers and fillings.
5. Arrange the gyozas in the pan and spritz with cooking spray.
6. Put the air fryer basket on sheet pan and place into oven. Select Air Fry, set temperature to 360ºF (182ºC) and set time to 10 minutes.
7. Flip the gyozas halfway through the cooking time.
8. When cooked, the gyozas will be golden brown.
9. Serve immediately.

Montreal Steak and Seeds Burgers

Prep time: 15 minutes | Cook time: 10 minutes | Serves 4

1 teaspoon cumin seeds
1 teaspoon mustard seeds
1 teaspoon coriander seeds
1 teaspoon dried minced garlic
1 teaspoon dried red pepper flakes
1 teaspoon kosher salt
2 teaspoons ground black pepper
1 pound (454 g) 85% lean ground beef
2 tablespoons Worcestershire sauce
4 hamburger buns
Mayonnaise, for serving
Cooking spray

1. Spritz the air fryer basket with cooking spray.
2. Put the seeds, garlic, red pepper flakes, salt, and ground black pepper in a food processor. Pulse to coarsely ground the mixture.
3. Put the ground beef in a large bowl. Pour in the seed mixture and drizzle with Worcestershire sauce. Stir to mix well.
4. Divide the mixture into four parts and shape each part into a ball, then bash each ball into a patty. Arrange the patties in the basket.
5. Put the air fryer basket on sheet pan and place into oven. Select Air Fry, set temperature to 350ºF (180ºC) and set time to 10 minutes.
6. Flip the patties with tongs halfway through the cooking time.
7. When cooked, the patties will be well browned.
8. Assemble the buns with the patties, then drizzle the mayo over the patties to make the burgers. Serve immediately.

Chapter 9: Wraps and Sandwiches | 107

Turkey, Leek, and Pepper Hamburger

Prep time: 10 minutes | Cook time: 20 minutes | Serves 4

1 cup leftover turkey, cut into bite-sized chunks
1 leek, sliced
1 Serrano pepper, deveined and chopped
2 bell peppers, deveined and chopped
2 tablespoons Tabasco sauce
½ cup sour cream
1 heaping tablespoon fresh cilantro, chopped
1 teaspoon hot paprika
¾ teaspoon kosher salt
½ teaspoon ground black pepper
4 hamburger buns
Cooking spray

1. Spritz the sheet pan with cooking spray.
2. Mix all the ingredients, except for the buns, in a large bowl. Toss to combine well.
3. Pour the mixture in the sheet pan.
4. Place the sheet pan on wire rack and slide into oven. Select Bake, set temperature to 385ºF (196ºC) and set time to 20 minutes.
5. When done, the turkey will be well browned and the leek will be tender.
6. Assemble the hamburger buns with the turkey mixture and serve immediately.

Bulgogi Burgers

Prep time: 15 minutes | Cook time: 10 minutes | Serves 4

Burgers:
1 pound (454 g) 85% lean ground beef
2 tablespoons gochujang
¼ cup chopped scallions
2 teaspoons minced garlic
2 teaspoons minced fresh ginger
1 tablespoon soy sauce
1 tablespoon toasted sesame oil
2 teaspoons sugar
½ teaspoon kosher salt
4 hamburger buns
Cooking spray
Korean Mayo:
1 tablespoon gochujang
¼ cup mayonnaise
2 teaspoons sesame seeds
¼ cup chopped scallions
1 tablespoon toasted sesame oil

1. Combine the ingredients for the burgers, except for the buns, in a large bowl. Stir to mix well, then wrap the bowl in plastic and refrigerate to marinate for at least an hour.
2. Spritz the air fryer basket with cooking spray.
3. Divide the meat mixture into four portions and form into four balls. Bash the balls into patties.
4. Arrange the patties in the pan and spritz with cooking spray.
5. Put the air fryer basket on sheet pan and place into oven. Select Air Fry, set temperature to 350ºF (180ºC) and set time to 10 minutes.
6. Flip the patties halfway through the cooking time.
7. Meanwhile, combine the ingredients for the Korean mayo in a small bowl. Stir to mix well.
8. When cooking is complete, the patties should be golden brown.
9. Remove the patties from the oven and assemble with the buns, then spread the Korean mayo over the patties to make the burgers. Serve immediately.

Eggplant Hoagies

Prep time: 15 minutes | Cook time: 12 minutes | Makes 3 hoagies

6 peeled eggplant slices (about ½ inch thick and 3 inches in diameter)
¼ cup jarred pizza sauce
6 tablespoons grated
Parmesan cheese
3 Italian sub rolls, split open lengthwise, warmed
Cooking spray

1. Spritz the air fryer basket with cooking spray.
2. Arrange the eggplant slices in the pan and spritz with cooking spray.
3. Put the air fryer basket on sheet pan and place into oven. Select Air Fry, set temperature to 350ºF (180ºC) and set time to 10 minutes.
4. Flip the slices halfway through the cooking time.
5. When cooked, the eggplant slices should be lightly wilted and tender.
6. Divide and spread the pizza sauce and cheese on top of the eggplant slice
7. Put the air fryer basket on sheet pan and place into oven. Select Air Fry, set temperature to 375ºF (190ºC) and set time to 2 minutes.
8. When cooked, the cheese will be melted.
9. Assemble each sub roll with two slices of eggplant and serve immediately.

Cheesy Shrimp Sandwich

Prep time: 10 minutes | Cook time: 6 minutes | Serves 4

1¼ cups shredded Colby, Cheddar, or Havarti cheese
1 (6-ounce / 170-g) can tiny shrimp, drained
3 tablespoons mayonnaise
2 tablespoons minced green onion
4 slices whole grain or whole-wheat bread
2 tablespoons softened butter

1. Preheat the air fryer oven to 400°F (204°C).
2. In a medium bowl, combine the cheese, shrimp, mayonnaise, and green onion, and mix well.
3. Spread this mixture on two of the slices of bread. Top with the other slices of bread to make two sandwiches. Spread the sandwiches lightly with butter.
4. Lay the sandwiches in the air fryer basket. Put the air fryer basket on sheet pan and place into oven. Select Air Fry and set time to 6 minutes, or until the bread is browned and crisp and the cheese is melted.
5. Cut in half and serve warm.

Turkey Sliders with Chive Mayo

Prep time: 10 minutes | Cook time: 15 minutes | Serves 6

12 burger buns
Turkey Sliders:
¾ pound (340 g) turkey, minced
1 tablespoon oyster sauce
¼ cup pickled jalapeno, chopped
2 tablespoons chopped
Chive Mayo:
1 tablespoon chives
1 cup mayonnaise
Cooking spray

scallions
1 tablespoon chopped fresh cilantro
1 to 2 cloves garlic, minced
Sea salt and ground black pepper, to taste

Zest of 1 lime
1 teaspoon salt

1. Spritz the air fryer basket with cooking spray.
2. Combine the ingredients for the turkey sliders in a large bowl. Stir to mix well. Shape the mixture into 6 balls, then bash the balls into patties.
3. Arrange the patties in the basket and spritz with cooking spray.

4. Put the air fryer basket on sheet pan and place into oven. Select Air Fry, set temperature to 365°F (185°C) and set time to 15 minutes.
5. Flip the patties halfway through the cooking time.
6. Meanwhile, combine the ingredients for the chive mayo in a small bowl. Stir to mix well.
7. When cooked, the patties will be well browned.
8. Smear the patties with chive mayo, then assemble the patties between two buns to make the sliders. Serve immediately.

Smoky Chicken Sandwich

Prep time: 10 minutes | Cook time: 11 minutes | Serves 2

2 boneless, skinless chicken breasts (8 ounces / 227 g each), sliced horizontally in half and separated into 4 thinner cutlets
Kosher salt and freshly ground black pepper, to taste
½ cup all-purpose flour
3 large eggs, lightly beaten
½ cup dried bread crumbs
1 tablespoon smoked paprika
Cooking spray
½ cup marinara sauce
6 ounces (170 g) smoked Mozzarella cheese, grated
2 store-bought soft, sesame-seed hamburger or Italian buns, split

1. Preheat the air fryer oven to 350°F (177°C).
2. Season the chicken cutlets all over with salt and pepper. Set up three shallow bowls: Place the flour in the first bowl, the eggs in the second, and stir together the bread crumbs and smoked paprika in the third. Coat the chicken pieces in the flour, then dip fully in the egg. Dredge in the paprika bread crumbs, then transfer to a wire rack set over a baking sheet and spray both sides liberally with cooking spray.
3. Transfer the chicken cutlets to the air fryer basket.
4. Put the air fryer basket on sheet pan and place into oven. Select Air Fry and set time to 6 minutes, or until the chicken begins to brown.
5. Spread each cutlet with 2 tablespoons of the marinara sauce and sprinkle with one-quarter of the smoked Mozzarella.
6. Increase the temperature to 400°F (204°C) and air fry for 5 minutes more, or until the chicken is cooked through and crisp and the cheese is melted and golden brown.
7. Transfer the cutlets to a plate and place two cutlets inside each of two buns. Serve the sandwiches warm.

Chapter 9: Wraps and Sandwiches | 109

Salsa Verde Golden Chicken Empanadas

Prep time: 25 minutes | Cook time: 12 minutes | Makes 12 empanadas

1 cupboneless, skinless rotisserie chicken breast meat, chopped finely
¼ cup salsa verde
⅔ cupshredded Cheddar cheese
1 teaspoonground cumin
1 teaspoonground black pepper
2purchased refrigerated pie crusts, from a minimum 14.1-ounce (400 g) box
1 large egg
2 tablespoonswater
Cooking spray

1. Spritz the air fryer basket with cooking spray. Set aside.
2. Combine the chicken meat, salsa verde, Cheddar, cumin, and black pepper in a large bowl. Stir to mix well. Set aside.
3. Unfold the pie crusts on a clean work surface, then use a large cookie cutter to cut out 3½-inch circles as much as possible.
4. Roll the remaining crusts to a ball and flatten into a circle which has the same thickness of the original crust. Cut out more 3½-inch circles until you have 12 circles in total.
5. Make the empanadas: Divide the chicken mixture in the middle of each circle, about 1½ tablespoons each. Dab the edges of the circle with water. Fold the circle in half over the filling to shape like a half-moon and press to seal, or you can press with a fork.
6. Whisk the egg with water in a small bowl.
7. Arrange the empanadas in the pan and spritz with cooking spray. Brush with whisked egg.
8. Put the air fryer basket on sheet pan and place into oven. Select Air Fry, set temperature to 350°F (180°C) and set time to 12 minutes.
9. Flip the empanadas halfway through the cooking time.
10. When cooking is complete, the empanadas will be golden and crispy.
11. Serve immediately.

Mexican Flavor Chicken Burgers

Prep time: 15 minutes | Cook time: 20 minutes | Serves 6 to 8

4 skinless and boneless chicken breasts
1 small head of cauliflower, sliced into florets
1 jalapeño pepper
3 tablespoons smoked paprika
1 tablespoon thyme
1 tablespoon oregano
1 tablespoon mustard powder
1 teaspoon cayenne pepper
1 egg
Salt and ground black pepper, to taste
2 tomatoes, sliced
2 lettuce leaves, chopped
6 to 8 brioche buns, sliced lengthwise
¾ cup taco sauce
Cooking spray

1. Spritz the air fryer basket with cooking spray. Set aside.
2. In a blender, add the cauliflower florets, jalapeño pepper, paprika, thyme, oregano, mustard powder and cayenne pepper and blend until the mixture has a texture similar to bread crumbs.
3. Transfer ¾ of the cauliflower mixture to a medium bowl and set aside. Beat the egg in a different bowl and set aside.
4. Add the chicken breasts to the blender with remaining cauliflower mixture. Sprinkle with salt and pepper. Blend until finely chopped and well mixed.
5. Remove the mixture from the blender and form into 6 to 8 patties. One by one, dredge each patty in the reserved cauliflower mixture, then into the egg. Dip them in the cauliflower mixture again for additional coating.
6. Place the coated patties into the pan and spritz with cooking spray.
7. Put the air fryer basket on sheet pan and place into oven. Select Air Fry, set temperature to 350°F (180°C) and set time to 20 minutes.
8. Flip the patties halfway through the cooking time.
9. When cooking is complete, the patties should be golden and crispy.
10. Transfer the patties to a clean work surface and assemble with the buns, tomato slices, chopped lettuce leaves and taco sauce to make burgers. Serve and enjoy.

Pea and Potato Samosas with Chutney

Prep time: 30 minutes | Cook time: 22 minutes | Makes 16 samosas

Dough:

4 cups all-purpose flour, plus more for flouring the work surface

¼ cup plain yogurt

½ cup cold unsalted butter, cut into cubes

2 teaspoons kosher salt

1 cup ice water

Filling:

2 tablespoons vegetable oil

1 onion, diced

1½ teaspoons coriander

1½ teaspoons cumin

1 clove garlic, minced

1 teaspoon turmeric

1 teaspoon kosher salt

½ cup peas, thawed if frozen

2 cups mashed potatoes

2 tablespoons yogurt

Cooking spray

Chutney:

1 cup mint leaves, lightly packed

2 cups cilantro leaves, lightly packed

1 green chile pepper, deseeded and minced

½ cup minced onion

Juice of 1 lime

1 teaspoon granulated sugar

1 teaspoon kosher salt

2 tablespoons vegetable oil

1. Put the flour, yogurt, butter, and salt in a food processor. Pulse to combine until grainy. Pour in the water and pulse until a smooth and firm dough forms.
2. Transfer the dough on a clean and lightly floured working surface. Knead the dough and shape it into a ball. Cut in half and flatten the halves into 2 discs. Wrap them in plastic and let sit in refrigerator until ready to use.
3. Meanwhile, make the filling: Heat the vegetable oil in a saucepan over medium heat.
4. Add the onion and sauté for 5 minutes or until lightly browned.
5. Add the coriander, cumin, garlic, turmeric, and salt and sauté for 2 minutes or until fragrant.
6. Add the peas, potatoes, and yogurt and stir to combine well. Turn off the heat and allow to cool.
7. Meanwhile, combine the ingredients for the chutney in a food processor. Pulse to mix well until glossy. Pour the chutney in a bowl and refrigerate until ready to use.
8. Make the samosas: Remove the dough discs from the refrigerator and cut each disc into 8 parts. Shape each part into a ball, then roll the ball into a 6-inch circle. Cut

the circle in half and roll each half into a cone.
9. Scoop up 2 tablespoons of the filling into the cone, press the edges of the cone to seal and form into a triangle. Repeat with remaining dough and filling.
10. Spritz the air fryer basket with cooking spray. Arrange the samosas in the pan and spritz with cooking spray.
11. Put the air fryer basket on sheet pan and place into oven. Select Air Fry, set temperature to 360ºF (182ºC) and set time to 15 minutes.
12. Flip the samosas halfway through the cooking time.
13. When cooked, the samosas will be golden brown and crispy.
14. Serve the samosas with the chutney.

Classic Sloppy Joes

Prep time: 10 minutes | Cook time: 19 minutes | Makes 4 large sandwiches or 8 sliders

1 pound (454 g) very lean ground beef

1 teaspoon onion powder

⅓ cup ketchup

¼ cup water

½ teaspoon celery seed

1 tablespoon lemon juice

1½ teaspoons brown sugar

1¼ teaspoons low-sodium

Worcestershire sauce

½ teaspoon salt (optional)

½ teaspoon vinegar

⅛ teaspoon dry mustard

Hamburger or slider buns, for serving

Cooking spray

1. Preheat the air fryer oven to 390ºF (199ºC). Spray the air fryer basket with cooking spray.
2. Break raw ground beef into small chunks and pile into the basket.
3. Put the air fryer basket on sheet pan and place into oven. Select Air Fry and set time to 12 minutes. Stir the meat twice during cooking, or until meat is well done.
4. Remove the meat from the oven, drain, and use a knife and fork to crumble into small pieces.
5. Place all the remaining ingredients, except for the buns, in a sheet pan and mix together. Add the meat and stir well.
6. Place the sheet pan on wire rack and slide into oven. Select Bake, set temperature to 330ºF (166ºC) and set time to 7 minutes.
7. After 5 minutes, remove from the oven. Stir and return to the oven to continue cooking.
8. Scoop onto buns and serve hot.

Veggie Pita Sandwich

Prep time: 10 minutes | Cook time: 12 minutes | Serves 4

1 baby eggplant, peeled and chopped
1 red bell pepper, sliced
½ cup diced red onion
½ cup shredded carrot
1 teaspoon olive oil
⅓ cup low-fat Greek yogurt
½ teaspoon dried tarragon
2 low-sodium whole-wheat pita breads, halved crosswise

1. Preheat the air fryer oven to 390ºF (199ºC).
2. In a sheet pan, stir together the eggplant, red bell pepper, red onion, carrot, and olive oil.
3. Put the sheet pan on wire rack and slide into the oven. Select Bake and set time to 9 minutes, stirring once, or until the vegetables are tender. Drain if necessary.
4. In a small bowl, thoroughly mix the yogurt and tarragon until well combined. Stir the yogurt mixture into the vegetables. Stuff one-fourth of this mixture into each pita pocket.
5. Place the sheet pan with the pita sandwiches back into oven and bake for an additional 3 minutes, or until the bread is toasted.
6. Serve immediately.

Chicken Pita Sandwich

Prep time: 10 minutes | Cook time: 10 minutes | Serves 4

2 boneless, skinless chicken breasts, cut into 1-inch cubes
1 small red onion, sliced
1 red bell pepper, sliced
⅓ cup Italian salad
dressing, divided
½ teaspoon dried thyme
4 pita pockets, split
2 cups torn butter lettuce
1 cup chopped cherry tomatoes

1. Preheat the air fryer oven to 380ºF (193ºC).
2. Place the chicken, onion, and bell pepper in the air fryer basket. Drizzle with 1 tablespoon of the Italian salad dressing, add the thyme, and toss.
3. Put the air fryer basket on sheet pan and place into oven. Select Air Fry and set time to 10 minutes, or until the chicken is 165ºF (74ºC) on a meat thermometer, stirring once during cooking time.
4. Transfer the chicken and vegetables to a bowl and toss with the remaining salad dressing.
5. Assemble sandwiches with the pita pockets, butter lettuce, and cherry tomatoes. Serve immediately.

Chapter 10   Fast and Easy Everyday Favorites

Apple Fritters with Sugary Glaze

Prep time: 10 minutes | Cook time: 8 minutes | Makes 15 fritters

Apple Fritters:
2 firm apples, peeled, cored, and diced
½ teaspoon cinnamon
Juice of 1 lemon
1 cup all-purpose flour
1½ teaspoons baking powder
½ teaspoon kosher salt
Glaze:
½ teaspoon vanilla extract
1¼ cups powdered sugar,

2 eggs
¼ cup milk
2 tablespoons unsalted butter, melted
2 tablespoons granulated sugar
Cooking spray

sifted
¼ cup water

1. Line the air fryer basket with parchment paper.
2. Combine the apples with cinnamon and lemon juice in a small bowl. Toss to coat well.
3. Combine the flour, baking powder, and salt in a large bowl. Stir to mix well.
4. Whisk the egg, milk, butter, and sugar in a medium bowl. Stir to mix well.
5. Make a well in the center of the flour mixture, then pour the egg mixture into the well and stir to mix well. Mix in the apple until a dough forms.
6. Use an ice cream scoop to scoop 15 balls from the dough onto the pan. Spritz with cooking spray.
7. Put the air fryer basket on sheet pan and place into oven. Select Air Fry, set temperature to 360ºF (182ºC) and set time to 8 minutes.
8. Flip the apple fritters halfway through the cooking time.
9. Meanwhile, combine the ingredients for the glaze in a separate small bowl. Stir to mix well.
10. When cooking is complete, the apple fritters will be golden brown. Serve the fritters with the glaze on top or use the glaze for dipping.

Hot Wings

Prep time: 5 minutes | Cook time: 15 minutes | Makes 16 wings

16 chicken wings
3 tablespoons hot sauce

Cooking spray

1. Spritz the air fryer basket with cooking spray.
2. Arrange the chicken wings in the basket.
3. Put the air fryer basket on sheet pan and place into oven. Select Air Fry, set temperature to 360ºF (182ºC) and set time to 15 minutes.
4. Flip the wings at lease three times during cooking.
5. When cooking is complete, the chicken wings will be well browned. Remove from the oven.
6. Transfer the air fried wings to a plate and serve with hot sauce.

Lemony and Garlicky Asparagus

Prep time: 5 minutes | Cook time: 10 minutes | Makes 10 spears

10 spears asparagus (about ½ pound / 227 g in total), snap the ends off
1 tablespoon lemon juice

2 teaspoons minced garlic
½ teaspoon salt
¼ teaspoon ground black pepper
Cooking spray

1. Line the air fryer basket with parchment paper.
2. Put the asparagus spears in a large bowl. Drizzle with lemon juice and sprinkle with minced garlic, salt, and ground black pepper. Toss to coat well.
3. Transfer the asparagus to the basket and spritz with cooking spray.
4. Put the air fryer basket on sheet pan and place into oven. Select Air Fry, set temperature to 400ºF (205ºC) and set time to 10 minutes.
5. Flip the asparagus halfway through cooking.
6. When cooked, the asparagus should be wilted and soft. Remove from the oven and serve immediately.

Chapter 10: Fast and Easy Everyday Favorites | 113

Parsnip Fries with Garlic-Yogurt Dip

Prep time: 10 minutes | Cook time: 10 minutes | Serves 4

3 medium parsnips, peeled, cut into sticks
¼ teaspoon kosher salt
Dip:
¼ cup plain Greek yogurt
⅛ teaspoon garlic powder
1 tablespoon sour cream
1 teaspoon olive oil
1 garlic clove, unpeeled
Cooking spray
¼ teaspoon kosher salt
Freshly ground black pepper, to taste

1. Spritz the air fryer basket with cooking spray.
2. Put the parsnip sticks in a large bowl, then sprinkle with salt and drizzle with olive oil.
3. Transfer the parsnip into the basket and add the garlic.
4. Put the air fryer basket on sheet pan and place into oven. Select Air Fry, set temperature to 360ºF (182ºC) and set time to 10 minutes.
5. Stir the parsnip halfway through the cooking time.
6. Meanwhile, peel the garlic and crush it. Combine the crushed garlic with the ingredients for the dip. Stir to mix well.
7. When cooked, the parsnip sticks should be crisp. Remove the parsnip fries from the oven and serve with the dipping sauce.

Air Fried Okra Chips

Prep time: 5 minutes | Cook time: 16 minutes | Serves 6

2 pounds (907 g) fresh okra pods, cut into 1-inch pieces
2 tablespoons canola oil
1 teaspoon coarse sea salt

1. Stir the oil and salt in a bowl to mix well. Add the okra and toss to coat well. Place the okra in the air fryer basket.
2. Put the air fryer basket on sheet pan and place into oven. Select Air Fry, set temperature to 400ºF (205ºC) and set time to 16 minutes.
3. Flip the okra at least three times during cooking.
4. When cooked, the okra should be lightly browned. Remove from the oven and serve immediately.

Sweet and Sour Peanuts

Prep time: 5 minutes | Cook time: 5 minutes | Serves 9

3 cups shelled raw peanuts
1 tablespoon hot red pepper sauce
3 tablespoons granulated white sugar

1. Put the peanuts in a large bowl, then drizzle with hot red pepper sauce and sprinkle with sugar. Toss to coat well.
2. Pour the peanuts in the air fryer basket.
3. Put the air fryer basket on sheet pan and place into oven. Select Air Fry, set temperature to 400ºF (205ºC) and set time to 5 minutes.
4. Stir the peanuts halfway through the cooking time.
5. When cooking is complete, the peanuts will be crispy and browned. Remove from the oven and serve immediately.

Cheesy Shrimps

Prep time: 10 minutes | Cook time: 8 minutes | Serves 4 to 6

⅔ cup grated Parmesan cheese
4 minced garlic cloves
1 teaspoon onion powder
½ teaspoon oregano
1 teaspoon basil
1 teaspoon ground black pepper
2 tablespoons olive oil
2 pounds (907 g) cooked large shrimps, peeled and deveined
Lemon wedges, for topping
Cooking spray

1. Spritz the air fryer basket with cooking spray.
2. Combine all the ingredients, except for the shrimps, in a large bowl. Stir to mix well.
3. Dunk the shrimps in the mixture and toss to coat well. Shake the excess off. Arrange the shrimps in the basket.
4. Put the air fryer basket on sheet pan and place into oven. Select Air Fry, set temperature to 350ºF (180ºC) and set time to 8 minutes.
5. Flip the shrimps halfway through the cooking time.
6. When cooking is complete, the shrimps should be opaque. Transfer the cooked shrimps onto a large plate and squeeze the lemon wedges over before serving.

Spanakopita

Prep time: 10 minutes | Cook time: 8 minutes | Serves 6

½ (10-ounce / 284-g) package frozen spinach, thawed and squeezed dry
1 egg, lightly beaten
¼ cup pine nuts, toasted
¼ cup grated Parmesan cheese
¾ cup crumbled feta cheese
⅛ teaspoon ground nutmeg
½ teaspoon salt
Freshly ground black pepper, to taste
6 sheets phyllo dough
½ cup butter, melted

1. Combine all the ingredients, except for the phyllo dough and butter, in a large bowl. Whisk to combine well. Set aside.
2. Place a sheet of phyllo dough on a clean work surface. Brush with butter then top with another layer sheet of phyllo. Brush with butter, then cut the layered sheets into six 3-inch-wide strips.
3. Top each strip with 1 tablespoon of the spinach mixture, then fold the bottom left corner over the mixture towards the right strip edge to make a triangle. Keep folding triangles until each strip is folded over.
4. Brush the triangles with butter and repeat with remaining strips and phyllo dough.
5. Place the triangles in the sheet pan.
6. Put the air fryer basket on sheet pan and place into oven. Select Air Fry, set temperature to 350°F (180°C) and set time to 8 minutes.
7. Flip the triangles halfway through the cooking time.
8. When cooking is complete, the triangles should be golden brown. Remove from the oven and serve immediately.

Spicy Air Fried Old Bay Shrimp

Prep time: 10 minutes | Cook time: 10 minutes | Makes 2 cups

½ teaspoon Old Bay Seasoning
1 teaspoon ground cayenne pepper
½ teaspoon paprika
1 tablespoon olive oil
⅛ teaspoon salt
½ pound (227 g) shrimps, peeled and deveined
Juice of half a lemon

1. Combine the Old Bay Seasoning, cayenne pepper, paprika, olive oil, and salt in a large bowl, then add the shrimps and toss to coat well.
2. Put the shrimps in the air fryer basket.
3. Put the air fryer basket on sheet pan and place into oven. Select Air Fry, set temperature to 390°F (199°C) and set time to 10 minutes.
4. Flip the shrimps halfway through the cooking time.
5. When cooking is complete, the shrimps should be opaque. Serve the shrimps with lemon juice on top.

Garlicky Spiralized Zucchini and Squash

Prep time: 10 minutes | Cook time: 10 minutes | Serves 4

2 large zucchini, peeled and spiralized
2 large yellow summer squash, peeled and spiralized
1 tablespoon olive oil, divided
½ teaspoon kosher salt
1 garlic clove, whole
2 tablespoons fresh basil, chopped
Cooking spray

1. Spritz the air fryer basket with cooking spray.
2. Combine the zucchini and summer squash with 1 teaspoon of the olive oil and salt in a large bowl. Toss to coat well.
3. Transfer the zucchini and summer squash to the basket and add the garlic.
4. Put the air fryer basket on sheet pan and place into oven. Select Air Fry, set temperature to 360°F (182°C) and set time to 10 minutes.
5. Stir the zucchini and summer squash halfway through the cooking time.
6. When cooked, the zucchini and summer squash will be tender and fragrant. Transfer the cooked zucchini and summer squash onto a plate and set aside.
7. Remove the garlic from the oven and allow to cool for 5 minutes. Mince the garlic and combine with remaining olive oil in a small bowl. Stir to mix well.
8. Drizzle the spiralized zucchini and summer squash with garlic oil and sprinkle with basil. Toss to serve.

Chapter 10: Fast and Easy Everyday Favorites | 115

Southwest Corn and Bell Pepper Roast

Prep time: 10 minutes | Cook time: 10 minutes | Serves 4

Corn:

1½ cups thawed frozen corn kernels
1 cup mixed diced bell peppers
1 jalapeño, diced
1 cup diced yellow onion
½ teaspoon ancho chile powder
1 tablespoon fresh lemon juice
1 teaspoon ground cumin
½ teaspoon kosher salt
Cooking spray

For Serving:

¼ cup feta cheese
¼ cup chopped fresh cilantro
1 tablespoon fresh lemon juice

1. Spritz the air fryer basket with cooking spray.
2. Combine the ingredients for the corn in a large bowl. Stir to mix well.
3. Pour the mixture into the basket.
4. Put the air fryer basket on sheet pan and place into oven. Select Air Fry, set temperature to 375ºF (190ºC) and set time to 10 minutes.
5. Stir the mixture halfway through the cooking time.
6. When done, the corn and bell peppers should be soft.
7. Transfer them onto a large plate, then spread with feta cheese and cilantro. Drizzle with lemon juice and serve.

Golden Salmon and Carrot Croquettes

Prep time: 15 minutes | Cook time: 10 minutes | Serves 6

2 egg whites
1 cup almond flour
1 cup panko bread crumbs
1 pound (454 g) chopped salmon fillet
⅔ cup grated carrots
2 tablespoons minced garlic cloves
½ cup chopped onion
2 tablespoons chopped chives
Cooking spray

1. Spritz the air fryer basket with cooking spray.
2. Whisk the egg whites in a bowl. Put the flour in a second bowl. Pour the bread crumbs in a third bowl. Set aside.
3. Combine the salmon, carrots, garlic, onion, and chives in a large bowl. Stir to mix well.
4. Form the mixture into balls with your hands. Dredge the balls into the flour, then egg, and then bread crumbs to coat well.
5. Arrange the salmon balls on the basket and spritz with cooking spray.
6. Put the air fryer basket on sheet pan and place into oven. Select Air Fry, set temperature to 350ºF (180ºC) and set time to 10 minutes.
7. Flip the salmon balls halfway through cooking.
8. When cooking is complete, the salmon balls will be crispy and browned. Remove from the oven and serve immediately.

Purple Potato Chips with Rosemary

Prep time: 10 minutes | Cook time: 12 minutes | Serves 6

1 cup Greek yogurt
2 chipotle chiles, minced
2 tablespoons adobo sauce
1 teaspoon paprika
1 tablespoon lemon juice
10 purple fingerling potatoes
1 teaspoon olive oil
2 teaspoons minced fresh rosemary leaves
⅛ teaspoon cayenne pepper
¼ teaspoon coarse sea salt

1. Preheat the air fryer oven to 400ºF (204ºC).
2. In a medium bowl, combine the yogurt, minced chiles, adobo sauce, paprika, and lemon juice. Mix well and refrigerate.
3. Wash the potatoes and dry them with paper towels. Slice the potatoes lengthwise, as thinly as possible. You can use a mandoline, a vegetable peeler, or a very sharp knife.
4. Combine the potato slices in a medium bowl and drizzle with the olive oil; toss to coat. Transfer to the air fryer basket.
5. Put the air fryer basket on sheet pan and place into oven. Select Air Fry and set time to 12 minutes. Use tongs to gently rearrange the chips halfway during cooking time.
6. Sprinkle the chips with the rosemary, cayenne pepper, and sea salt. Serve with the chipotle sauce for dipping.

Baked Cherry Tomatoes with Basil

Prep time: 5 minutes | Cook time: 5 minutes | Serves 2

2 cups cherry tomatoes
1 clove garlic, thinly sliced
1 teaspoon olive oil
⅛ teaspoon kosher salt
1 tablespoon freshly chopped basil, for topping
Cooking spray

1. Spritz the sheet pan with cooking spray and set aside.
2. In a large bowl, toss together the cherry tomatoes, sliced garlic, olive oil, and kosher salt. Spread the mixture in an even layer in the prepared pan.
3. Place the sheet pan on wire rack and slide into oven. Select Bake, set temperature to 360°F (182°C) and set time to 5 minutes.
4. When cooking is complete, the tomatoes should be the soft and wilted.
5. Transfer to a bowl and rest for 5 minutes. Top with the chopped basil and serve warm.

Air Fried Crispy Brussels Sprouts

Prep time: 5 minutes | Cook time: 20 minutes | Serves 4

¼ teaspoon salt
⅛ teaspoon ground black pepper
1 tablespoon extra-virgin olive oil
1 pound (454 g) Brussels sprouts, trimmed and halved
Lemon wedges, for garnish

1. Combine the salt, black pepper, and olive oil in a large bowl. Stir to mix well.
2. Add the Brussels sprouts to the bowl of mixture and toss to coat well. Arrange the Brussels sprouts in the air fryer basket.
3. Put the air fryer basket on sheet pan and place into oven. Select Air Fry, set temperature to 350°F (180°C) and set time to 20 minutes.
4. Stir the Brussels sprouts two times during cooking.
5. When cooked, the Brussels sprouts will be lightly browned and wilted. Transfer the cooked Brussels sprouts to a large plate and squeeze the lemon wedges on top to serve.

Herb-Fried Veggies

Prep time: 10 minutes | Cook time: 16 minutes | Serves 4

1 red bell pepper, sliced
1 (8-ounce / 227-g) package sliced mushrooms
1 cup green beans, cut into 2-inch pieces
⅓ cup diced red onion
3 garlic cloves, sliced
1 teaspoon olive oil
½ teaspoon dried basil
½ teaspoon dried tarragon

1. Preheat the air fryer oven to 350°F (177°C).
2. In a medium bowl, mix the red bell pepper, mushrooms, green beans, red onion, and garlic. Drizzle with the olive oil. Toss to coat.
3. Add the herbs and toss again. Place the vegetables in the air fryer basket.
4. Put the air fryer basket on sheet pan and place into oven. Select Air Fry and set time to 16 minutes, or until tender.
5. Serve immediately.

Indian Masala Omelet

Prep time: 10 minutes | Cook time: 12 minutes | Serves 2

4 large eggs
½ cup diced onion
½ cup diced tomato
¼ cup chopped fresh cilantro
1 jalapeño, deseeded and finely chopped
½ teaspoon ground turmeric
½ teaspoon kosher salt
½ teaspoon cayenne pepper
Olive oil, for greasing the pan

1. Preheat the air fryer oven to 250°F (121°C). Generously grease a sheet pan.
2. In a large bowl, beat the eggs. Stir in the onion, tomato, cilantro, jalapeño, turmeric, salt, and cayenne.
3. Pour the egg mixture into the prepared pan.
4. Put the sheet pan on wire rack and slide into the oven. Select Bake and set time to 12 minutes, or until the eggs are cooked through. Carefully unmold and cut the omelet into four pieces.
5. Serve immediately.

Chapter 10: Fast and Easy Everyday Favorites | 117

Peppery Brown Rice Fritters

Prep time: 10 minutes | Cook time: 10 minutes | Serves 4

1 (10-ounce / 284-g) bag frozen cooked brown rice, thawed
1 egg
3 tablespoons brown rice flour
⅓ cup finely grated carrots
⅓ cup minced red bell pepper
2 tablespoons minced fresh basil
3 tablespoons grated Parmesan cheese
2 teaspoons olive oil

1. Preheat the air fryer oven to 380°F (193°C).
2. In a small bowl, combine the thawed rice, egg, and flour and mix to blend.
3. Stir in the carrots, bell pepper, basil, and Parmesan cheese.
4. Form the mixture into 8 fritters and drizzle with the olive oil. Put the fritters carefully into the air fryer basket.
5. Put the air fryer basket on sheet pan and place into oven. Select Air Fry and set time to 10 minutes, or until the fritters are golden brown and cooked through.
6. Serve immediately.

South Carolina Shrimp and Corn Bake

Prep time: 10 minutes | Cook time: 18 minutes | Serves 2

1 ear corn, husk and silk removed, cut into 2-inch rounds
8 ounces (227 g) red potatoes, unpeeled, cut into 1-inch pieces
2 teaspoons Old Bay Seasoning, divided
2 teaspoons vegetable oil, divided
¼ teaspoon ground black pepper
8 ounces (227 g) large shrimps (about 12 shrimps), deveined
6 ounces (170 g) andouille or chorizo sausage, cut into 1-inch pieces
2 garlic cloves, minced
1 tablespoon chopped fresh parsley

1. Put the corn rounds and potatoes in a large bowl. Sprinkle with 1 teaspoon of Old Bay seasoning and drizzle with vegetable oil. Toss to coat well.
2. Transfer the corn rounds and potatoes into the sheet pan.
3. Place the sheet pan on wire rack and slide into oven. Select Bake, set temperature to 400°F (205°C) and set time to 18 minutes.
4. After 6 minutes, remove from the oven. Stir the corn rounds and potatoes. Return the pan to the oven and continue cooking.
5. Meanwhile, cut slits into the shrimps but be careful not to cut them through. Combine the shrimps, sausage, remaining Old Bay seasoning, and remaining vegetable oil in the large bowl. Toss to coat well.
6. After 6 minutes, remove the pan from the oven. Add the shrimps and sausage to the pan. Return the pan to the oven and continue cooking for 6 minutes. Stir the shrimp mixture halfway through the cooking time.
7. When done, the shrimps should be opaque. Transfer the dish to a plate and spread with parsley before serving.

Indian-Style Sweet Potato Fries

Prep time: 5 minutes | Cook time: 8 minutes | Makes 20 fries

Seasoning Mixture:
¾ teaspoon ground coriander
½ teaspoon garam masala
½ teaspoon garlic powder
½ teaspoon ground cumin
¼ teaspoon ground cayenne pepper
Fries:
2 large sweet potatoes, peeled
2 teaspoons olive oil

1. Preheat the air fryer oven to 400°F (204°C).
2. In a small bowl, combine the coriander, garam masala, garlic powder, cumin, and cayenne pepper.
3. Slice the sweet potatoes into ¼-inch-thick fries.
4. In a large bowl, toss the sliced sweet potatoes with the olive oil and the seasoning mixture.
5. Transfer the seasoned sweet potatoes to the air fryer basket.
6. Put the air fryer basket on sheet pan and place into oven. Select Air Fry and set time to 8 minutes, until crispy.
7. Serve warm.

118 | Chapter 10: Fast and Easy Everyday Favorites

Pomegranate Avocado Fries

Prep time: 5 minutes | Cook time: 8 minutes | Serves 4

1 cup panko bread crumbs
1 teaspoon kosher salt, plus more for sprinkling
1 teaspoon garlic powder
½ teaspoon cayenne pepper
2 ripe but firm avocados
1 egg, beaten with 1 tablespoon water
Cooking spray
Pomegranate molasses, for serving

1. Preheat the air fryer oven to 375°F (191°C).
2. Whisk together the panko, salt, and spices on a plate. Cut each avocado in half and remove the pit. Cut each avocado half into 4 slices and scoop the slices out with a large spoon, taking care to keep the slices intact.
3. Dip each avocado slice in the egg wash and then dredge it in the panko. Place the breaded avocado slices on a plate.
4. Arrange the avocado slices in a single layer in the air fryer basket. Spray lightly with oil.
5. Put the air fryer basket on sheet pan and place into oven. Select Air Fry and set time to 8 minutes, turning once halfway through.
6. Remove the cooked slices to a platter. Sprinkle the warm avocado slices with salt and drizzle with pomegranate molasses. Serve immediately.

Rosemary and Orange Chickpeas

Prep time: 5 minutes | Cook time: 12 minutes | Makes 4 cups

4 cups cooked chickpeas
2 tablespoons vegetable oil
1 teaspoon kosher salt
1 teaspoon cumin
1 teaspoon paprika
Zest of 1 orange
1 tablespoon chopped fresh rosemary

1. Preheat the air fryer oven to 400°F (204°C).
2. Make sure the chickpeas are completely dry prior to cooking. In a medium bowl, toss the chickpeas with oil, salt, cumin, and paprika.
3. Spread the chickpeas in a single layer in the air fryer basket.
4. Put the air fryer basket on sheet pan and place into oven. Select Air Fry and set time to 12 minutes, until crisp. Shake the basket once halfway through.
5. Transfer the warm chickpeas to the bowl and toss with the orange zest and rosemary. Allow to cool completely before serving.

Scalloped Veggie Mix

Prep time: 10 minutes | Cook time: 15 minutes | Serves 4

1 Yukon Gold potato, thinly sliced
1 small sweet potato, peeled and thinly sliced
1 medium carrot, thinly sliced
¼ cup minced onion
3 garlic cloves, minced
¾ cup 2 percent milk
2 tablespoons cornstarch
½ teaspoon dried thyme

1. Preheat the air fryer oven to 380°F (193°C).
2. In a sheet pan, layer the potato, sweet potato, carrot, onion, and garlic.
3. In a small bowl, whisk the milk, cornstarch, and thyme until blended. Pour the milk mixture evenly over the vegetables in the pan.
4. Put the sheet pan on wire rack and slide into the oven. Select Bake and set time to 15 minutes. It should be golden brown on top, and the vegetables should be tender.
5. Serve immediately.

Pea Delight

Prep time: 5 minutes | Cook time: 15 minutes | Serves 2 to 4

1 cup flour
1 teaspoon baking powder
3 eggs
1 cup coconut milk
1 cup cream cheese
3 tablespoons pea protein
½ cup chicken or turkey strips
Pinch of sea salt
1 cup Mozzarella cheese

1. Preheat the air fryer oven to 390°F (199°C).
2. In a large bowl, mix all ingredients together using a large wooden spoon.
3. Spoon equal amounts of the mixture into muffin cups. Place the muffin cups in a sheet pan.
4. Put the sheet pan on wire rack and slide into the oven. Select Bake and set time to 15 minutes.
5. Serve immediately.

Chapter 10: Fast and Easy Everyday Favorites | 119

Croutons

Prep time: 5 minutes | Cook time: 8 minutes | Serves 4

2 slices friendly bread
1 tablespoon olive oil

Hot soup, for serving

1. Preheat the air fryer oven to 390°F (199°C).
2. Cut the slices of bread into medium-size chunks.
3. Brush the air fryer basket with the oil. Place the chunks in the air fryer basket.
4. Put the air fryer basket on sheet pan and place into oven. Select Air Fry and set time to 8 minutes.
5. Serve with hot soup.

Sweet Potato Soufflé

Prep time: 10 minutes | Cook time: 30 minutes | Serves 4

1 sweet potato, baked and mashed
2 tablespoons unsalted butter, divided

1 large egg, separated
¼ cup whole milk
½ teaspoon kosher salt

1. Preheat the air fryer oven to 330°F (166°C).
2. In a medium bowl, combine the sweet potato, 1 tablespoon of melted butter, egg yolk, milk, and salt. Set aside.
3. In a separate medium bowl, whisk the egg white until stiff peaks form.
4. Using a spatula, gently fold the egg white into the sweet potato mixture.
5. Coat the inside of four ramekins with the remaining 1 tablespoon of butter, then fill each ramekin halfway full.
6. Place the ramekins on wire rack and slide into oven. Select Bake and set time to 15 minutes.
7. Remove the ramekins from the oven and allow to cool on a wire rack for 10 minutes before serving

Chicken Wings

Prep time: 5 minutes | Cook time: 15 minutes | Serves 6

2 pounds (907 g) chicken wings, tips removed

⅛ teaspoon salt

1. Preheat the air fryer oven to 400°F (204°C).
2. Season the wings with salt. Put the chicken wings in the air fryer basket.
3. Put the air fryer basket on sheet pan and place into oven. Select Air Fry and set time to 15 minutes, or until the skin is browned and cooked through, turning the wings with tongs halfway through cooking.
4. Transfer to a large bowl and serve immediately.

Spinach and Carrot Balls

Prep time: 10 minutes | Cook time: 10 minutes | Serves 4

2 slices toasted bread
1 carrot, peeled and grated
1 package fresh spinach, blanched and chopped
½ onion, chopped
1 egg, beaten
½ teaspoon garlic powder

1 teaspoon minced garlic
1 teaspoon salt
½ teaspoon black pepper
1 tablespoon nutritional yeast
1 tablespoon flour

1. Preheat the air fryer oven to 390°F (199°C).
2. In a food processor, pulse the toasted bread to form bread crumbs. Transfer into a shallow dish or bowl.
3. In a bowl, mix together all the other ingredients.
4. Use your hands to shape the mixture into small-sized balls. Roll the balls in the bread crumbs, ensuring to cover them well.
5. Put them in the air fryer basket. Put the air fryer basket on sheet pan and place into oven. Select Air Fry and set time to 10 minutes.
6. Serve immediately.

Sweet Corn and Carrot Fritters

Prep time: 10 minutes | Cook time: 10 minutes | Serves 4

1 medium-sized carrot, grated
1 yellow onion, finely chopped
4 ounces (113 g) canned sweet corn kernels, drained
1 teaspoon sea salt flakes
1 tablespoon chopped fresh cilantro
1 medium-sized egg, whisked
2 tablespoons plain milk
1 cup grated Parmesan cheese
¼ cup flour
⅓ teaspoon baking powder
⅓ teaspoon sugar
Cooking spray

1. Preheat the air fryer oven to 350°F (177°C).
2. Place the grated carrot in a colander and press down to squeeze out any excess moisture. Dry it with a paper towel.
3. Combine the carrots with the remaining ingredients.
4. Mold 1 tablespoon of the mixture into a ball and press it down with your hand or a spoon to flatten it. Repeat until the rest of the mixture is used up.
5. Spritz the balls with cooking spray. Arrange them in a sheet pan, taking care not to overlap any balls.
6. Put the sheet pan on wire rack and slide into the oven. Select Bake and set time to 10 minutes, or until they're firm.
7. Serve warm.

Traditional Queso Fundido

Prep time: 10 minutes | Cook time: 25 minutes | Serves 4

4 ounces (113 g) fresh Mexican chorizo, casings removed
1 medium onion, chopped
3 cloves garlic, minced
1 cup chopped tomato
2 jalapeños, deseeded and diced
2 teaspoons ground cumin
2 cups shredded Oaxaca or Mozzarella cheese
½ cup half-and-half
Celery sticks or tortilla chips, for serving

1. Preheat the air fryer oven to 400°F (204°C).
2. In a sheet pan, combine the chorizo, onion, garlic, tomato, jalapeños, and cumin. Stir to combine.
3. Put the sheet pan on wire rack and slide into the oven. Select Bake and set time to 15 minutes, or until the sausage is cooked, stirring halfway through the cooking time to break up the sausage.
4. Add the cheese and half-and-half; stir to combine. Bake for an additional 10 minutes, or until the cheese has melted.
5. Serve with celery sticks or tortilla chips.

Chapter 11   Holiday Specials

Lush Snack Mix

Prep time: 10 minutes | Cook time: 12 minutes | Serves 10

½ cup honey
3 tablespoons butter, melted
1 teaspoon salt
2 cups sesame sticks
2 cup pumpkin seeds
2 cups granola
1 cup cashews
2 cups crispy corn puff cereal
2 cup mini pretzel crisps

1. In a bowl, combine the honey, butter, and salt.
2. In another bowl, mix the sesame sticks, pumpkin seeds, granola, cashews, corn puff cereal, and pretzel crisps.
3. Combine the contents of the two bowls.
4. Preheat the air fryer oven to 370ºF (188ºC).
5. Put the mixture in the air fryer basket. Put the air fryer basket on sheet pan and place into oven. Select Air Fry and set time to 12 minutes. Shake the basket frequently during cooking.
6. Put the snack mix on a cookie sheet and allow it to cool completely. Serve immediately.

Jewish Blintzes

Prep time: 5 minutes | Cook time: 10 minutes | Makes 8 blintzes

2 (7½-ounce / 213-g) packages farmer cheese, mashed
¼ cup cream cheese
¼ teaspoon vanilla extract
¼ cup granulated white sugar
8 egg roll wrappers
4 tablespoons butter, melted

1. Combine the farmer cheese, cream cheese, vanilla extract, and sugar in a bowl. Stir to mix well.
2. Unfold the egg roll wrappers on a clean work surface, spread ¼ cup of the filling at the edge of each wrapper and leave a ½-inch edge uncovering.
3. Wet the edges of the wrappers with water and fold the uncovered edge over the filling. Fold the left and right sides in the center, then tuck the edge under the filling and fold to wrap the filling.
4. Brush the wrappers with melted butter, then arrange the wrappers in a single layer in the air fryer basket, seam side down. Leave a little space between each two wrappers.
5. Put the air fryer basket on sheet pan and place into oven. Select Air Fry, set temperature to 375ºF (190ºC) and set time to 10 minutes.
6. When cooking is complete, the wrappers will be golden brown.
7. Serve immediately.

Air Fried Spicy Olives

Prep time: 10 minutes | Cook time: 5 minutes | Serves 4

12 ounces (340 g) pitted black extra-large olives
¼ cup all-purpose flour
1 cup panko bread crumbs
2 teaspoons dried thyme
1 teaspoon red pepper
flakes
1 teaspoon smoked paprika
1 egg beaten with 1 tablespoon water
Vegetable oil for spraying

1. Preheat the air fryer oven to 400ºF (204ºC).
2. Drain the olives and place them on a paper towel–lined plate to dry.
3. Put the flour on a plate. Combine the panko, thyme, red pepper flakes, and paprika on a separate plate. Dip an olive in the flour, shaking off any excess, then coat with egg mixture. Dredge the olive in the panko mixture, pressing to make the crumbs adhere, and place the breaded olive on a platter. Repeat with the remaining olives.
4. Spray the olives with oil and place them in a single layer in the air fryer basket.
5. Put the air fryer basket on sheet pan and place into oven. Select Air Fry and set time to 5 minutes, or until the breading is browned and crispy. Serve warm

Pão de Queijo

Prep time: 37 minutes | Cook time: 12 minutes | Makes 12 balls

2 tablespoons butter, plus more for greasing	½ teaspoon salt
½ cup milk	1 large egg
1½ cups tapioca flour	⅔ cup finely grated aged Asiago cheese

1. Put the butter in a saucepan and pour in the milk, heat over medium heat until the liquid boils. Keep stirring.
2. Turn off the heat and mix in the tapioca flour and salt to form a soft dough. Transfer the dough in a large bowl, then wrap the bowl in plastic and let sit for 15 minutes.
3. Break the egg in the bowl of dough and whisk with a hand mixer for 2 minutes or until a sanity dough forms. Fold the cheese in the dough. Cover the bowl in plastic again and let sit for 10 more minutes.
4. Grease the sheet pan with butter.
5. Scoop 2 tablespoons of the dough into the sheet pan. Repeat with the remaining dough to make dough 12 balls. Keep a little distance between each two balls.
6. Place the sheet pan on wire rack and slide into oven. Select Bake, set temperature to 375ºF (190ºC) and set time to 12 minutes.
7. Flip the balls halfway through the cooking time.
8. When cooking is complete, the balls should be golden brown and fluffy.
9. Remove the balls from the oven and allow to cool for 5 minutes before serving.

Classic Churros

Prep time: 35 minutes | Cook time: 10 minutes | Makes 12 churros

4 tablespoons butter	2 teaspoons ground cinnamon
¼ teaspoon salt	
½ cup water	¼ cup granulated white sugar
½ cup all-purpose flour	
2 large eggs	Cooking spray

1. Put the butter, salt, and water in a saucepan. Bring to a boil until the butter is melted on high heat. Keep stirring.
2. Reduce the heat to medium and fold in the flour to form a dough. Keep cooking and stirring until the dough

is dried out and coat the pan with a crust.
3. Turn off the heat and scrape the dough in a large bowl. Allow to cool for 15 minutes.
4. Break and whisk the eggs into the dough with a hand mixer until the dough is sanity and firm enough to shape.
5. Scoop up 1 tablespoon of the dough and roll it into a ½-inch-diameter and 2-inch-long cylinder. Repeat with remaining dough to make 12 cylinders in total.
6. Combine the cinnamon and sugar in a large bowl and dunk the cylinders into the cinnamon mix to coat.
7. Arrange the cylinders on a plate and refrigerate for 20 minutes.
8. Spritz the air fryer basket with cooking spray. Place the cylinders in the basket and spritz with cooking spray.
9. Put the air fryer basket on sheet pan and place into oven. Select Air Fry, set temperature to 375ºF (190ºC) and set time to 10 minutes.
10. Flip the cylinders halfway through the cooking time.
11. When cooked, the cylinders should be golden brown and fluffy.
12. Serve immediately.

Pigs in a Blanket

Prep time: 10 minutes | Cook time: 8 minutes | Makes 16 rolls

1 can refrigerated crescent roll dough	dry
	2 tablespoons melted butter
1 small package mini smoked sausages, patted	2 teaspoons sesame seeds
	1 teaspoon onion powder

1. Place the crescent roll dough on a clean work surface and separate into 8 pieces. Cut each piece in half and you will have 16 triangles.
2. Make the pigs in the blanket: Arrange each sausage on each dough triangle, then roll the sausages up.
3. Brush the pigs with melted butter and place of the pigs in the blanket in the sheet pan. Sprinkle with sesame seeds and onion powder.
4. Place the sheet pan on wire rack and slide into oven. Select Bake, set temperature to 330ºF (166ºC) and set time to 8 minutes.
5. Flip the pigs halfway through the cooking time.
6. When cooking is complete, the pigs should be fluffy and golden brown.
7. Serve immediately.

Chapter 11: Holiday Specials | 123

Milky Pecan Tart

Prep time: 2 hours 25 minutes | Cook time: 26 minutes | Serves 8

Tart Crust:

¼ cup firmly packed brown sugar

⅓ cup butter, softened

1 cup all-purpose flour

¼ teaspoon kosher salt

Filling:

¼ cup whole milk

4 tablespoons butter, diced

½ cup packed brown sugar

¼ cup pure maple syrup

1½ cups finely chopped

pecans

¼ teaspoon pure vanilla extract

¼ teaspoon sea salt

1. Line the sheet pan with aluminum foil, then spritz the pan with cooking spray.

2. Stir the brown sugar and butter in a bowl with a hand mixer until puffed, then add the flour and salt and stir until crumbled.

3. Pour the mixture in the prepared sheet pan and tilt the pan to coat the bottom evenly.

4. Place the sheet pan on wire rack and slide into oven. Select Bake, set temperature to 350°F (180°C) and set time to 13 minutes.

5. When done, the crust will be golden brown.

6. Meanwhile, pour the milk, butter, sugar, and maple syrup in a saucepan. Stir to mix well. Bring to a simmer, then cook for 1 more minute. Stir constantly.

7. Turn off the heat and mix the pecans and vanilla into the filling mixture.

8. Pour the filling mixture over the golden crust and spread with a spatula to coat the crust evenly.

9. Select Bake and set time to 12 minutes. When cooked, the filling mixture should be set and frothy.

10. Remove the sheet pan from the oven and sprinkle with salt. Allow to sit for 10 minutes or until cooled.

11. Transfer the pan to the refrigerator to chill for at least 2 hours, then remove the aluminum foil and slice to serve.

Garlicky Olive Stromboli

Prep time: 25 minutes | Cook time: 25 minutes | Serves 8

4 large cloves garlic, unpeeled

3 tablespoons grated Parmesan cheese

½ cup packed fresh basil leaves

½ cup marinated, pitted green and black olives

¼ teaspoon crushed red pepper

½ pound (227 g) pizza dough, at room temperature

4 ounces (113 g) sliced provolone cheese (about 8 slices)

Cooking spray

1. Spritz the air fryer basket with cooking spray. Put the unpeeled garlic in the basket.

2. Put the air fryer basket on sheet pan and place into oven. Select Air Fry, set temperature to 370°F (188°C) and set time to 10 minutes.

3. When cooked, the garlic will be softened completely. Remove from the oven and allow to cool until you can handle.

4. Peel the garlic and place into a food processor with 2 tablespoons of Parmesan, basil, olives, and crushed red pepper. Pulse to mix well. Set aside.

5. Arrange the pizza dough on a clean work surface, then roll it out with a rolling pin into a rectangle. Cut the rectangle in half.

6. Sprinkle half of the garlic mixture over each rectangle half, and leave ½-inch edges uncover. Top them with the provolone cheese.

7. Brush one long side of each rectangle half with water, then roll them up. Spritz the basket with cooking spray. Transfer the rolls to the basket. Spritz with cooking spray and scatter with remaining Parmesan.

8. Select Air Fry and set time to 15 minutes.

9. Flip the rolls halfway through the cooking time. When done, the rolls should be golden brown.

10. Remove the rolls from the oven and allow to cool for a few minutes before serving.

Supplì al Telefono (Risotto Croquettes)

Prep time: 1 hour 40 minutes | Cook time: 54 minutes | Serves 6

Risotto Croquettes:

4 tablespoons unsalted butter
1 small yellow onion, minced
1 cup Arborio rice
3½ cups chicken stock
½ cup dry white wine
3 eggs
Zest of 1 lemon
½ cup grated Parmesan cheese

2 ounces (57 g) fresh Mozzarella cheese
¼ cup peas
2 tablespoons water
½ cup all-purpose flour
1½ cups panko bread crumbs
Kosher salt and ground black pepper, to taste
Cooking spray

Tomato Sauce:

2 tablespoons extra-virgin olive oil
4 cloves garlic, minced
¼ teaspoon red pepper flakes
1 (28-ounce / 794-g) can

crushed tomatoes
2 teaspoons granulated sugar
Kosher salt and ground black pepper, to taste

1. Melt the butter in a pot over medium heat, then add the onion and salt to taste. Sauté for 5 minutes or until the onion in translucent.
2. Add the rice and stir to coat well. Cook for 3 minutes or until the rice is lightly browned. Pour in the chicken stock and wine.
3. Bring to a boil. Then cook for 20 minutes or until the rice is tender and liquid is almost absorbed.
4. Make the risotto: When the rice is cooked, break the egg into the pot. Add the lemon zest and Parmesan cheese. Sprinkle with salt and ground black pepper. Stir to mix well.
5. Pour the risotto in a baking sheet, then level with a spatula to spread the risotto evenly. Wrap the baking sheet in plastic and refrigerate for1 hour.
6. Meanwhile, heat the olive oil in a saucepan over medium heat until shimmering.
7. Add the garlic and sprinkle with red pepper flakes. Sauté for a minute or until fragrant.
8. Add the crushed tomatoes and sprinkle with sugar. Stir to mix well. Bring to a boil. Reduce the heat to low and simmer for 15 minutes or until lightly thickened. Sprinkle with salt and pepper to taste. Set aside until ready to serve.
9. Remove the risotto from the refrigerator. Scoop the risotto into twelve 2-inch balls, then flatten the balls with your hands.
10. Arrange a about ½-inch piece of Mozzarella and 5 peas in the center of each flattened ball, then wrap them back into balls.
11. Transfer the balls to a baking sheet lined with parchment paper, then refrigerate for 15 minutes or until firm.
12. Whisk the remaining 2 eggs with 2 tablespoons of water in a bowl. Pour the flour in a second bowl and pour the panko in a third bowl.
13. Dredge the risotto balls in the bowl of flour first, then into the eggs, and then into the panko. Shake the excess off.
14. Transfer the balls to the sheet pan and spritz with cooking spray.
15. Place the sheet pan on wire rack and slide into oven. Select Bake, set temperature to 400ºF (205ºC) and set time to 10 minutes.
16. Flip the balls halfway through the cooking time.
17. When cooking is complete, the balls should be until golden brown.
18. Serve the risotto balls with the tomato sauce.

Teriyaki Shrimp Skewers

Prep time: 10 minutes | Cook time: 6 minutes | Makes 12 skewered shrimp

1½ tablespoons mirin
1½ teaspoons ginger juice
1½ tablespoons soy sauce
12 large shrimp (about 20

shrimps per pound), peeled and deveined
1 large egg
¾ cup panko bread crumbs
Cooking spray

1. Combine the mirin, ginger juice, and soy sauce in a large bowl. Stir to mix well.
2. Dunk the shrimp in the bowl of mirin mixture, then wrap the bowl in plastic and refrigerate for 1 hour to marinate.
3. Spritz the air fryer basket with cooking spray.
4. Run twelve 4-inch skewers through each shrimp.
5. Whisk the egg in the bowl of marinade to combine well. Pour the bread crumbs on a plate.
6. Dredge the shrimp skewers in the egg mixture, then shake the excess off and roll over the bread crumbs to coat well.
7. Arrange the shrimp skewers in the basket and spritz with cooking spray.
8. Put the air fryer basket on sheet pan and place into oven. Select Air Fry, set temperature to 400ºF (205ºC) and set time to 6 minutes.
9. Flip the shrimp skewers halfway through the cooking time.
10. When done, the shrimp will be opaque and firm.
11. Serve immediately.

Golden Nuggets

Prep time: 15 minutes | Cook time: 4 minutes | Makes 20 nuggets

1 cup all-purpose flour, plus more for dusting
1 teaspoon baking powder
½ teaspoon butter, at room temperature, plus more for brushing
¼ teaspoon salt
¼ cup water
⅛ teaspoon onion powder
¼ teaspoon garlic powder
⅛ teaspoon seasoning salt
Cooking spray

1. Line the air fryer basket with parchment paper.
2. Mix the flour, baking powder, butter, and salt in a large bowl. Stir to mix well. Gradually whisk in the water until a sanity dough forms.
3. Put the dough on a lightly floured work surface, then roll it out into a ½-inch thick rectangle with a rolling pin.
4. Cut the dough into about twenty 1- or 2-inch squares, then arrange the squares in a single layer in the basket. Spritz with cooking spray.
5. Combine onion powder, garlic powder, and seasoning salt in a small bowl. Stir to mix well, then sprinkle the squares with the powder mixture.
6. Put the air fryer basket on sheet pan and place into oven. Select Air Fry, set temperature to 370ºF (188ºC) and set time to 4 minutes.
7. Flip the squares halfway through the cooking time.
8. When cooked, the dough squares should be golden brown.
9. Remove the golden nuggets from the oven and brush with more butter immediately. Serve warm.

Bourbon Monkey Bread

Prep time: 15 minutes | Cook time: 25 minutes | Serves 6 to 8

1 (16.3-ounce / 462-g) can store-bought refrigerated biscuit dough
¼ cup packed light brown sugar
1 teaspoon ground cinnamon
½ teaspoon freshly grated nutmeg
½ teaspoon ground ginger
½ teaspoon kosher salt
¼ teaspoon ground allspice
⅛ teaspoon ground cloves
4 tablespoons (½ stick) unsalted butter, melted
½ cup powdered sugar
2 teaspoons bourbon
2 tablespoons chopped candied cherries
2 tablespoons chopped pecans

1. Preheat the air fryer oven to 310ºF (154ºC).
2. Open the can and separate the biscuits, then cut each into quarters. Toss the biscuit quarters in a large bowl with the brown sugar, cinnamon, nutmeg, ginger, salt, allspice, and cloves until evenly coated. Transfer the dough pieces and any sugar left in the bowl to a round cake pan, metal cake pan, or foil pan and drizzle evenly with the melted butter.
3. Place the pan on wire rack and slide into oven. Select Bake and set time to 25 minutes, or until the monkey bread is golden brown and cooked through in the center.
4. Transfer the pan to a wire rack and let cool completely. Unmold from the pan.
5. In a small bowl, whisk the powdered sugar and the bourbon into a smooth glaze. Drizzle the glaze over the cooled monkey bread and, while the glaze is still wet, sprinkle with the cherries and pecans to serve.

Kale Salad Sushi Rolls with Sriracha Mayo

Prep time: 10 minutes | Cook time: 10 minutes | Serves 12

Kale Salad:
1½ cups chopped kale
1 tablespoon sesame seeds
¾ teaspoon soy sauce
¾ teaspoon toasted sesame
oil
½ teaspoon rice vinegar
¼ teaspoon ginger
⅛ teaspoon garlic powder

Sushi Rolls:
3 sheets sushi nori
1 batch cauliflower rice
½ avocado, sliced

Sriracha Mayonnaise:
¼ cup Sriracha sauce
¼ cup vegan mayonnaise

Coating:
½ cup panko bread crumbs

1. In a medium bowl, toss all the ingredients for the salad together until well coated and set aside.
2. Place a sheet of nori on a clean work surface and spread the cauliflower rice in an even layer on the nori. Scoop 2 to 3 tablespoon of kale salad on the rice and spread over. Place 1 or 2 avocado slices on top. Roll up the sushi, pressing gently to get a nice, tight roll. Repeat to make the remaining 2 rolls.
3. In a bowl, stir together the Sriracha sauce and mayonnaise until smooth. Add bread crumbs to a separate bowl.
4. Dredge the sushi rolls in Sriracha Mayonnaise, then roll in bread crumbs till well coated.
5. Place the coated sushi rolls in the air fryer basket.
6. Put the air fryer basket on sheet pan and place into oven. Select Air Fry, set temperature to 390ºF (199ºC) and set time to 10 minutes.
7. Flip the sushi rolls halfway through the cooking time.
8. When cooking is complete, the sushi rolls will be golden brown and crispy. .
9. Transfer to a platter and rest for 5 minutes before slicing each roll into 8 pieces. Serve warm.

Honey Yeast Rolls

Prep time: 10 minutes | Cook time: 12 minutes | Makes 8 rolls

¼ cup whole milk, heated to 115ºF (46ºC) in the microwave
½ teaspoon active dry yeast
1 tablespoon honey
⅔ cup all-purpose flour,
plus more for dusting
½ teaspoon kosher salt
2 tablespoons unsalted butter, at room temperature, plus more for greasing
Flaky sea salt, to taste

1. In a large bowl, whisk together the milk, yeast, and honey and let stand until foamy, about 10 minutes.
2. Stir in the flour and salt until just combined. Stir in the butter until absorbed. Scrape the dough onto a lightly floured work surface and knead until smooth, about 6 minutes. Transfer the dough to a lightly greased bowl, cover loosely with a sheet of plastic wrap or a kitchen towel, and let sit until nearly doubled in size, about 1 hour.
3. Uncover the dough, lightly press it down to expel the bubbles, then portion it into 8 equal pieces. Prep the work surface by wiping it clean with a damp paper towel (if there is flour on the work surface, it will prevent the dough from sticking lightly to the surface, which helps it form a ball). Roll each piece into a ball by cupping the palm of the hand around the dough against the work surface and moving the heel of the hand in a circular motion while using the thumb to contain the dough and tighten it into a perfectly round ball. Once all the balls are formed, nestle them side by side in the air fryer basket.
4. Cover the rolls loosely with a kitchen towel or a sheet of plastic wrap and let sit until lightly risen and puffed, 20 to 30 minutes.
5. Preheat the air fryer oven to 270ºF (132ºC).
6. Uncover the rolls and gently brush with more butter, being careful not to press the rolls too hard.
7. Put the air fryer basket on sheet pan and place into oven. Select Air Fry and set time to 12 minutes, until the rolls are light golden brown and fluffy.
8. Remove the rolls from the oven and brush liberally with more butter, if you like, and sprinkle each roll with a pinch of sea salt. Serve warm.

Chapter 12　Sauces, Dips, and Dressings

Lemony Tahini

Prep time: 5 minutes | Cook time: 0 minutes | Serves 4

¾ cup water
½ cup tahini
3 garlic cloves, minced
Juice of 3 lemons
½ teaspoon pink Himalayan salt

1. In a bowl, whisk together all the ingredients until mixed well.

Hummus

Prep time: 5 minutes | Cook time: 0 minutes | Serves 2

1 (19-ounce / 539-g) can chickpeas, drained and rinsed
¼ cup tahini
3 tablespoons cold water
2 tablespoons freshly squeezed lemon juice
1 garlic clove
½ teaspoon turmeric powder
⅛ teaspoon black pepper
Pinch pink Himalayan salt, to taste

1. Combine all the ingredients in a food processor and blend until smooth.

Dijon and Balsamic Vinaigrette

Prep time: 5 minutes | Cook time: 0 minutes | Makes 12 tablespoons

6 tablespoons water
4 tablespoons Dijon mustard
4 tablespoons balsamic vinegar
1 teaspoon maple syrup
½ teaspoon pink Himalayan salt
¼ teaspoon freshly ground black pepper

1. In a bowl, whisk together all the ingredients.

Cashew Mayo

Prep time: 5 minutes | Cook time: 0 minutes | Makes 18 tablespoons

1 cup cashews, soaked in hot water for at least 1 hour
¼ cup plus 3 tablespoons milk
1 tablespoon apple cider vinegar
1 tablespoon freshly squeezed lemon juice
1 tablespoon Dijon mustard
1 tablespoon aquafaba
⅛ teaspoon pink Himalayan salt

1. In a food processor, combine all the ingredients and blend until creamy and smooth.

Classic Marinara Sauce

Prep time: 15 minutes | Cook time: 30 minutes | Makes about 3 cups

¼ cup extra-virgin olive oil
3 garlic cloves, minced
1 small onion, chopped (about ½ cup)
2 tablespoons minced or puréed sun-dried tomatoes (optional)
1 (28-ounce / 794-g) can
crushed tomatoes
½ teaspoon dried basil
½ teaspoon dried oregano
¼ teaspoon red pepper flakes
1 teaspoon kosher salt or ½ teaspoon fine salt, plus more as needed

1. Heat the oil in a medium saucepan over medium heat.
2. Add the garlic and onion and sauté for 2 to 3 minutes, or until the onion is softened. Add the sun-dried tomatoes (if desired) and cook for 1 minute until fragrant. Stir in the crushed tomatoes, scraping any brown bits from the bottom of the pot. Fold in the basil, oregano, red pepper flakes, and salt. Stir well.
3. Bring to a simmer. Cook covered for about 30 minutes, stirring occasionally.
4. Turn off the heat and allow the sauce to cool for about 10 minutes.
5. Taste and adjust the seasoning, adding more salt if needed.
6. Use immediately.

Pico de Gallo

Prep time: 5 minutes | Cook time: 0 minutes | Serves 2

3 large tomatoes, chopped
½ small red onion, diced
⅛ cup chopped fresh cilantro
3 garlic cloves, chopped

2 tablespoons chopped pickled jalapeño pepper
1 tablespoon lime juice
¼ teaspoon pink Himalayan salt (optional)

1. In a medium bowl, combine all the ingredients and mix with a wooden spoon.

Hemp Dressing

Prep time: 5 minutes | Cook time: 0 minutes | Makes 12 tablespoons

½ cup white wine vinegar
¼ cup tahini
¼ cup water
1 tablespoon hemp seeds
½ tablespoon freshly squeezed lemon juice
1 teaspoon garlic powder
1 teaspoon dried oregano

1 teaspoon dried basil
1 teaspoon red pepper flakes
½ teaspoon onion powder
½ teaspoon pink Himalayan salt
½ teaspoon freshly ground black pepper

1. In a bowl, combine all the ingredients and whisk until mixed well.

Cashew Ranch Dressing

Prep time: 15 minutes | Cook time: 0 minutes | Serves 12

1 cup cashews, soaked in warm water for at least 1 hour
½ cup water
2 tablespoons freshly

squeezed lemon juice
1 tablespoon vinegar
1 teaspoon garlic powder
1 teaspoon onion powder
2 teaspoons dried dill

1. In a food processor, combine the cashews, water, lemon juice, vinegar, garlic powder, and onion powder. Blend until creamy and smooth. Add the dill and pulse a few times until combined.

Avocado Dressing

Prep time: 5 minutes | Cook time: 0 minutes | Makes 12 tablespoons

1 large avocado, pitted and peeled
½ cup water
2 tablespoons tahini
2 tablespoons freshly squeezed lemon juice
1 teaspoon dried basil

1 teaspoon white wine vinegar
1 garlic clove
¼ teaspoon pink Himalayan salt
¼ teaspoon freshly ground black pepper

1. Combine all the ingredients in a food processor and blend until smooth.

Mushroom Apple Gravy

Prep time: 5 minutes | Cook time: 10 minutes | Serves 4

2 cups vegetable broth
½ cup finely chopped mushrooms
2 tablespoons whole wheat flour
1 tablespoon unsweetened applesauce

1 teaspoon onion powder
½ teaspoon dried thyme
¼ teaspoon dried rosemary
⅛ teaspoon pink Himalayan salt
Freshly ground black pepper, to taste

1. In a nonstick saucepan over medium-high heat, combine all the ingredients and mix well. Bring to a boil, stirring frequently, reduce the heat to low, and simmer, stirring constantly, until it thickens.

Balsamic Dressing

Prep time: 5 minutes | Cook time: 0 minutes | Makes 1 cup

2 tablespoons Dijon mustard

¼ cup balsamic vinegar
¾ cup olive oil

1. Put all ingredients in a jar with a tight-fitting lid. Put on the lid and shake vigorously until thoroughly combined. Refrigerate until ready to use and shake well before serving.

Chapter 12: Sauces, Dips, and Dressings | 129

Asian Dipping Sauce

Prep time: 15 minutes | Cook time: 0 minutes | Makes about 1 cup

¼ cup rice vinegar
¼ cup hoisin sauce
¼ cup low-sodium chicken or vegetable stock
3 tablespoons soy sauce
1 tablespoon minced or grated ginger
1 tablespoon minced or pressed garlic
1 teaspoon chili-garlic sauce or sriracha (or more to taste)

1. Stir together all the ingredients in a small bowl, or place in a jar with a tight-fitting lid and shake until well mixed.
2. Use immediately.

Caesar Salad Dressing

Prep time: 5 minutes | Cook time: 0 minutes | Makes about ⅔ cup

½ cup extra-virgin olive oil
2 tablespoons freshly squeezed lemon juice
1 teaspoon anchovy paste
¼ teaspoon kosher salt or
⅛ teaspoon fine salt
¼ teaspoon minced or pressed garlic
1 egg, beaten

1. Add all the ingredients to a tall, narrow container.
2. Purée the mixture with an immersion blender until smooth.
3. Use immediately.

Southwest Seasoning

Prep time: 5 minutes | Cook time: 0 minutes | Makes about ¾ cups

3 tablespoons ancho chile powder
3 tablespoons paprika
2 tablespoons dried oregano
2 tablespoons freshly ground black pepper
2 teaspoons cayenne
2 teaspoons cumin
1 tablespoon granulated onion
1 tablespoon granulated garlic

1. Stir together all the ingredients in a small bowl.
2. Use immediately or place in an airtight container in the pantry.

Appendix 1 Measurement Conversion Chart

VOLUME EQUIVALENTS(DRY)

US STANDARD	METRIC (APPROXIMATE)
1/8 teaspoon	0.5 mL
1/4 teaspoon	1 mL
1/2 teaspoon	2 mL
3/4 teaspoon	4 mL
1 teaspoon	5 mL
1 tablespoon	15 mL
1/4 cup	59 mL
1/2 cup	118 mL
3/4 cup	177 mL
1 cup	235 mL
2 cups	475 mL
3 cups	700 mL
4 cups	1 L

VOLUME EQUIVALENTS(LIQUID)

US STANDARD	US STANDARD (OUNCES)	METRIC (APPROXIMATE)
2 tablespoons	1 fl.oz.	30 mL
1/4 cup	2 fl.oz.	60 mL
1/2 cup	4 fl.oz.	120 mL
1 cup	8 fl.oz.	240 mL
1 1/2 cup	12 fl.oz.	355 mL
2 cups or 1 pint	16 fl.oz.	475 mL
4 cups or 1 quart	32 fl.oz.	1 L
1 gallon	128 fl.oz.	4 L

TEMPERATURES EQUIVALENTS

FAHRENHEIT(F)	CELSIUS(C) (APPROXIMATE)
225 °F	107 °C
250 °F	120 °C
275 °F	135 °C
300 °F	150 °C
325 °F	160 °C
350 °F	180 °C
375 °F	190 °C
400 °F	205 °C
425 °F	220 °C
450 °F	235 °C
475 °F	245 °C
500 °F	260 °C

WEIGHT EQUIVALENTS

US STANDARD	METRIC (APPROXIMATE)
1 ounce	28 g
2 ounces	57 g
5 ounces	142 g
10 ounces	284 g
15 ounces	425 g
16 ounces (1 pound)	455 g
1.5 pounds	680 g
2 pounds	907 g

Appendix 2 Air Fryer Cooking Chart

Beef

Item	Temp (°F)	Time (mins)	Item	Temp (°F)	Time (mins)
Beef Eye Round Roast (4 lbs.)	400 °F	45 to 55	Meatballs (1-inch)	370 °F	7
Burger Patty (4 oz.)	370 °F	16 to 20	Meatballs (3-inch)	380 °F	10
Filet Mignon (8 oz.)	400 °F	18	Ribeye, bone-in (1-inch, 8 oz)	400 °F	10 to 15
Flank Steak (1.5 lbs.)	400 °F	12	Sirloin steaks (1-inch, 12 oz)	400 °F	9 to 14
Flank Steak (2 lbs.)	400 °F	20 to 28			

Chicken

Item	Temp (°F)	Time (mins)	Item	Temp (°F)	Time (mins)
Breasts, bone in (1 ¼ lb.)	370 °F	25	Legs, bone-in (1 ¾ lb.)	380 °F	30
Breasts, boneless (4 oz)	380 °F	12	Thighs, boneless (1 ½ lb.)	380 °F	18 to 20
Drumsticks (2 ½ lb.)	370 °F	20	Wings (2 lb.)	400 °F	12
Game Hen (halved 2 lb.)	390 °F	20	Whole Chicken	360 °F	75
Thighs, bone-in (2 lb.)	380 °F	22	Tenders	360 °F	8 to 10

Pork & Lamb

Item	Temp (°F)	Time (mins)	Item	Temp (°F)	Time (mins)
Bacon (regular)	400 °F	5 to 7	Pork Tenderloin	370 °F	15
Bacon (thick cut)	400 °F	6 to 10	Sausages	380 °F	15
Pork Loin (2 lb.)	360 °F	55	Lamb Loin Chops (1-inch thick)	400 °F	8 to 12
Pork Chops, bone in (1-inch, 6.5 oz)	400 °F	12	Rack of Lamb (1.5 – 2 lb.)	380 °F	22

Fish & Seafood

Item	Temp (°F)	Time (mins)	Item	Temp (°F)	Time (mins)
Calamari (8 oz)	400 °F	4	Tuna Steak	400 °F	7 to 10
Fish Fillet (1-inch, 8 oz)	400 °F	10	Scallops	400 °F	5 to 7
Salmon, fillet (6 oz)	380 °F	12	Shrimp	400 °F	5
Swordfish steak	400 °F	10			

Appendix 3 Index

Vegetables					
INGREDIENT	AMOUNT	PREPARATION	OIL	TEMP	COOK TIME
Asparagus	2 bunches	Cut in half, trim stems	2 Tbsp	420°F	12-15 mins
Beets	1½ lbs	Peel, cut in ½-inch cubes	1Tbsp	390°F	28-30 mins
Bell peppers (for roasting)	4 peppers	Cut in quarters, remove seeds	1Tbsp	400°F	15-20 mins
Broccoli	1 large head	Cut in 1-2-inch florets	1Tbsp	400°F	15-20 mins
Brussels sprouts	1lb	Cut in half, remove stems	1Tbsp	425°F	15-20 mins
Carrots	1lb	Peel, cut in ¼-inch rounds	1 Tbsp	425°F	10-15 mins
Cauliflower	1 head	Cut in 1-2-inch florets	2 Tbsp	400°F	20-22 mins
Corn on the cob	7 ears	Whole ears, remove husks	1 Tbps	400°F	14-17 mins
Green beans	1 bag (12 oz)	Trim	1 Tbps	420°F	18-20 mins
Kale (for chips)	4 oz	Tear into pieces,remove stems	None	325°F	5-8 mins
Mushrooms	16 oz	Rinse, slice thinly	1 Tbps	390°F	25-30 mins
Potatoes, russet	1½ lbs	Cut in 1-inch wedges	1 Tbps	390°F	25-30 mins
Potatoes, russet	1lb	Hand-cut fries, soak 30 mins in cold water, then pat dry	½ -3 Tbps	400°F	25-28 mins
Potatoes, sweet	1lb	Hand-cut fries, soak 30 mins in cold water, then pat dry	1 Tbps	400°F	25-28 mins
Zucchini	1lb	Cut in eighths lengthwise, then cut in half	1 Tbps	400°F	15-20 mins

A

All-purpose flour
Banana Bread   13
Black and White Brownies   88
Apple Fritters   88
Orange Cake   94
Pea and Potato Samosas with Chutney   111
Apple Fritters with Sugary Glaze   113
Classic Churros   123
Milky Pecan Tart   124
Golden Nuggets   126
Honey Yeast Rolls   127
Oatmeal Raisin Bars   91
Almond
Almond Crusted Fish   37
Almond flour
Ricotta Lemon Poppy Seed Cake   89
Spice Cookies   93
Keto Cheese Quiche   100
Ancho chile powder
Southwest Seasoning   130
Apple
Spicy Apple Turnovers   7
Cinnamon Apple Wedges   78
Spiced Apple Chips   78
Glazed Apples   91
Pear and Apple Crisp   95
Pecan and Cherry Stuffed Apples   96
Apple Fritters with Sugary Glaze   113
Chicken Breakfast Sausages   7
Apple Turnovers   96
Applesauce
Lemony Apple Butter   92
Apple and Walnut Muffins   11
Arborio rice
Supplì al Telefono (Risotto Croquettes)   125
Artichoke heart
Cripsy Artichoke Bites   82
Cheesy Artichoke-Mushroom Frittata   7
Asparagus
Asparagus and Cheese Strata   5
Lemony and Garlicky Asparagus   113
Goat Cheese and Asparagus Frittata   99
Avocado
Baked Avocado with Eggs   9
Avocado Chips   79
Pomegranate Avocado Fries   119
Avocado Dressing   129
Egg and Avocado Burrito   6
Avocado Quesadillas   11

B

Baby spinach
Turkey, Hummus, and Cheese Wraps   57
Bacon
Bacon and Bell Pepper Sandwich   105
All-in-One Toast   8
Cheesy Bacon Quiche   102
Bacon-Wrapped Scallops   34
Sweet Bacon Tater Tots   84
Balsamic vinegar
Dijon and Balsamic Vinaigrette   128
Balsamic Dressing   129
Banana
Sweet Banana Bread Pudding   10
Breaded Bananas with Chocolate Sauce   94
Banana Bread   13
Basil
Green Curry Shrimp   36
Bruschetta with Tomato and Basil   80
basmati rice
Basmati Risotto   22
beef cube steak
Beef Steak Fingers   75
Beef schnitzel
Beef Schnitzel   74
Beet
Chermoula Beet   19
Bell pepper
Cream Cheese Stuffed Bell Peppers   18
Bacon and Bell Pepper Sandwich   105
Fajita Chicken Strips   50
Southwest Corn and Bell Pepper Roast   116
Cheesy Rice and Olives Stuffed Peppers   19
Sirloin Steak and Pepper Fajitas   67
Berry
Coconut Chip Mixed Berry Crisp   90
Berry Crumble   93
Biscuit
Jelly Doughnuts   92
Biscuit dough
Bourbon Monkey Bread   126
Bisquick
Blueberry Cake   12
Black bean
Black Bean and Tomato Chili   23
Corn and Black Bean Salsa   79
Turkey Stuffed Bell Peppers   55
Lime-Chili Shrimp Bowl   40

134 | Appendix 3 Index

Sweet Potato and Black Bean Burritos   106

Black olive
Air Fried Spicy Olives   122
Italian Rice Balls   80

Blackberry
Blackberry and Peach Cobbler   89
Lemony Blackberry Crisp   90
Summer Berry Crisp   90
Blueberry Cake   12
Whole-Wheat Muffins with Blueberries   9
Breakfast Blueberry Cobbler   6
Whole-Wheat Blueberry Scones   8

Bosc pear
Lemony Pear Chips   85

Bread
All-in-One Toast   8
Mushroom and Squash Toast   13
Croutons   120

Bread crumb
Breaded Scallops   33

Bread dough
Creamy Cinnamon Rolls   10

Broccoli
Sweet and Spicy Broccoli   16
Cheesy Broccoli Tots   17
Chicken Divan   98
Sriracha Beef and Broccoli   65
Herbed Scallops with Vegetables   30
Beef and Vegetable Cubes   71

Broccoli floret
Broccoli, Carrot, and Tomato Quiche   102

Brown rice
Mini Brown Rice Quiches   9
Peppery Brown Rice Fritters   118

Brussels sprout
Lemony Brussels Sprouts and Tomatoes   16
Balsamic Brussels Sprouts   21
Air Fried Crispy Brussels Sprouts   117

Butter lettuce
Spicy Pork Lettuce Wraps   66

butternut squash
Pork with Butternut Squash and Apples   67

Button mushroom
Turkey and Mushroom Meatballs   44

C

Cabbage
Super Veg Rolls   21
Air Fried Spring Rolls   38

Calamari ring
Breaded Calamari with Lemon   32

Calf's liver
Calf's Liver Golden Strips   63

Carrot
Carrot Chips   78
Pork Chops with Carrots and Mushrooms   63
Golden Salmon and Carrot Croquettes   116
Lush Summer Rolls   21
Spinach and Carrot Balls   120
Sweet Corn and Carrot Fritters   121
Seafood Spring Rolls   27
Carrot Banana Muffin   5
Scalloped Veggie Mix   119

Cashew
Cashew Mayo   128
Cashew Ranch Dressing   129

Cauliflower
Paprika Cauliflower   18
Cauliflower, Chickpea, and Avocado Mash   22
Turkey and Cauliflower Meatloaf   42

Cauliflower floret
Spicy Cauliflower   25

Cauliflower rice
Kale Salad Sushi Rolls with Sriracha Mayo   127

Celery
Celery Chicken   52
Air Fried Vegetables   20

Celery root
Cinnamon Celery Roots   15

Cheddar cheese
Herbed Cheddar Frittata   97
Cheesy Turkey Burgers   44
Mac and Cheese   102
Grit and Ham Fritters   13

Cheese ravioli
Ravioli with Beef-Marinara Sauce   66

Cheese tortellini
Tortellini with Spicy Dipping Sauce   86

Cherry tomato
Baked Cherry Tomatoes with Basil   117
Chicken Shawarma   48
Shrimp and Cherry Tomato Kebabs   31
Mediterranean Air Fried Veggies   23

Chicken breast
Chicken Breakfast Sausages   7
Italian Chicken Breasts with Tomatoes   45
Pineapple Chicken   46

Appendix 3 Index | 135

Peach and Cherry Chicken   46
Chicken Skewers with Corn Salad   47
Super Lemon Chicken   49
Gnocchi with Chicken and Spinach   51
Israeli Chicken Schnitzel   53
Potato Cheese Crusted Chicken   54
Lemon Parmesan Chicken   55
Blackened Chicken Breasts   56
Dill Chicken Strips   58
Honey Rosemary Chicken   59
Peppery Chicken Meatballs   82
Chicken Divan   98
Smoky Chicken Sandwich   109
Salsa Verde Golden Chicken Empanadas   110
Mexican Flavor Chicken Burgers   110
Chicken Pita Sandwich   112

Chicken breast tender
Air Fried Naked Chicken Tenders   53

Chicken drumstick
Glazed Chicken Drumsticks   49
Sweet-and-Sour Drumsticks   54
Crisp Paprika Chicken Drumsticks   57
Lemony Chicken Drumsticks   85

Chicken parts
Spanish Chicken and Pepper Baguette   42

Chicken tender
Golden Chicken Fries   46
Fried Chicken Tenders with Veggies   52
Chicken Satay with Peanut Sauce   53
Nutty Chicken Tenders   56

Chicken tenderloin
Fajita Chicken Strips   50
Celery Chicken   52

Chicken thigh
Yakitori   43
Braised Chicken with Hot Peppers   47
Chicken Shawarma   48
Chicken Thighs with Radish Slaw   48
Chicken and Sweet Potato Curry   49
Chicken with Potatoes and Corn   50
Piri-Piri Chicken Thighs   52

Chicken wing
Air Fried Chicken Wings   42
Air Fried Chicken Wings   82
Honey Sriracha Chicken Wings   83
Spicy Chicken Wings   83
Hot Wings   113
Chicken Wings   120

Chickpea
Stuffed Peppers with Beans and Rice   16
Crispy Spiced Chickpeas   83
Rosemary and Orange Chickpeas   119
Hummus   128
Cauliflower, Chickpea, and Avocado Mash   22
Spinach and Chickpea Casserole   98

Chocolate
Chocolate Cheesecake   88

chocolate chip
Rich Chocolate Cookie   95

Chorizo
Chorizo, Corn, and Potato Frittata   99

Cinnamon graham cracker
Cinnamon S'mores   91

Cocktail smoked sausage
Pigs in a Blanket   85

Cocoa powder
Fudgy Chocolate Brownies   95

Coconut
Pineapple Sticks   87
Coconut Pineapple Sticks   87

Coconut flour
Chocolate Cheesecake   88
Fudgy Chocolate Brownies   95

Cod fillet
Crispy Cod Cakes with Salad Greens   34
Glazed Cod with Sesame Seeds   36
Crispy Cod Fingers   81

Cooked chicken
Fried Buffalo Chicken Taquitos   55
Chicken and Yogurt Taquitos   104
Cheesy Chicken Sandwich   106

Corn
Corn and Black Bean Salsa   79
Chicken Skewers with Corn Salad   47

Corn kernel
Southwest Corn and Bell Pepper Roast   116

Corn puff cereal
Sweet and Salty Snack Mix   79

Corn tortilla
Tortilla Chips   83

Corn tortilla chip
Veggie Salmon Nachos   79

Cornish hen
Herbed Hens   50
Creole Hens   51

Crab stick
Panko Crab Sticks with Mayo Sauce   31

Cream cheese
Cream Cheese Stuffed Bell Peppers   18
Creamy Cinnamon Rolls   10

136 | Appendix 3 Index

Crispy Crab and Cream Cheese Wontons   105
Air Fried Cream Cheese Wontons   106
crescent roll dough
Pigs in a Blanket   123
Cucumber
Blackened Salmon   37

D

Dark cherry
Peach and Cherry Chicken   46
Deli turkey
Turkey, Hummus, and Cheese Wraps   57
Dijon mustard
Dijon and Balsamic Vinaigrette   128
Duck breast
Duck Breasts with Balsamic Glaze   45
Orange and Honey Glazed Duck   57
Duck leg quarter
Deep Fried Duck Leg Quarters   43

E

Egg
Egg and Avocado Burrito   6
Cheesy Artichoke-Mushroom Frittata   7
Egg Florentine with Spinach   8
Scotch Eggs   9
Avocado Quesadillas   11
Lush Vegetable Omelet   12
Greek Frittata   97
Herbed Cheddar Frittata   97
Chorizo, Corn, and Potato Frittata   99
Goat Cheese and Asparagus Frittata   99
Sumptuous Vegetable Frittata   99
Kale Frittata   100
Shrimp Spinach Frittata   100
Mediterranean Quiche   101
Mini Quiche Cups   101
Broccoli, Carrot, and Tomato Quiche   102
Vegetable Frittata   102
Cheesy Bacon Quiche   102
Shrimp Quiche   103
Indian Masala Omelet   117
Classic Churros   123
Ricotta Lemon Poppy Seed Cake   89
Keto Cheese Quiche   100
Asparagus and Cheese Strata   5
Baked Avocado with Eggs   9
Breaded Calamari with Lemon   32
Caesar Salad Dressing   130
Pea Delight   119

Rosemary Turkey Breast   43
Rosemary Turkey Scotch Eggs   45
Salmon Patty Bites   37
Spinach with Scrambled Eggs   10
Sweet Potato Soufflé   120
Eggplant
Ratatouille   20
Eggplant Hoagies   108
Veggie Pita Sandwich   112
Rice and Eggplant Bowl   23
Ratatouille   14
Endive
Lemony Endive in Curried Yogurt   81
Enoki mushroom
Teriyaki Pork and Mushroom Rolls   71
Extra-virgin olive oil
Caesar Salad Dressing   130

F

Farmer cheese
Jewish Blintzes   122
Fat-free cream cheese
Fried Buffalo Chicken Taquitos   55
Feta cheese
Mediterranean Quiche   101
Fish
Coconut Chili Fish Curry   26
Crispy Crab and Fish Cakes   30
Fish fillet
Almond Crusted Fish   37
Homemade Fish Sticks   39
Flank steak
Miso Marinated Steak   68
Mongolian Flank Steak   72
Flat iron steak
Sriracha Beef and Broccoli   65
Flour
Apple and Walnut Muffins   11
Rich Chocolate Cookie   95
Pineapple and Chocolate Cake   96
Pea Delight   119
Panko Crab Sticks with Mayo Sauce   31

G

Goat cheese
Goat Cheese Shrimp   28
Granny Smith apple
Apple Fritters   88
Granola
Lush Snack Mix   122

Appendix 3 Index | 137

Lemony Blackberry Crisp   90
Green bean
Herb-Fried Veggies   117
Green cabbage
Tortilla Shrimp Tacos   41
Green chili
Mini Brown Rice Quiches   9
Ground beef
Beef and Spinach Meatloaves   64
Ravioli with Beef-Marinara Sauce   66
Spaghetti Squash Lasagna   68
Classic Spring Rolls   69
Cheesy Beef Meatballs   72
Mushroom and Beef Meatloaf   73
Provolone Stuffed Beef and Pork Meatballs   73
Swedish Beef Meatballs   77
Sumptuous Beef and Bean Chili Casserole   97
Montreal Steak and Seeds Burgers   107
Bulgogi Burgers   108
Classic Sloppy Joes   111
Ground chicken
Crispy Chicken Egg Rolls   105
Ground lamb
Lamb Meatballs   71
Lamb and Feta Hamburgers   107
Ground pork
Pork Meatballs with Red Chili   63
Pork and Pinto Bean Gorditas   74
Pork Momos   104
Thai Pork Sliders   104
Cabbage and Pork Gyoza   107
Provolone Stuffed Beef and Pork Meatballs   73
Ground turkey
Turkey and Cauliflower Meatloaf   42
Rosemary Turkey Breast   43
Turkey and Mushroom Meatballs   44
Cheesy Turkey Burgers   44
Rosemary Turkey Scotch Eggs   45
Asian Turkey Meatballs   54
Turkey Stuffed Bell Peppers   55
Turkey Hoisin Burgers   59

I

Imitation crab meat
Crispy Crab and Fish Cakes   30
Italian sausage
Italian Sausages and Red Grapes   64
Mushroom and Sausage Calzones   65

J

Jalapeño pepper
Jalapeño Poppers   23

Jumbo lump crab meat
Crab Cakes with Bell Peppers   31
Jumbo shrimp
Fired Shrimp with Mayonnaise Sauce   29
Shrimp and Cherry Tomato Kebabs   31

K

Kale
Kale and Potato Nuggets   12
Kale Chips with Sesame   78
Kale Salad Sushi Rolls with Sriracha Mayo   127
Kale Frittata   100
king prawn
Piri-Piri King Prawns   32

L

Lamb chop
Lollipop Lamb Chops   70
Lamb rib
Air Fried Lamb Ribs   69
Lamb steak
Fast Lamb Satay   68
Leek
Turkey, Leek, and Pepper Hamburger   108
Lemon juice
Super Lemon Chicken   49
London broil
Air Fried London Broil   69
Lump crab meat
Crab Cake Sandwich   41
Crispy Crab and Cream Cheese Wontons   105

M

Macaroni
Mac and Cheese   102
Mascarpone cheese
Mascarpone Mushrooms   24
Mexican chorizo
Traditional Queso Fundido   121
Miniature bell pepper
Braised Chicken with Hot Peppers   47
Mozzarella cheese
Chicken and Yogurt Taquitos   104
Cheese-Walnut Stuffed Mushrooms   19
Mozzarella Arancini   84
Mushroom
Golden Garlicky Mushrooms   14
Mascarpone Mushrooms   24
Herb-Fried Veggies   117
Mushroom Apple Gravy   129
Mushroom and Squash Toast   13

Mushroom and Spinach Calzones 81

N

Napa cabbage
Spicy Thai-Style Vegetables 17
Cabbage and Pork Gyoza 107
Nectarine
Caramelized Fruit Kebabs 93

O

Oat
Maple and Pecan Granola 15
Oatmeal Raisin Bars 91
Oatmeal
Oatmeal and Carrot Cookie Cups 90
Okra pod
Air Fried Okra Chips 114
Orange juice
Orange Cake 94
Oyster mushroom
Mushroom and Pepper Pizza Squares 15

P

Paprika
Southwest Seasoning 130
Parsley
Garlic Shrimp with Parsley 26
Classic Shrimp Empanadas 33
Parsnip
Air Fried Vegetables 20
Parsnip Fries with Garlic-Yogurt Dip 114
Peach
Baked Peaches and Blueberries 87
Caramelized Fruit Kebabs 93
Blackberry and Peach Cobbler 89
Peanut
Sweet and Sour Peanuts 114
Pear
Pear and Apple Crisp 95
Pecan
Milky Pecan Tart 124
Nutty Chicken Tenders 56
Maple and Pecan Granola 15
Chocolate Pecan Pie 92
Pepperoni
Pepperoni and Bell Pepper Pockets 69
Sumptuous Pizza Tortilla Rolls 70
Phyllo dough
Apple Turnovers 96
Pickle spear
Tangy Fried Pickle Spears 80

Pie crust
Chocolate Pecan Pie 92
Pineapple
Crispy Pineapple Rings 87
Pineapple Sticks 87
Coconut Pineapple Sticks 87
Pineapple Chicken 46
Pineapple and Chocolate Cake 96
Gold Cutlets with Aloha Salsa 60
Pork with Aloha Salsa 72
Pineapple Galette 94
Pink salmon
Salmon Patty Bites 37
Pinto bean
Pork and Pinto Bean Gorditas 74
Pita
Herbed Pita Chips 84
Pizza dough
Mushroom and Pepper Pizza Squares 15
Mushroom and Sausage Calzones 65
Garlicky Olive Stromboli 124
Pork
Sweet and Sour Pork 76
Pork belly
Lechon Kawali 62
Teriyaki Pork and Mushroom Rolls 71
Pork chop
Pork Chops with Carrots and Mushrooms 63
Pork Chop Roast 68
Vietnamese Pork Chops 75
Pork cutlet
Gold Cutlets with Aloha Salsa 60
Pork with Aloha Salsa 72
Pork loin chop
Pork with Butternut Squash and Apples 67
Pork loin roast
Citrus Pork Loin Roast 75
Pork rib
Homemade Teriyaki Pork Ribs 61
Citrus Carnitas 61
Barbecue Pork Ribs 74
Pork sausage
Scotch Eggs 9
Mini Quiche Cups 101
Pork schnitzel
Classic Walliser Schnitzel 62
Pork shoulder
Char Siu 60

Appendix 3 Index | 139

Pork shoulder butt
Char Siew   75
Pork steak
Pork and Tricolor Vegetables Kebabs   61
Pork tenderloin
Dijon Pork Tenderloin   64
Spicy Pork Lettuce Wraps   66
Orange Pork Tenderloin   70
Pulled Pork   73
Creamy Pork Gratin   98
Portobello mushroom
Stuffed Portobellos with Peppers and Cheese   18
Cheese-Walnut Stuffed Mushrooms   19
Stuffed Portobello Mushrooms with Vegetables   20
Potato
Super Veg Rolls   21
Ricotta Potatoes   24
Potato and Prosciutto Salad   73
Pea and Potato Samosas with Chutney   111
Kale and Potato Nuggets   12
Potatoes with Zucchinis   20
Potato chip
Dill Chicken Strips   58
Prawn
Coconut-Crusted Prawns   28
Chili Prawns   29
Pretzel crisp
Sweet and Salty Snack Mix   79
Prosciutto
Potato and Prosciutto Salad   73
Puff pastry
Pineapple Galette   94
Spicy Apple Turnovers   7
Pumpkin purée
Pumpkin Pudding and Vanilla Wafers   91
Pumpkin Pudding   92
Pumpkin seeds
Lush Snack Mix   122
Purple fingerling potato
Purple Potato Chips with Rosemary   116

Q

Quick-cooking grits
Grit and Ham Fritters   13

R

Rack of pork
Macadamia Nuts Crusted Pork Rack   62
Radish
Chicken Thighs with Radish Slaw   48

Raspberry jam
Jelly Doughnuts   92
Ravioli
Gold Ravioli   24
Red grape
Italian Sausages and Red Grapes   64
Red potato
Fried Potatoes with Peppers and Onions   5
Potato and Broccoli with Tofu Scramble   21
Fried Chicken Tenders with Veggies   52
Chicken with Potatoes and Corn   50
Garlic-Butter Shrimp with Vegetables   28
South Carolina Shrimp and Corn Bake   118
Ribeye steak
Worcestershire Ribeye Steaks   66
Rosemary Ribeye Steaks   76
Rice
Cheesy Rice and Olives Stuffed Peppers   19
Mozzarella Arancini   84
Shrimp and Vegetable Paella   29
Rice vinegar
Asian Dipping Sauce   130
Ricotta cheese
Ricotta Potatoes   24
Roast beef
Smoked Beef   76
Roma tomato
Italian Chicken Breasts with Tomatoes   45
Romaine lettuce heart
Caesar Shrimp Salad   27
Russet potato
Potatoes Lyonnaise   11

S

Salmon fillet
Salmon Burgers   36
Blackened Salmon   37
Marinated Salmon Fillets   40
Lime-Chili Shrimp Bowl   40
Veggie Salmon Nachos   79
Golden Salmon and Carrot Croquettes   116
Scallop
Breaded Scallops   33
Air-Fried Scallops   35
Sea scallop
Herbed Scallops with Vegetables   30
Easy Scallops   32
Bacon-Wrapped Scallops   34
Roasted Scallops with Snow Peas   35

Shallot

Air-Fried Scallops   35

Shelf-stable gnocchi

Gnocchi with Chicken and Spinach   51

shiitake mushroom

Lush Summer Rolls   21

Shrimp

Spicy Orange Shrimp   26

Garlic Shrimp with Parsley   26

Caesar Shrimp Salad   27

Goat Cheese Shrimp   28

Garlic-Butter Shrimp with Vegetables   28

Paprika Shrimp   29

Shrimp and Vegetable Paella   29

Browned Shrimp Patties   30

Lemony Shrimp   32

Garlic Butter Shrimp Scampi   33

Classic Shrimp Empanadas   33

Crispy Coconut Shrimp   35

Green Curry Shrimp   36

Blackened Shrimp Tacos   38

Country Shrimp   38

Spicy Orange Shrimp   39

Seasoned Breaded Shrimp   39

Lemony Shrimp and Zucchini   40

Tortilla Shrimp Tacos   41

Veggie Shrimp Toast   84

Cheesy Shrimp Sandwich   109

Cheesy Shrimps   114

Spicy Air Fried Old Bay Shrimp   115

South Carolina Shrimp and Corn Bake   118

Teriyaki Shrimp Skewers   125

Shrimp Spinach Frittata   100

Shrimp Quiche   103

Skirt steak

Skirt Steak Fajitas   77

smoked sausage

Pigs in a Blanket   123

Smoked trout

Smoked Trout and Crème Fraiche Frittata   101

Smoked turkey sausage

Country Shrimp   38

Snow pea

Spicy Thai-Style Vegetables   17

Roasted Scallops with Snow Peas   35

Spaghetti squash

Spaghetti Squash Lasagna   68

Spinach

Spinach with Scrambled Eggs   10

Creamy and Cheesy Spinach   22

Mushroom and Spinach Calzones   81

Spinach and Chickpea Casserole   98

Spanakopita   115

Spinach and Carrot Balls   120

Egg Florentine with Spinach   8

Greek Frittata   97

Beef and Spinach Meatloaves   64

Squash

Pork and Tricolor Vegetables Kebabs   61

Sticky rice

Italian Rice Balls   80

Strawberry

Summer Berry Crisp   90

Summer squash

Garlicky Spiralized Zucchini and Squash   115

Sushi rice

Rice and Eggplant Bowl   23

Browned Shrimp Patties   30

Sweet corn kernel

Sweet Corn and Carrot Fritters   121

Sweet pepper

Spanish Chicken and Pepper Baguette   42

Sweet potato

Sweet Potatoes with Zucchini   17

Sweet Potatoes with Tofu   22

Sweet Potato and Black Bean Burritos   106

Indian-Style Sweet Potato Fries   118

Chicken and Sweet Potato Curry   49

T

Tahini

Lemony Tahini   128

Hemp Dressing   129

Tapioca flour

Pão de Queijo   123

Tart apple

Orange and Honey Glazed Duck   57

Tart cherry

Pecan and Cherry Stuffed Apples   96

Tater tot

Sweet Bacon Tater Tots   84

Tilapia fillet

Cajun-Style Fish Tacos   34

Tiny shrimp

Seafood Spring Rolls   27

Air Fried Spring Rolls   38

Appendix 3 Index | 141

Tofu
Spicy Kung Pao Tofu   15
Potato and Broccoli with Tofu Scramble   21
Sweet Potatoes with Tofu   22
Tomato
Bruschetta with Tomato and Basil   80
Classic Marinara Sauce   128
Pico de Gallo   129
Supplì al Telefono (Risotto Croquettes)   125
Black Bean and Tomato Chili   23
Lemony Brussels Sprouts and Tomatoes   16
Coconut Chili Fish Curry   26
Sumptuous Beef and Bean Chili Casserole   97
Lamb Meatballs   71
Stuffed Portobello Mushrooms with Vegetables   20
Top round steak
Beef and Vegetable Cubes   71
Top sirloin steak
Sirloin Steak and Pepper Fajitas   67
Tuna
Tuna Patty Sliders   34
Turkey
Turkey, Leek, and Pepper Hamburger   108
Turkey Sliders with Chive Mayo   109
Turkey breast
Turkey and Cranberry Quesadillas   56
Herbed Turkey Breast   58
Mini Turkey Meatloaves with Carrot   59
Turkey cutlet
Pecan-Crusted Turkey Cutlets   58
Turkey thigh
Cajun Turkey   56

V

Vidalia onion
Potatoes Lyonnaise   11

W

Waffle cut fry
Poutine with Waffle Fries   86
Weet potato
Sweet Potato Soufflé   120
White bread
Peanut Butter-Chocolate Bread Pudding   89
White cabbage
Crispy Chicken Egg Rolls   105

White chocolate chip
Black and White Brownies   88
White mushroom
Sumptuous Pizza Tortilla Rolls   70
White rice
Stuffed Peppers with Beans and Rice   16
White wine
Herbed Hens   50
White wine vinegar
Hemp Dressing   129
Whole chicken
Chicken Roast   51
Whole milk
Honey Yeast Rolls   127
Whole-grain bread
Sweet Banana Bread Pudding   10
Whole-wheat bread
French Toast Sticks   6
Whole-wheat flour
Carrot Banana Muffin   5
Whole-Wheat Muffins with Blueberries   9
Whole-wheat pastry flour
Breakfast Blueberry Cobbler   6
Whole-Wheat Blueberry Scones   8
Oatmeal and Carrot Cookie Cups   90
Wonton wrapper
Air Fried Cream Cheese Wontons   106

Y

Yellow cornmeal
Ham and Corn Muffins   12
Yukon Gold potato
Scalloped Veggie Mix   119

Z

Zucchini
Ratatouille   14
Zucchini Crisps   14
Potatoes with Zucchinis   20
Mediterranean Air Fried Veggies   23
Garlicky Spiralized Zucchini and Squash   115
Sumptuous Vegetable Frittata   99
Vegetable Frittata   102
Ratatouille   20
Lemony Shrimp and Zucchini   40
Sweet Potatoes with Zucchini   17

Made in the USA
Middletown, DE
12 December 2021